Storytelling in the Pulps,
Comics, and Radio

To the uncultured Philistines of Friday snack-time

Storytelling in the Pulps, Comics, and Radio

How Technology Changed Popular Fiction in America

by TIM DEFOREST

x

McFarland & Company, Inc., Publishers
Jefferson, North Carolina, and London

Special thanks to Allen Novak for photographing or scanning the many pulp covers and comic strips reproduced in this book.

The *G-8 and His Battle Aces* cover reprinted in this volume is used with permission. The distinctive logo and composite cover design, and all related elements, are trademarks and are the property of Argosy Communications, Inc.

Images from *Astounding Science Fiction* used with permission of Dell Magazines.

The Shadow character, copyrights and trademarks are owned by The Condé Nast Publications. Used with permission.

LIBRARY OF CONGRESS CATALOGUING-IN-PUBLICATION DATA

DeForest, Tim, 1960–
    Storytelling in the pulps, comics, and radio : how technology
changed popular fiction in America / by Tim DeForest.
      p.   cm.
    Includes bibliographical references and index.

    ISBN 0-7864-1902-4 (softcover : 50# alkaline paper) ∞

    1. Storytelling in mass media.   2. Mass media — United
States.   3. Mass media and technology — United States.   I.
Title.
P96.S782U63   2004
302.23'0973 — dc22   2004008620

British Library cataloguing data are available

Cover art ©2004 Wood River Gallery.

Manufactured in the United States of America

*McFarland & Company, Inc., Publishers
  Box 611, Jefferson, North Carolina 28640
  www.mcfarlandpub.com*

Contents

Preface

The process of how we tell stories to one another has changed drastically over the last couple of centuries. With the advent of industrialization, we've gone from an oral tradition to popular literature to radio to television in an historical blink of an eye. We've embraced new methods of storytelling, hung on to them for a while, and then left them behind.

This book is about a few of those things left behind. My interest in pulp fiction, adventure comic strips and old-time radio began before I reached my teens, fed by paperback reprints and long-playing records. While I was in high school, a local radio station briefly ran *Lone Ranger* reruns on weekday evenings—and I was hooked forever. By the time I reached adulthood, my personal pop culture references all came from several decades before I was born.

I'd always been a history buff as well, so I eventually began investigating the history of storytelling. I soon realized that all the stuff I loved as a kid and still loved as a grown-up had been made possible by technological advancements. Artists and writers in the first half of the 20th century had taken advantage of new technologies to tell stories in vibrant new ways. Eventually, it occurred to me that a study of the connection between storytelling and technology might be worthwhile. "New" hasn't always meant "better"—television isn't automatically superior to radio—and I was convinced that a look back at what our parents and grandparents had gotten right was important.

Researching this book was a pleasure, since much of work consisted of reading stories and comics I'd have been reading for fun anyway. The same thing applied to old-time radio shows—researching the chapter on *Gunsmoke*, for example, consisted largely of listening to multiple episodes of that literate and powerful drama, then applying the techniques of critical analysis to its thematic overtones, plots and characters. It was a challenge, but an enormously enjoyable one.

Getting hold of everything I need to read occasionally presented another challenge, but online used book and auction services helped a lot. I'd get the original pulp magazine containing each story I would use whenever possible. I'd settle for a reprint only when I could reasonably confirm that the story had not been significantly changed since its original appearance in the pulps.

A lot of classic comic strips were reprinted, sometimes in their entire runs, during the 1980s and '90s, while the advent of MP3 meant it was now practical to get most surviving episodes of specific radio shows with relative ease. Technology was making my task of writing about technology easier.

Gathering background information about these mediums was made possible by the excellent scholarship that had already been done by many other writers. Rick Marschall's *America's Great Comic Strip Artists* is the Ur-book about comics— anyone who claims an interest in the subject but has not read this should simply be taken outside and shot. *The Great American Broadcast*, by Leonard Maltin, and John Dunning's *On the Air: The Encyclopedia of Old-Time Radio* were among the more valuable books on that subject. There are so many great books on the history of pulps that it's difficult to pick a particular standout, but Lee Server's *Danger is My Business: An Illustrated History of the Fabulous Pulp Magazines* is one of my favorites. Most of the original writers, artists and actors from the pre-television years are no longer with us, but the authors of the above works had interviewed them and chronicled their accomplishments. My own book would not have been possible without these entertaining and valuable sources of information.

Introduction

The human race is always leaving stuff behind, tossed into a cultural or technological junk heap. Somebody thinks of something new, the great unwashed decide they like whatever it is, and, presto, we all live a little differently than we did before.

For instance: We used to live in caves and paint on the walls. Then we invented towns and cities and moved out of the caves. We painted on the city walls for a while, and then we invented paper and canvas and so on. In the process, we stopped painting on cave walls. Mankind's first form of artistic expression was left behind.

Now this isn't necessarily bad. We needed to move out of the caves in order to eventually have a Renaissance. We needed to have a Renaissance in order for Pope Julius II to hire Michelangelo to paint the ceiling of the Sistine Chapel. We left cave painting behind because we had found more profound and meaningful ways of expressing ourselves.

Sometimes, though, when we leave something behind, it's to our detriment. Sometimes the item we've just tossed on the cultural junk heap still has value. It still serves a unique purpose that can't be adequately fulfilled by whatever new thing replaces it.

This has happened for more often in the last century or two than it did in the previous six or seven thousand years.

For most of human history, change happens very, very slowly. A peasant (or a knight or a blacksmith) in medieval Latvia lived much the same life as his great-grandfather lived. Assuming everyone wasn't hacked to death by marauding Huns, his own kids would follow in his footsteps. When someone invented (or rediscovered) the horse collar or algebra, it did change things, often profoundly. But these changes were relatively gradual and most people never really noticed them at the time.

But then, along about the end of the 18th century, we had an industrial revolution. All of a sudden we could invent new tools and machines and devices and what-have-you on a seemingly daily basis. We could distribute said devices quickly and efficiently. Soon each generation was living a life significantly different from the previous generation. In fact, life would change significantly within a single decade, or a single year.

To use an obvious example: Twenty years ago, few of us had computers in our homes. Ten years ago, most of us had acquired computers. Now, along with computers, most of us (at least in the wealthier nations) have Internet access and all that entails in terms of changes in culture and methods of communication.

Here's another example that may seem a little silly but ties in with the theme of this book. When I was a kid, I would have to anxiously scan the TV listings to see if this week's Creature Feature was finally showing *King Kong* again, and then make a point of being in front of the TV at the right time to watch it. Now I *own* a copy of *King Kong* and can watch it pretty much whenever I please.

This last example demonstrates both the good and the bad of change. On the one hand, I can watch my favorite movie whenever I want to. This would seem to be a good thing (at least for those of us with good taste in films).

On the other hand, one might argue that this easy access to *Kong* takes away some of the thrill of watching it. Growing up, I was fortunate to see it maybe once every two or three years. This made it a much more special experience. It was a rare treat rather than a common occurrence. I could see *A Charlie Brown Christmas* just once each December and looked forward to doing so with great anticipation. Now I can watch it in July if I want to.

Things change. This isn't a bad thing. It's the decisions we make about what to leave behind (and they're nearly always decisions, not requirements) that are good or bad.

I can choose to watch *A Charlie Brown Christmas* just once each December. And this is what I do, thus preserving an important part of the experience. It's my decision.

In general, technological change comes first, followed by (often unexpected) cultural change.

For instance: Mass-production of the automobile was the catalyst for monumental transformations within Western society. People had more options regarding where they could live in relation to where they worked. The car was a major factor in reducing strong feelings of regionalism (the sense that you're a Virginian first and an American second) as the population shifted about the country with relative speed and ease. The concepts of courtship and dating changed radically. No one expected most of these changes. They just sort of sneaked up on everybody.

Industrialization also spurred a growth in literacy and increased educational opportunities, brought on in part by improvements in printing technology. It became practical to mass-produce newspapers and pamphlets that the general population was now able to read. Other even more radical changes in communication have followed — radio, television, etc. All this resulted in some quite unexpected fallout. It changed the nature of politics. It changed the nature of organized religion.

It changed, too, the nature of storytelling. *That* is what I'll be talking about. In the last few centuries we've come to tell each other stories using completely different processes than in days of yore. Many of the old ways have been largely supplanted and, though not necessarily forgotten, they are rare enough so as to be effectively absent from the lives of the general population. On top of this, many of the more worthwhile new storytelling techniques brought about by industrialization lasted only a few decades, then faded away when something else came along. This is not a good thing.

Storytelling, of course, has been around since the beginning of time. After all, Adam and Eve certainly had some pretty good tales to tell their kids. Storytelling developed into an important part of every early culture, usually following similar evolutions in both subject material and storytelling genres. Perhaps the most common genre was heroic poetry; stories of danger and adventure and monsters and shipwrecks and whatever else could be thrown in to make the hero's life significantly miserable so as to entertain those listening to the poem.

Tales of heroism grew organically out of early myth, which often presented the world as a wild and uncontrollable place where gods and monsters would squash you flat without blinking an eye. When the hero of a story killed a monster or stood up to the gods, he exerted some level of control over his own fate, a control that many people felt was absent from their own lives. His story would provide a sense of hope to others. But the dangers he faced and the failures he suffered would serve as a reminder that few accomplishments come without sacrifices — and that often the sacrifice being made should not be for oneself, but for others. Joseph Campbell, author of the seminal *Hero with a Thousand Faces*, described the hero as someone who had "given his life to something bigger than himself." Campbell's book traces this theme through the myths of many diverse cultures — it's a common thread linking all of humanity.

As myths gradually moved from attempts to explain the mysteries of the world to stories of men standing up against the world, the third-person narrative became predominant. Also contributing to this were civilization's early technical advancements as food production methods improved and it took less time and manpower to bring in the crops. Consequently, people found themselves with more free time, and the demand for entertainment increased. One of the primary methods for sating this demand was storytelling. The heroic epic, already in place for numerous cultural reasons, became a really good way to enjoy an evening out with the wife and kids.

Over the centuries there have been the Homeric poems of early Greece (*The Iliad* and *The Odyssey*); the Teutonic poems of the early Christian era (*Beowulf*); the Norse sagas that flourished from the 9th through 13th Centuries; the beast or totem tales of various Native American cultures; and so on and so on. These stories still reflected important aspects of the cultures that produced them, but they also kept their audiences on the edge of their collective seat and always had them coming back for more. They were, above all else, fun. Otherwise no one would have bothered to listen.

As history progressed, bards and poets continued to tell stories. Actually, more often than not, they sang the stories. Usually, narrative poems were constructed in a uniform metrical pattern (though this pattern changes from culture to culture), and recited to the accompaniment of primitive musical instruments or rhythmic dances. Patterns like this were a mnemonic device, helping aspiring poets to learn or compose lengthy epics. By the time Thebes and Babylon were built, storytelling was an established profession, and if you wanted to be a poet when you grew up, you needed to get the hang of memorization while you were still young.

While cultures continued to evolve, so, to an extent, did storytelling, though the basic ingredients of the heroic epic remained. Twelfth century Europe, for example, saw the development of chivalric literature. These stories often dealt with romantic love, which was a new direction for Western culture. Where love had in the past been presented as little different than lust (Odysseus catted around quite a lot during the ten years it took him to get home to his faithful wife), now it became something more intense and more special — though it was also usually presented as unrequited or unattainable. But the protagonists were still heroes (in this case, knights) who would encounter significant villains and dragons and such to keep things interesting while they mooned over their lost loves.

It was from the medieval troubadours, by the way, that we got the stories of Charlemagne and Arthur that shaped the modern view of knights and chivalry.

Eventually, the musical accompaniment for oral storytelling disappeared, and as printed literature became more accessible, oral storytelling became less and less of a formalized profession. But it remained —for a time — a big part of Western culture.

Of course, the heroic tale wasn't the only sort of story being told. Political oratory is nearly as old as storytelling, and one can make a case that a good storyteller and a good orator employ pretty much the same skills.

In November of 1863, when the cemetery at Gettysburg, Pennsylvania, was to be dedicated, several people were invited to give speeches. The main speaker was Edward Everett, a 69-year-old orator who had also been a minister, a professor of Greek literature at Harvard, a member of Congress and a diplomat. He spoke for two hours and by all accounts kept his audience spellbound. He recounted the course of the three-day battle that had raged nearby a few months before, gesturing dramatically towards various parts of the battlefield as he did so. He drew parallels between the United States and ancient Athens, where the Western world's original democracy had defended itself against powerful enemies.

Everett's speech is largely forgotten today, mostly because he was followed by Abraham Lincoln, whose brief but brilliant remarks have been justifiably immortalized as *the* Gettysburg Address. But Everett is a prime example of how people were entertained in the days before television and motion pictures. People loved going to hear someone speak, and a skilled orator could always draw a big crowd and grab hold of their collective imagination. A quarter-century after Gettysburg, a singer and monologist named William De Wolf Hopper added a recitation of the poem "Casey at the Bat" to his act. He ended up reciting it on stage some 10,000 times over the course of his career. While his subject matter may have lacked the depth and importance of Everett's speech, both men had one thing in common — they knew how to tell a story.

People loved this stuff. And it wasn't because the average 19th century guy or gal was less sophisticated than any of us today, or that we're all a little smarter than they were. I suspect a conversation with Edward Everett would make most of us today feel like uneducated rubes.

It wasn't purely because of a lack of entertainment choices either. Even as cultures came up with other ways of entertaining themselves— games, knightly tournaments, music, printed literature — storytelling remained a big deal.

People loved this stuff because human civilization got at least one thing right on its first try. Listening to a real live storyteller — someone standing right there where you can see them while they talk —can be a very intense and exciting experience. In the book *The Storyteller's Journey: An American Revival*, author Joseph Daniel Sobol makes this point better than I can: "The storyteller's presence embodies a concentration of physical, emotional, mental and unconscious faculties, through which an audience is transported away from the physical plane."[1]

This is not to imply that early civilizations were havens of primitive bliss. After all, people back then were lucky to live into their thirties, their children as often as not died in infancy, and they hadn't invented deodorant yet. But they *did* get some things right, like storytelling.

Now keep in mind that until we get into the last couple of centuries, we've been dealing with cultures in which only a very small percentage of the population could read. The oldest written record of a story comes from Egypt, about 6,000 years ago. "Tales of the Magicians" involve the sons of the Pharaoh Cheops trying to outdo one another with increasingly wild stories— a sort of early version of the Arabian Nights tales that would eventually appear in Muslim culture.

But for most of human history, recording stories in writing served no immediate purpose for the average farmer or ditch digger. The general masses still depended on oral storytelling.

The printing press and the gradual increase in average educational levels made printed fiction more accessible. This would eventually lead to the explosion of popular literature that we'll discuss a little later, which led to the development of the modern novel. Not surprisingly, this new literary device continued to use the same elements of danger, suspense, romance and violence that had been providing storytelling fodder since the beginning of time.

In 1719, Daniel Defoe published *Robinson Crusoe*, in which he stuck his unfortunate protagonist on a desert island for 28-plus years. Crusoe's perseverance and ingenuity keeps him alive, allows him to preserve his faith and integrity, and makes for a nifty story that still reads well today.

The 19th century ushered in an extraordinary series of modern literary accomplishments. James Fenimore Cooper's *Leatherstocking Tales* were enormously successful, helping to codify some of the conventions of the adventure genre and making him a major influence on popular literature for the rest of the century — though for today's reader, his stilted and wordy prose makes him difficult to enjoy.

But things soon got better. In 1883, Robert Louis Stevenson published the template for great adventure stories: *Treasure Island*. Stevenson's tale of mutiny and maps and buried treasure defined the modern popular view of piracy. Adding spice to its well-described action sequences was the psychological depth Stevenson gave to his chief villain, Long John Silver. Silver is, in fact, a lot more interesting than some of the novel's somewhat one-dimensional protagonists. Silver's relationship with young Jim Hawkins provides the plot with a true emotional center. *Treasure Island* was written for younger readers, but it demonstrated that the adventure novel was growing up.

It was not adventure alone that drove popular literature forward. In 1841, Edgar Allan Poe published "The Murders in the Rue Morgue," the first modern detective story. "Rue Morgue's" protagonist, C. August Dupin, was the first true literary detective and the direct fictional ancestor of Sherlock Holmes, Nero Wolfe, Hercule Poirot and (quite literally) every other fictional crime-solver who followed. Nearly every convention of the genre — the brilliant detective, the not-quite-so-smart friend and narrator, the feats of clever deduction, the unlikely suspect — was introduced by Poe in this or his later mysteries.

Poe, of course, was also very good at scaring people, as were Mary Shelley, Nathaniel Hawthorne, Sheridan La Fanu, and others who throughout the 19th century began to infuse the horror story with intelligence and style, leavening it all with a mixture of both graphic and subtle frights.

Finally, there's science fiction. One can argue that this particular genre arose long before the 19th century, tracing its roots to Homer's *Odyssey* or Cyrano de Bergerac's 17th century romances about trips to the sun and the moon. But the true fathers of the genre have to be Jules Verne and H.G. Wells, who melded fanciful plots with realism and strong characterizations. Both men were brilliant writers, and both brought a different attitude to their novels. Verne was concerned with what might be possible and tried to keep the science part of his fiction accurate. Wells, on the other hand, took up more obviously fantastic subjects, such as time travel and invisibility, without worrying as much about what was actually possible. Also, where Verne was optimistic about the benefits of new technology, Wells portrayed the destruction (or at least unpleasant disruption) of civilization on a fairly regular basis. Between them, Verne and Wells opened up an infinite range of possibilities for future writers.

Adventure, mystery, horror and fantasy —from these genres would spring the new storytelling outlets that we'll be dealing with: pulp magazines, radio drama and adventure comic strips. All three mediums took elements both as old as mankind and brand new, and, aided by new technology, gave us a few brief decades of entertainment and escapism. Then they faded, to be set aside and nearly forgotten by all but a few aficionados. In the case of the pulps, this was mostly the result of economic factors outside the average person's control, plus the legitimate evolution of literary tastes. But radio drama and adventure strips died from abandonment, when we as a culture chose to leave them behind after we found something new. Television killed them, or at least fired the final bullet. Keep reading and find out what you're missing.

Part I

The Pulps; or, One Darn Thing After Another

The pulps were wonderful things. Magazines produced on inexpensive pulpy paper (hence the name) that were usually seven inches by ten inches and sold for a dime, the pulps provided their readers with fiction of all conceivable types. Love stories, westerns, science fiction, horror, adventure — you name it and they published it. Some pulps featured specific characters like the Shadow or Doc Savage. Others specialized in specific genres like mystery or horror. Certain pulps chose their stories with extraordinary specificity. If you wrote a war story, you'd send it to *Over the Top* or perhaps *Under Fire* magazine. If your narrative featured buccaneers and buried treasure, *Pirate Stories* might buy it. If your newest adventure epic involved a zeppelin, then (and I'm not making this up) *Zeppelin Stories* could be the right home for it.

Pulps first appeared in the late 19th century and faded away in the 1950s. During their heyday, any newsstand in the country was overflowing with pulps, with their garish and often bizarre covers competing for the attention of eager readers. It was a new and vital outlet for storytelling that helped develop several important literary genres. Individual stories ranged in quality from brilliant to truly horrible, but almost all accomplished the same purpose — to provide their readers with a short period of enjoyment and escapism. And some few pulp stories were among the best American fiction ever produced.

1. Story Papers

Pulps grew out of the dime novel, one of the first truly successful forms of popular literature, which in turn was fathered by industrialization.

Prior to the 19th century, reading for pleasure was an activity confined mostly to the wealthy. In general, no one else had the money, leisure time or education. But several disparate products of the modern world would combine to change this.

The steam-powered printing press, first used in 1814 by the London *Times*, made it possible to mass-produce the written word quickly and cheaply.[1] At the same time, improved roads, railroads and other transportation advancements were creating conditions for efficient postal systems, allowing books and periodicals to be quickly distributed on a national level. Finally, industrialization was spawning the rapid growth of a middle class—people who had at least a modicum of leisure time, spending money and education.[2] The middle class knew how to read and had money with which to buy something to read.

It wasn't long before publishers realized they had a huge new market on their hands. The early 1800s saw the emergence of story papers. These were four-to-eight-page tabloids with names like *New York Ledger* or *Saturday Night*—newspapers that printed double-columns of fiction rather than news. Published weekly, usually on Saturdays when people were finishing their workweeks, the story papers soon gained enormous popularity, with the most popular achieving a circulation of 400,000.

Because they were issued on a regular basis and were consecutively numbered, the story papers qualified for cheaper postal rates. Publishers were anxious to keep costs down—an understandable goal, but some of their cost-cutting methods could stray onto ethically shaky ground. Many story papers routinely plagiarized fiction from other sources or from each other. One trick in the American papers was to reprint work published in England, thus bypassing the loose copyright laws of the era. Another trick was to change the title and character names of a story and print it a second or third or fourth time.

But the success of the story papers forced publishers to eventually seek out more and more original material. In 1859, the *New York Ledger* paid Charles Dickens $5,000 for the rights to his newest work. Writers of lesser renown but of proven popularity were also paid reasonably well, although many publishers saved money by paying very little or, if they could get away with it, nothing at all.[3] Most often, though, they did pay, and the professional popular fiction writer was born.

In England, story papers were known as "bloods" or "penny dreadfuls," names that reflected the lurid nature of much early popular fiction. One of the best known of the penny dreadfuls was *Varney the Vampire*, published in 109 blood-soaked installments between 1845 and 1847. Written by James Malcolm Rymer,[4] *Varney* typifies the appeal this sort of storytelling can often exude. It's a fun read that succeeds in generating a sustained level of horror and suspense as the story follows its undead title character through a series of chases, false identities, escapes and murders. In other words, it skillfully gave the readers exactly what they wanted, as the following excerpt from early in the story demonstrates:

> The figure turns half round, and the light falls upon the face. It was perfectly white — perfectly bloodless. The eyes look like polished tin; the lips were drawn back, and the principle feature next to those dread eyes is the teeth — the fearful-looking teeth — projecting like those of some wild animal, hideously, glaringly white and fang-like.

Not as good as Bram Stoker and later authors would do it, but still pretty good. There's even a nifty twist at the end as Varney, becoming self-aware of his own evil, throws himself into Mount Vesuvius.

2. Dime Novels

The story papers were soon joined by another important outlet of popular fiction. By 1860, mass-marketing techniques were being developed (still another result of industrialization), and one particular publisher quickly demonstrated just how effective these techniques could be.

In 1858, Erastus F. Beadle, along with his brother Irwin and partner Robert Adams, founded a publishing company with the intention of offering inexpensive books for the general public. Their editor, Orville J. Victor, would soon prove to have an excellent sense of what the public wanted, and in 1860 the first dime novel was published.

"BOOKS FOR THE MILLION!" shouted an advertisement in the *New York Tribune* on June 7 of that year. "A DOLLAR BOOK FOR A DIME!!!" The book being advertised was Beadle's Dime Novels No. 1: *Malaeska, the Indian Wife of the White Hunter*, by Ann S. Stephens. The book, actually a reprint of an 1839 magazine serial, was an immediate success, selling 300,000 copies in its first year of print. It was cheap — ten cents when most novels cost at least a quarter — and it was compact, easily fitting into someone's pocket. Most importantly, it was about the early American frontier, a subject that James Fenimore Cooper had already proven the American public would go mad over. Stephens' 128-page novel begins when white hunter William Danforth marries the Indian woman Malaeska. But the Indians and whites are soon at war; Danforth and Malaeska's father end up killing each other. Malaeska, along with her infant son, goes to live with her in-laws in the East. The in-laws insist that Malaeska never reveal to her son that she is his mother, thus sparing him the shame of knowing he's half Indian. The son grows up, finds out anyway and, after a lot of melodramatic goings-on, everything ends tragically for everybody.

Beadle and Adams continued to produce dime novels on a regular schedule, each one sequentially numbered to take advantage of second class postal rates. The subjects were chiefly pioneer life, the American Revolution and other aspects of American history — Beadle had no incentive to be innovative in terms of story material. He was, though, willing to try new advertising techniques.

Dime Novel #8, published in October 1860, was preceded by an advertising blitz. Newspaper ads and posters plastered all over New York City blared out the question: "Who is Seth Jones?" This cryptic question continued to pop up everywhere until, just as the risk of seriously annoying people grew too great, it was followed by a new series of posters and ads. These featured an illustration of a stalwart Fenimore Cooper–style frontiersman, with "I am Seth Jones" in large type alongside.

Seth Jones; or, the Captives of the Frontier was still another big hit, eventually selling 400,000 copies. Written by a young New Jersey schoolteacher named Edward S. Ellis, the novel involved a series of kidnappings by Indians, escapes, false identities and romantic misunderstandings.

It was obvious that the dime novel was a highly successful format for popular literature. After the start of the Civil War, sales rose even higher. The cheap and easy-to-carry books proved popular among soldiers. At the time, wars were still fought almost entirely during the spring and summer, when the weather permitted large armies to travel. During the winter months, soldiers had little to do other than sit around camp fires and die of diphtheria. Dime novels were one of their major sources of entertainment. By the end of the war, Beadle and Adams had sold nearly five million copies of their various novels.

Other publishers soon got into the act. Dime novels supplanted the story papers, and "dime novel" became the term for any sort of fiction published on a regular schedule, though the format and price would vary. They usually weren't novels in any real sense, generally running less than 30,000 words. The most common format was probably a 32-page pamphlet costing a nickel, but a 100-page story costing ten or fifteen cents wasn't unusual.

Not surprisingly, publishers continued to stick with proven, reliable subject matter. By the end of the dime novel era, millions of words of fiction had been printed, but most of it would fit into just a few different genres. It was this limitation of subject matter that prevented the dime novels from producing anything that approached literary greatness.

Frontier stories and Westerns remained enormously popular.[1] Purely fictional characters abounded, but some of the most popular dime novel series featured historical characters— Buffalo Bill, Kit Carson, Grizzly Adams, Calamity Jane and so on. Few, if any, of their printed adventures had anything to do with their real lives. A Kit Carson novel, for example, included an illustration of Carson battling Indians with one hand while holding an unconscious girl in the other. When the aged Carson saw the illustration, he said, "That there may have happened, but I ain't got no recollection of it."

Of these characters, Buffalo Bill and Jesse James are appropriate ones to briefly examine and contrast. The Buffalo Bill series is a good example of the type of empty but fun storytelling that dime novels did best, while the various series featuring Jesse James, despite the popularity they enjoyed more than a century ago, are models of storytelling ineptitude — dime novel writing at its worst.

Buffalo Bill Cody was one of the first real-life figures to jump into a fictional world. He entered the dime novel canon in 1869 with the publication of *Buffalo Bill, the King of the Border Men*, written by Ned Buntline.

Buntline was a pen name used by Edward Zane Carrol Judson, who had been a successful writer of popular fiction since the 1840s. His selection of William Cody as the newest dime novel hero was pretty much by chance. In 1869, Judson traveled west to meet Major Frank North, a famous scout. It was North whom Judson wanted to use as a new hero in a series for the publishing firm of Street and Smith. North wasn't interested, but he recommended Cody (then a scout attached to North's command) as a more likely subject. After meeting Cody, Judson agreed. Cody, who would eventually demonstrate a tremendous flair for self-promotion and showmanship, had no objections to having his life fictionalized.

The dime novel version of Buffalo Bill (Judson gave him the nickname) remained enormously popular for over half a century. Over the years, the make-believe Bill appeared in scores of novels, many of them reprinted multiple times, and fought and killed enough Indians, outlaws and spies to depopulate the West several times over, all for the enjoyment of his fans.

And the Buffalo Bill novels *were* kind of enjoyable, especially the later ones written by Colonel Prentiss Ingraham.[2] Like all dime novels, there were no real characterizations, but the action was well-described and often exciting. If the plots had little to do with reality, they made reasonable sense in the context of their own world. Even today, it's not too hard to suspend disbelief for the half-hour or so it takes to read through one of them.

Not all dime novel heroes were actually asked if they wanted to be dime novel heroes. Not all of them were heroes, either. Tales of Jesse James rivaled Buffalo Bill in popularity. Nearly every dime novel publisher produced their own versions of his adventures, many of them coming out

while James was still alive and active as an outlaw. Regardless of the publisher, though, many of the James stories suffer from a sort of literary
schizophrenia that makes them all but unreadable today. Dime novelists
couldn't seem to make up their minds whether James should be a hero or
a villain, and they'd jump back and forth between the two extremes, often
within the same story. In one paragraph Jesse might be ruthlessly tortur-
ing an enemy to death to satisfy his own crazed blood-lust. In the next
paragraph he'd be a Robin Hood figure, rescuing widows and orphans from
evil bankers or some other form of certain doom. If you ever want to experience something truly annoying, try reading a Jesse James dime novel.
The failure to consistently establish even a one-dimensional characterization of the outlaw weighs the stories down, stripping them of any pleasure
they might otherwise have generated.

   With the popularity of dime novels continuing to rise, Westerns and
related stories did not by themselves meet the demands of readers. A few
other genres gradually established themselves, one of which spun off directly
from the Westerns. In 1865, Beadle and Adams published *The Steam Man
of the Prairies*, written by Edward S. Ellis (the author of *Seth Jones*). This
was the story of a teenaged boy named Johnny Brainerd, a hunchbacked
dwarf blessed with astounding mechanical genius. Young Johnny demonstrates this genius by building a steam-powered mechanical man. Before
long, he has brought his invention out West, where he assists a trio of
miners in defending their claim against Indians and outlaws.

   The Steam Man is a well-constructed yarn. Ellis avoids using the
mechanical man as a *duex ex machina* by giving it reasonable limitations,
such as a constant need for fuel and an inability to walk up or down inclines
without tipping over. The Indians are at first terrified at the sight of the
steam man, but soon get used to it and continue to threaten the miners.
Johnny, in the meantime, is anxious to prove himself and takes his invention off on his own, leading to encounters with buffalo and a bad-tempered
grizzly bear. Later, he and the miners use the steam man as a mobile gun
platform to fight off an Indian attack. At the story's climax, Johnny blows
up his creation (by over-pressurizing the boiler) in order to blast an exit
out of a box canyon, allowing the miners and himself to escape with their
hard-won gold.

   The Steam Man proved extremely popular and was reprinted at least
six times under different titles. Oddly, Beadle and Adams never capitalized
on its success by producing similar stories, but other publishers didn't hesitate to do so. By the 1890s, a legion of young inventors were creating a del-
uge of mechanical men, horses, submarines and flying machines, powered

FOURTH EDITION.

$2.50 a year.   Entered at the Post Office at New York, N. Y., at Second Class Mail Rates.   Copyrighted in 1882 by BEADLE AND ADAMS.   October 3, 1882.

Vol. XI.   Single Number.   PUBLISHED WEEKLY BY BEADLE AND ADAMS,
No. 98 WILLIAM STREET, NEW YORK.   Price, 5 Cents.   No. 271.

THE HUGE HUNTER; or, THE STEAM MAN OF THE PRAIRIES.

BY EDWARD S. ELLIS.

AUTHOR OF "THE BOY MINERS," "SETH JONES," "BILL BIDDON," ETC., ETC., ETC.

"BEGORRAH, BUT IT'S THE OULD DIVIL, HITCHED TO HIS THROTTIN' WAGING, WID HIS OULD WIFE BOWLDING THE REINS!" EXCLAIMED MICKEY.

An odd combination of the western and science fiction story, Edward Ellis' *The Steam Man of the Prairies* introduced the young inventors genre to the dime novel universe.

at first by steam and later by electricity.[3] With these fantastic devices, secret treasure troves were uncovered, lost cities found and evil villains foiled. These stories reflected the attitude of 19th century Western culture towards technological advances. As the next century approached, new inventions such as the telephone and electric lights seemed to bring nothing but good. Pollution was only just starting to impact the largest cities, and no one seemed to fully appreciate that the high body counts of the Civil War were due to technological improvements in weaponry. The common view was that technology was unequivocally beneficial and would inevitably lead mankind into a utopia — a view that would remain prevalent until shattered by the horrors of the First World War. The young inventor stories played into this optimism and filled the pockets of publishers with nickels and dimes.

The most successful of the young inventors was Frank Reade, Jr., whose long series of adventures were printed by publisher Frank Tousey. Young Reade was the son of a famous inventor who carried on the family tradition himself by inventing countless numbers of bizarre devices, beginning with his own version of a steam-powered man in his premiere adventure. Another Reade invention was an electric horse armed with torpedoes, which he used to hunt for treasure in Peru. Other characters from this genre included Jack Wright (who once pursued Jesse James in an electric carriage equipped with pneumatic weapons) and, of course, Tom Edison, Jr. (who once destroyed an undersea pirate base with his submersible "Sea Spider").

All these inventors were young because many dime novel readers (though certainly not all) were young as well. Though no reliable statistics exist, in general, children and teenagers devoured dime novels as eagerly as adults.[4] Boy geniuses, dictated the logic of the publishing world, gave younger readers someone with whom they could more easily identify.

Youthful heroes also began to pop up elsewhere in the dime novel universe. In 1866, a young Unitarian minister named Horatio Alger, Jr., suffering from depression and under the shadow of a sex scandal, was forced to leave the ministry. He turned to writing to support himself, and became one of the most widely read wordsmiths of his time. Alger wrote over 100 dime novels, each of them a variation of the same theme. A young boy or girl (or one of each), orphaned or homeless (or both), and more often than not pursued by criminals, overcomes all adversity by remaining honest and optimistic and often fortuitously rescuing some rich guy from beneath the hooves of a runaway horse.

Alger's stories today seem plodding and styleless, but at the time he struck a nerve in his readers and an estimated 100 to 300 million copies of his books sold during his 30-year writing career. Whatever his moral failings when he was a minister, Alger really believed in the virtues of honesty and generosity stressed in his novels. Certainly he lived by what he wrote. His novels brought him a lot of money, but he died in near poverty — in part because he gave away so much of what he earned to those who seemed to need it more.

Perhaps the single most successful young hero was Frank Merriwell, whose career lasted beyond the dime novels into comic strips, films and radio. The first Merriwell story was "Frank Merriwell, or First Days at Fardale," published in April 1896 by Street and Smith. It was a huge success and was followed by about 1,000 sequels[5] that often sold 200,000 copies per week.

Merriwell was a student, attending first a prep school and later Yale. He was a star athlete, playing just about every sport. He was also an honor student, honest, brave, resourceful, and prone to getting kidnapped a lot.

Often he was kidnapped by gamblers just before the big game. He'd always escape, of course, arriving at the game just in time to kick a field goal or hit a home run. Frank stumbled into all sorts of other adventures as well, both at school or during his fairly regular travels abroad. He foiled the evil plans of many a thief and saboteur, showed many an errant youth the error of their ways, and was such an all-around fine fellow that you find yourself guiltily wishing he'd just once lose his temper and cuss someone out.

About 900 of the 1,000 Merriwell stories were penned by William Gilbert Patten, a prototypical professional writer who could regularly and competently give a publisher something publishable. Like Alger, Patten seemed to take the moral tone of his work seriously. A better writer than Alger, he endowed the Merriwell stories with occasional moments of real emotional impact. In "Frank Merriwell's Nobility, or the Tragedy of the Ocean Tramp" (April 22, 1899), Frank risks his life to rescue from a sinking ship a man who had several times tried to murder him. Despite stilted dialogue and a contrived situation, the incident still manages to come across as just a little bit touching. Frank was a gosh darn good guy, and his stories can still be fun to read.

Congruent with the settlement of the American West was the increasingly rapid growth of cities. Small cities grew large, and large cities grew huge, as the Industrial Age brought with it the seemingly endless construction of factories, warehouses and transportation systems, thus creating new jobs by the thousands. So, while Westerns remained popular, it wasn't long before the dime novel universe felt the need for an urban hero. There was no conscious decision by any of the publishers to fill this need, or to choose what sort of hero the cities would be given, but the evolution of popular fiction sometimes follows an inevitable logic. Growing urban populations brought growing urban crime rates, so new villains— muggers, smugglers and gang leaders— were now available as fodder for new stories. The hero, then, would be someone dedicated to fighting such men; someone who could bring the marvelous benefits of modern technology to bear on this fight. And so the detective story, created out of Edgar Allan Poe's blood-red imagination just a few decades before, gained a permanent niche in the public consciousness.

Detectives actually began popping up in dime novels fairly quickly, usually within Western or frontier stories. Edward Ellis contributed a couple of these, though no one story in this growing trend was as influential as *The Steam Man of the Prairies*. It was more of a steady build-up, like water against a dam, as the detective hero population continued to grow. Eventually, detective fiction burst forth into a separate genre that would soon outsell the Western.

The first regular series featuring a detective began in June 1872, when "Old Sleuth, the Detective" appeared in *The Fireside Companion* #241. The Old Sleuth (not actually old— that was simply his favorite disguise) was typical of the dime novel detective. He was fearless, strong, able to outfight half-a-dozen bad guys at a time, and— most importantly— he was a master of disguise. With a quick dab of putty, a fake beard and a reversible coat, the Old Sleuth could change identities in the space of a few seconds. He could become a non-entity, unnoticed as he tailed you across town, or he could become your best friend, imitating voice and mannerisms so perfectly you are fooled completely up until the moment he pulls off the disguise and arrests you.

During the 1880s and 1890s, Old Sleuth was joined by hundreds of detective heroes, mostly male but occasionally female. There was Harlem Jack, the Office Boy Detective; Old Bullion; Young Sleuth (no relation); Old Cap Collier; Round Kate; the Bell-Boy Detective; Old Snap; Old Thunderbolt; and so on.[6] Most shared the same qualities of courage, skill and mastery of disguise. Many were private detectives, often independently wealthy and thus free to investigate any sort of crime they happened to stumble across.

Certain aspects of the modern urban environment were commonly used in many of these stories to help make them logistically believable. Railroads, mass transit and eventually automobiles made it possible for the

DOUBLE THE CIRCULATION OF ANY FIVE-CENT LIBRARY PUBLISHED

NICK CARTER
NICK CARTER IN VARIOUS DISGUISES
LIBRARY
The Best 5 Cent Library of Detective Stories.

PRICE 5 CENTS

PRICE 5 CENTS

Entered According to Act of Congress, in the Year 1892, by Street & Smith, in the Office of the Librarian of Congress, Washington, D. C.
Entered as Second-class Matter at the New York, N. Y., Post Office.   January 5, 1895.   Issued Weekly. Subscription Price, $2.50 per Year.   January 5, 1895

No. 179.   STREET & SMITH, Publishers,   NEW YORK.   29 Rose St., N. Y.   5 Cents.

The Counterfeiter's Gold Tooth;
Or, Nick Carter's Crooked Correspondent.

BY THE AUTHOR OF "NICK CARTER."

NICK TRIED TO SPRING ASIDE, AS A DARK PIT YAWNED AT HIS FEET, BUT BEFORE HE COULD FREE HIMSELF FROM THE
OUTLAW, BOTH WERE CARRIED DOWNWARD AT A TREMENDOUS RATE.

By the late 1870s, a new urban hero — the detective — had overtaken the cowboy and
frontiersman in popularity.

hero to travel quickly from Point A to Point B while following up clues or tailing suspects. Telegraphs and telephones simplified problems of communications and helped in the acquisition of information. All this made it possible to keep detective stories fast-paced and (hopefully) exciting.

Still another shared trait was the method of investigation used by the detectives. There was virtually never any Sherlock Holmes–style deductive reasoning, though some dime novels made a few poor attempts at this after the Holmes stories began appearing. Instead, the identities of the criminals were usually known as the story began, and it was just a matter of gathering evidence. This was done almost exclusively by following the suspects (in various disguises, of course) and eavesdropping on their conversations through keyholes and open windows. Most detectives would have to dodge several assassination attempts or escape from a death trap or two before finally bringing the bad guys to justice.

What's interesting is not that most of these stories today seem dull and repetitious, but that a small number of them are still mildly entertaining. With most of them at 32 pages or less in length, a well-written dime novel mystery can hold your interest just long enough to satisfy. Certainly they did so in the late 19th century, with some series running for decades.

Two of the most long-lived detective heroes were Nick Carter and Old King Brady. Carter, in particular, was an astonishing commercial success, running nearly three decades in several successive dime novel series, then crossing over into the pulps, radio, and both silent and sound movies. Nick was even resurrected in the 1960s as a James Bond clone in a paperback adventure series.

The first Nick Carter story, a multi-part serial entitled *The Old Detective's Pupil, or the Mysterious Crime of Madison Square*, began in the September 18, 1886, issue of the *New York Weekly*. When we first meet Nick, we learn that his father has been training him since boyhood to be the world's greatest detective, driving him to physical and mental perfection. (Fortunately, Nick did not develop any secret desires to play baseball or dance ballet while growing up, and was perfectly happy with his predestined lot in life.) But the elder Carter is soon murdered. Nick's first case involves finding the killers.

Nick was nicknamed the "little Hercules" because he was enormously strong (he could "fell an ox with one blow"), despite his diminutive stature. He was also a master of disguise (of course), fluent in many languages and an expert in a wide range of often obscure subjects. Week after week he employed his many talents to battle a wide variety of criminals. Most stories were set in or around New York City, and his most common adversaries were probably urban gang leaders. But Nick and his assistants traveled all over the world and went up against madmen and super-criminals of all sorts. Nick even acquired his own arch-enemy — an evil genius and serial killer named Doctor Quartz.

The bulk of the Nick Carter dime novels were written by Frederick van Rensselaer Dey. Like William Patten, Dey was one of those incredibly prolific writers capable of churning out a readable 30,000-word story in just a few days. Dey contributed over 1,000 Nick Carter stories.[7]

Unlike Nick Carter, Old King Brady only rarely left the Northeastern United States. First appearing in 1885, Brady was different from other detective heroes in several ways. He was a Roman Catholic, unusual for a fictional hero in those days of religious and racial stereotyping. He was not a master of disguise, using them only sparingly to hide his identity from casual observers. He wasn't super-strong and he made frequent mistakes. But he was intelligent and had a keen grasp of human nature. The Brady stories were primitive police procedurals, following the quick-thinking Irishman as he methodically hunted down his criminal prey.[8]

The most popular Brady adventures were written by Francis W. Doughty. Doughty was known for his realistic depictions of the locations he used in his stories. Whether Brady was in New York or Boston or elsewhere, that particular city would be accurately described, with the story unfolding along real streets and alleyways. Doughty was thus able to give the Brady stories an appreciable sense of realism, despite contrived dialogue and a typical dime novel over-dependence on coincidence to move the plot along.

3. Birth of the Pulps

By the time the 19th century rolled over into the 20th, the dime novel was in decline. A change in postal regulations delivered the most devastating blow to the format. Dime novels no longer qualified for 2nd Class postal rates, forcing the publishers to pay another one or two cents per issue to ship them. For an item that sold for a nickel or a dime, this was a ruinous rise in overhead. Dime novels began to fade away.

But the public's appetite for fiction was far from sated. In 1896, a publisher named Frank A. Munsey came up with a new and successful format through which to feed this appetite.

In 1882, Munsey began a weekly magazine for children called *The Golden Argosy*. At first, it didn't do well. Munsey stuck with it, though, shortening the name to *Argosy* and changing its format, size and target audience several times. For 13 years *Argosy* limped along, selling just enough issues to keep it financially afloat.

Eventually, Munsey tried still another format change. He realized the public was still clamoring for fiction, and he reasoned that nobody would care what a magazine looked like on the outside as long as they liked the stories inside. In October 1896, he published an all-fiction issue of *Argosy*, printed on cheap pulp paper with a nearly-bare yellow cover. It's only selling point was 135,000 words of fiction and poetry. That proved to be enough. *Argosy*'s circulation immediately doubled to 80,000 per week and eventually reached 700,000. The magazine would go on to enjoy a nearly fifty year run.

By 1919 the dime novel was just about gone. That year, Street and Smith converted the dime novel *Buffalo Bill Weekly* into the pulp *Western Story Weekly*. Four years earlier, a similar fate had been met by the seemingly immortal Nick Carter, when *Nick Carter Weekly* (dime novel) became

THE
RAILROAD
MAN'S
MAGAZINE

A Red-Hot Magazine for
the Railroad Man or for
any one else who knows a
Good Thing when he sees it

OCTOBER

THE FRANK A. MUNSEY COMPANY, NEW YORK

The premiere issue of *The Railroad Man's Magazine* introduced the idea of specialty
pulps.

Soon, other pulps, such as *Sea Stories Magazine*, were carving out their own literary niches.

Detective Story Weekly (pulp).[1] Two of the most popular dime novel heroes were gone, at least for the time being. But a new generation of heroes and anti-heroes were poised to take over.

Munsey followed up *Argosy*'s success by starting another all-fiction pulp entitled *All-Story*. Not surprisingly, other publishers quickly copied Munsey: *Adventure, The Popular Magazine, Top Notch, The Monthly Story Magazine, Tip Top* and many others soon crowded the newsstands.[2] Competition soon made it evident that it *did* sometimes matter what the magazine looked like on the outside. Publishers needed some visible hook to make their magazines stand out. The hook they used helped usher in an extraordinary, vibrant era of American illustration. Color covers, often done by talented artists such as N.C Wyeth and J. Allen St. John, became common, occasionally outshining the fiction they illustrated. But we, like Frank Munsey, will remain concerned primarily with what was inside the pulps—an endless variety of fiction designed purely to entertain its readers.

As well as introducing the first general fiction pulp, Frank Munsey was also the first to try a specialty fiction pulp. In October 1906 he published *The Railroad Man's Magazine*. Though a seemingly odd choice for subject material, it proved successful and once again started a trend. By the 1920s, specialty pulps ranging in subjects from sea stories to love stories to sports stories were common.

It was this variety that helped the pulps eventually produce fiction of a quality and cultural longevity that had eluded the dime novels. There were hundreds of magazines printing thousands of new stories each month; there were publishers willing to take chances on new genres in their efforts to attract readers; there were fresh takes on old ideas. Sooner or later, sheer chance would dictate that something truly excellent would see print. Innovative editors could not help but eventually stumble across a few masterful writers. In the end, American literature was forever enriched.

4. The Western and Max Brand

The Western remained a commercially viable genre, perhaps the most popular of the early pulps. It wasn't long before certain western writers began to rise above the pack. Zane Grey was one of the pulps' earliest success stories. His melodramatic but eagerly-read novels were being serialized in *Argosy*, *Popular* and other pulps by 1909, and it was soon apparent that his name on the cover would guarantee an increase in sales. By 1917, though, Grey had "graduated" to better paying slick magazines such as *Harpers* and *Ladies Home Journal*.[1] Pulp editors were sorry to lose access to his work, but other writers would soon show equal or greater skill in turning out exciting westerns. One of these scribes was a young man named Frederick Shiller Faust, who felt that writing for the pulps was beneath him but who did it better than nearly everybody else.

Frederick Faust was born in Seattle in 1892, the son of a failed attorney. As a child, Faust was a prodigious reader, having discovered Goethe, Walter Scott, Thomas Malory, and Greek and Roman mythology by age ten.

He was orphaned at thirteen and spent his teenage years earning a living as a laborer on farms and ranches. In 1911 he received a scholarship to Berkeley. His time in college proved valuable to him, as he was able to improve his writing skills. But he never received a diploma. Faust was prone to satirizing the faculty in campus publications and often led students on "drunken forays" into San Francisco. In 1915 he was tossed out of school.

Faust's classical education, reading preferences and writing talent had given him the drive to become a classical poet. But there's little money in poetry, laudable as the profession might otherwise be. In 1917, living in

New York and badly needing some ready cash, he gritted his teeth and began writing fiction for pulp magazines.

Faust was not proud of this and used a variety of pseudonyms to sign his work, saving his real name for his poetry. But he was good at it, as well as incredibly prolific. By the time of his death in 1944, he had produced at least 30,000,000 words of fiction for the pulps.[2] Even at one or two cents a word, that adds up. By 1925, Faust was no longer living in a New York City hovel, but in a villa in Florence, Italy.

His first western was written at the suggestion of Robert H. Davies, chief executive at Munsey Publications. Faust, using the pseudonym Max Brand, produced a novel entitled *Untamed*.

Untamed was first published in 1918 as a serial in *All-Story*. The following year it was republished as a best-selling book. In 1920 it was made into a Tom Mix film. Frederick Faust might have felt he was selling his literary soul, but as Max Brand his future as a writer of popular fiction was assured.[3]

What made *Untamed* and its two sequels stand out was a combination of atmosphere and characterization. All three books were drenched in a sense of foreboding that gave the tragic denouement of the third book a strong emotional impact. Added to this was a protagonist, Whistlin' Dan Barry, who would have been interesting even if stuck in a more standard story.

Whistlin' Dan is short and quiet and socially awkward. Men often mistake him as cowardly or just plain stupid until they tick him off. Dan was found as a child wandering in the desert. When asked where he came from, he just waved his hand about vaguely, taking in all the wilderness around him.

Dan, in fact, is a part of nature — a creature of myth separate from the rest of mankind. Brand compares him outright to the Greek god Pan; he's a feral being, with an affinity towards animals and an apathy towards much of the human race. His nickname derives from his tendency to whistle, producing "a thrilling and unearthly music" that seems to harmonize with the sounds of the wild.

By the time Dan grew up, he had acquired a pair of unusual companions: a wolf named Black Bart and a horse named Satan. Both animals are still wild, but both are devoted to Dan, obeying him in everything and able to understand him when he speaks to them. (This sounds a little silly when baldly stated, but it works in the context of the story.) Dan's also in love with Kate Cumberland, the daughter of the rancher who raised him.

But trouble starts when Dan meets an outlaw named Joe Silent. Silent

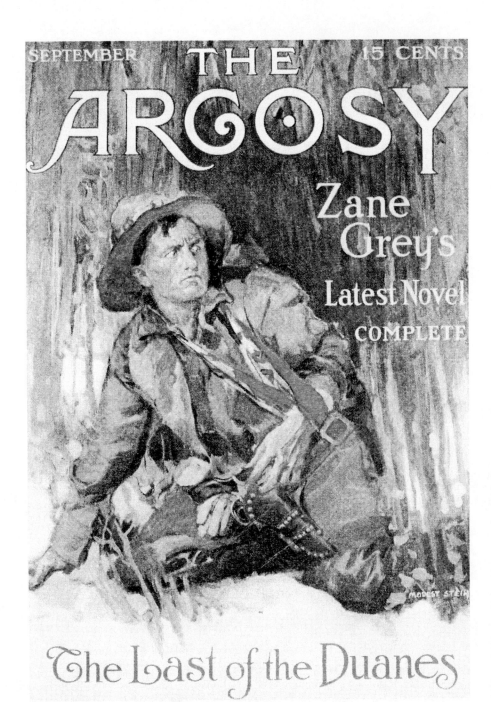

The September 1914 issue of *Argosy* featured one of Zane Grey's many pulp appearances. Westerns in general, and authors like Grey in particular, remained popular throughout the pulp era.

cold-cocks Dan, who is then driven to track down and kill Silent. Kate desperately urges him away from this course, but Dan has no choice. He is who he is—a child of nature who *must* follow his instincts. "I've never forgot the taste [of blood in my mouth]," he says. "It's goin' to be washed out ... or else made redder."

Dan pursues Silent and his gang, while Kate wiles away the time by getting kidnapped by those same outlaws. *Untamed* climaxes with a gruesome saloon encounter between Dan and Silent. After Silent's death, Dan rides off with his wolf and horse, unable to tame his wild instincts even for the woman he loves.

The second Whistlin' Dan novel, *The Night Horseman*, still portrays Dan as a slave to his wildness. The story is light on action but thick with emotional tension. It ends with Dan and Kate finally getting married; but Kate's dying father predicts trouble for them both: "...[Kate's] trail would go one way and Dan's would go another, and pretty soon your love wouldn't be nothin' but a big wind blowing between two mountains—and all it would do would be to freeze up the blood in your hearts."

He turns out to be right. The last novel in the series is *The Seventh Man*, published in 1921. This is easily the best of the three, with Brand's insights into his characters continuing to improve. The novel starts by introducing a new character, Vic Gregg, who returns to town after months in the wilderness, eager to see the girl he loves.

Brand realistically tracks Vic's thoughts and emotional state as he has a jealousy-induced argument with his girl, drinks a little too much, kills his supposed rival in a gun fight and abruptly finds himself a fugitive from a posse made up of men he considers his friends.

Dan and Kate, meanwhile, have been living in an isolated cabin and have a five-year-old daughter named Joan. Black Bart and Satan are both still around as well. In fact, Joan often climbs on the wolf's back and demands a ride—she has the same wild instincts as her dad.

Dan meets Vic by chance and impulsively decides to help him, riding Vic's horse to draw away the posse. But a member of the posse kills the borrowed horse. To Dan, this is as bad or worse as killing a man. He kills one of the posse in return and vows to hunt the rest of them down.

This makes Dan a wanted man and effectively ends his life with Kate. But, though he has lost his wife, he won't give up his daughter. He brings Joan into the mountains with him, making a cave their new home. Joan is perfectly happy with this arrangement, adapting to a feral life without effort or regret.

Kate and several friends manage to steal Joan back while Dan is busy hunting down members of the posse. Dan comes after them. In the end,

EVERY WEEK
APRIL 2, 1921

Western Story Magazine

Vol. 16
No. 2

15 Cents

BIG, CLEAN STORIES OF OUTDOOR LIFE

Street & Smith's *Western Story Magazine* was one of the better Western pulps. Max Brand's strong stories often appeared here.

Kate takes the only action left to her to save her daughter from a life as an animal. She guns down the man she loves.

The Seventh Man has a strong plot, a lot of tension and good characterizations. Some of its most notable points are:

1.) Little Joan. She's a believable little girl, which makes her descent into wildness downright creepy.

2.) The use of supporting characters. Some of the men Dan kills are not clear-cut villains and are often likable. We may understand that Dan has no choice in the actions he takes, but we're never allowed to feel unfettered empathy with him. Emotional issues generated by the story are complex and interesting.

3.) A climactic chase scene involves posses from several towns trying to run Dan down, organizing their efforts via newly-installed telephone lines. It's modern technology trying to rope in the god Pan. It's also an exciting action set piece.

Brand continued to produce both westerns and other fiction by the ton. In his westerns, he often returned to the concept of the feral man, though usually not to the extreme of Dan Barry.

In *Blood on the Sand*, published in 1935 in *Western Story Magazine*, the protagonist is Dave Reagan. Dave lives with his cousins, who treat him like dirt and consider him a half-wit, a view shared by the rest of the local community. Dave does all the chores and food-gathering for the household. His cousins also subcontract his services to the local blacksmith and keep all the pay for themselves.

Once again, Brand's characterizations are very good. Dave has very low self-esteem and does not recognize in himself the skill and intelligence he possesses. Even later on in the story, when he earns respect and admiration from others, he initially misinterprets their attitude as mockery. It's all perfectly believable given Dave's background.

The book opens by introducing us first to Gray Cloud, a wolf with a taste for cattle, who has avoided all hunters and killed or driven off every hunting dog sent after him. Gray Cloud is something of a legend, and there's a $2500 bounty on his pelt.

When Gray Cloud is finally caught in a trap, he's found by Dave. Dave recognizes the wolf; but rather than killing him, he saves him from the trap. He then saves the wolf from a grass fire and brings him home. When his cousins try to kill Gray Cloud for the bounty, Dave flees with the animal into the wilderness.

It's here we discover that Dave is significantly smarter than anyone, including the reader, thought. Dave's verbal awkwardness had made him seem like he really was one light bulb short of a well-lighted room, but now we learn differently. Without supplies or tools, Dave salvages some iron from a wrecked prairie schooner and fashions what he needs. He builds a cabin and is soon living a contented life as a hermit.

His only friend is Gray Cloud, who stays with him voluntarily. The two establish a rapport, and eventually Dave can communicate with the wolf silently, through gestures and expressions. Together they make an extremely effective hunting team.

Eventually, Dave's contentment is shattered by a couple of travelers, one of whom is a woman named Mary. Mary catches a fever and must be nursed back to health, giving Dave ample opportunity to fall in love with her. When she gets well, he follows her back home. Mary is perfectly happy with this; she recognizes his true worth. Her father, though, is *not* happy with the idea of her marrying some backwoods clod. He sets Dave up to be robbed and humiliated by outlaws.

Dave gets the better of the outlaws, earning their respect and forcing Mary's dad to realize he is indeed worthy of her.

Blood on the Sand flows quickly, with the action revolving around a number of brutal fist fights seeded throughout the story. Dave's gradual realization of his own worth comes across as a natural progression of real emotion. His unlikely relationship with Gray Cloud also seems natural.

Additional bits of good characterization are also present. Mary's father, for instance, is a bit of a blowhard, but he obviously loves his daughter and has the moral courage to admit his mistakes. Also noteworthy is Brand's recognition of the injustices suffered by Native Americans in the Old West, something relatively rare in Western fiction at that time. Dave befriends an Indian named Walking Thunder. At one point, he's complaining about his lot in life. Walking Thunder replies, "I am a man with red skin, and I live in a nation of white people. What is your curse compared to mine?" In the context of the conversation, Walking Thunder is not himself complaining or expressing bitterness, but simply putting things in proper perspective.[4]

Frederick Faust continued to produce quality fiction until the Second World War. He wasn't the only writer to add realistic characterizations and emotions to the Western. Others, both at the same time and later, did this as well or better. But he was an important part of the maturation of the genre, and his books have remained in print for most of a century.

Faust was killed in action while serving as a war correspondent in Italy.

5. *Adventure*: Pirates, Gladiators and Sudden Death for the Discerning Reader

In the long term, it was the editor rather than any one writer who would make or break a magazine. A good editor recognizes talented writers, of course, and would not hesitate to capitalize on the name of a successful scribe. But to maintain sales from issue to issue, an editor had to give his magazine its own voice, letting it speak to the readers in a way that would continue to bring them back for more.

Adventure most definitely had its own voice. It began publication in November 1910, but really took off the next year, when Albert Sullivan Hoffman became editor.

Adventure published, well, adventure stories— the sort of thing that many pulps were already doing with reasonable skill and that many literary critics automatically dismissed as dreck. But Hoffman believed that the adventure story, when done well, could equal any other sort of literature in quality. He would set high standards for the fiction he published, demanding character-driven plots and realistic settings. He bought fiction on the assumption that *Adventure*'s readers were as smart as he was. And he himself was awfully smart.

With a minuscule budget, Hoffman could not afford established writers, so he began to encourage new ones, building up what he would term his "Writers Brigade." He had a good eye for talent, and his Brigade consistently produced worthy material. W.C. Tuttle and Walt Coburn gave him Westerns. Harold Lamb created the blood-soaked character of Khlit the Cossack. Arthur O. Friel and Gordon Young took readers to the jungles of South America and the islands of the South Pacific, respectively.

Many of these writers are pretty much forgotten today, though their stories can still entertain enormously. In a moment, we'll look in detail at two other *Adventure* contributors who are unjustly forgotten. But let's first finish up with the magazine in general.

Even after attracting a pool of talented writers, Hoffman continued to build *Adventure* into something special. In June 1912 he introduced "The Camp Fire," a section where letters from readers were printed, along with comments from writers. Here arguments raged freely across the page. Was the geographical setting of a particular story described accurately? Did the sharpshooter in another story use the correct musket for the time period portrayed? Hoffman had attracted deeply loyal readers who themselves contributed intelligent, readable prose in the form of their letters.[1]

Other departments included "Ask Adventure," a question and answer section about outdoor life, and "Lost Trails," which assisted readers in renewing contact with old friends. All this helped make *Adventure* readers feel like they were in an exclusive club. They were never spoken down to; they were assumed to be intelligent; and they were always entertained.

Hoffman edited *Adventure* for sixteen commercially and artistically successful years, leaving the magazine in 1927. During the last half of his tenure, he helped introduce two important writers to American readers: Rafael Sabatini and Talbot Mundy.

Rafael Sabatini was born in Italy in 1875, the son of an Italian father and English mother. He learned to speak English at a young age, and learned to write English with remarkable style by the time he reached adulthood. In 1904, his first novel, *The Tavern Knight*, was published in England. Sabatini had a talent for producing fun historical romances. Over the next fifteen years he wrote over a dozen of them, as well as a couple of nonfiction biographies. His prose was just a little bit flowery, giving it a rhythm that seemed appropriate to the subject matter and forming passages that often beg to be read aloud. His dialogue was sharp and trenchant, often serving as much as the action set pieces to increase a story's level of tension or suspense. His characters were well-drawn. His heroes were men of honor and quick temper who were perfect fits for the situations into which Sabatini thrust them. His villains were appropriately evil, but had individual personalities of their own. His women were smart, vibrant and, inevitably, really good-looking.

Sabatini entered the American fiction market through *Adventure*, which in 1921 printed a nine-part serial about Captain Peter Blood.

If you have a name as dramatic-sounding as Peter Blood, I suppose you're going to end up living a life of danger and violence whether you want to or not.

This was certainly true of Sabatini's protagonist. Born in Ireland in the 17th century, Peter Blood trained as a doctor, but spent much of his early manhood giving in to his restless nature. He wandered around Europe, fighting as a soldier in a number of wars. He learned seamanship in the Dutch navy and spent a couple of years as a prisoner of war in Spain. Finally, having seen more than his share of bloodshed, he gave up adventuring and moved to the quiet English village of Bridgewater.

So determined was he to live the theoretically tranquil life of a country doctor that, when a rebellion against the tyrannical rule of James II rose up pretty much just outside his front door, he chose to ignore it.

But tranquility eluded him. When Blood treated a wounded man who happened to be a rebel, he was arrested for treason. Soon, Blood and a number of other men were transported to the West Indies to be sold as slaves.

All this happens in a few brief chapters, described in a prose that hurries the story along at just the right pace and includes a superbly written trial scene involving an embittered judge who— knowing that he himself is fatally ill — is determined to destroy as many lives as possible before his own painful end.

Arriving in Jamaica, Blood and most of his fellow prisoners are bought by the cold-hearted Colonel Bishop[2] and set to work on his sugar plantation. Blood's skill as a doctor brings him to the attention of the island's governor, who suffers from the gout. Soon, he's better dressed and fed than the plantation workers, and is allowed, to an extent, to move freely about the town.

But though Blood's lot is better than the other slaves, he's still a slave. He uses his relative freedom to plot a mass escape.

Oh yes, during this time he also meets Colonel Bishop's niece, a lovely, intelligent young woman named Arabella. The two are soon in love, though they spend much of the remainder of the story convinced they actually hate each other.[3]

Blood's original escape plan is foiled when a Spanish warship attacks and captures the town. Blood quickly improvises a new plan. He and his fellow slaves sneak aboard the warship while most of the Spaniards are ashore. By the next morning, Blood is in possession of a ship, a treasure (ransom that had been paid to the Spanish to spare the town), and a crew of wanted criminals.

There was really nothing to do after this but turn pirate. Blood does so and turns out to be really, really good at it. Much of the saga now traces his growing success as a buccaneer. His original ship, which he christens the *Arabella*, becomes the flagship of a small fleet. He directs his attention mostly against the Spanish, his piratical adventures culminating in a raid against the city of Maracaybo. Trapped inside the harbor there by a Spanish fleet, he uses several audacious strategies to fight his way free.

Soon after that, Blood becomes involved in some complex political maneuvering. He's recruited by the French in a war against the Spanish, betrayed by an arrogant French admiral, then recruited by the English (who have in the meantime deposed the evil King James) to save Jamaica from the same Frenchman. While all this is going on, he rescues Arabella from a Spanish ship, only to convince himself that she is in love with someone else. Even heroes need to be dope-slapped from time to time.

The story climaxes in a wonderfully described sea battle as Blood's flagship attacks two French ships in Port Royale's harbor. Afterwards, Blood and Arabella *finally* admit their love for each other, Colonel Bishop (who has been obsessively chasing Blood for most of the story) is disgraced, and the reader finds himself jumping back to re-read the climactic battle because it's just that good.

Captain Blood was a big hit with *Adventure*'s readers and was reprinted the next year as a best-selling novel.[4] Editor Hoffman had added another member to his Writer's Brigade. In 1922, Hoffman reprinted Sabatini's novel *The Sea Hawk*, first published in England seven years earlier, to equal acclaim.

Sabatini's commercial success soon priced him out of the pulps. By 1930 he had graduated to the better-paying slicks, with new Captain Blood stories appearing in *Cosmopolitan*. But it was the pulps that first introduced him to American readers. His skillful combination of blood and thunder and style and wit truly enriched the genre of adventure fiction.

Many of his books have, unfortunately, been out of print for years, though there is an occasional new edition of his better-known works. That's too bad, since his work stands up to the best modern action novels and still deserves to be read. Rafael Sabatini is an author most definitely in need of rediscovery.

Talbot Mundy's real name wasn't Talbot Mundy, but William Lancaster Gribbon. He left his old name behind around 1910 or so, about the same time he left behind a rather sordid life style.

Mundy (we'll leave his original name behind as well) had been an ivory poacher and a con artist, who at times seemed to have had one or two more wives than is strictly allowed by Western law. The details of his early life aren't always clear, but Mundy definitely was not the world's nicest person.

But then, while he was in New York City, someone gave him a cracked skull. Once again, the details of the event aren't clear. But whatever the original cause, the event itself seemed to have convinced Mundy to change his ways. He turned away from low-level crime and tried his hand at writing.[5]

His first published work was in *Adventure*—a nonfiction piece entitled "Pig-sticking in India," published in the February 1911 issue. He soon followed this up with fiction of excellent quality, becoming one of the most popular of Hoffman's Brigade.

Most of Mundy's stories were set in modern India or Africa, but his best effort was an epic set nearly 2000 years in the past—a series of stories recounting the adventures of Tros of Samothrace, a sailor who juggled trying to save a kingdom, foil the evil machinations of the world's most powerful and clever man, avenge his murdered father, and build a ship that would sail around the world. He sometimes succeeds and sometimes fails, but always over the course of a narrative that drips with realism and honest human emotion. It can be argued that the Tros saga was the best thing ever published in *Adventure*.

The first Tros story saw print in the February 10, 1925, issue. It begins with Tros newly arrived in Britain, accompanied by his one-eyed servant Conops. He has come reluctantly as a scout for Julius Caesar, who holds Tros' father captive to induce the sailor to do his will.

Caesar's will, in this case, was for Tros to cross the Channel from Gaul in a Roman ship and point out safe harbors for landing an invasion force. But good luck has allowed Tros and his servant to escape the Romans.

Tros makes contact with the local political and religious leaders, with whom he trades information. And so, in a few short chapters, Mundy expertly introduces us to the main characters, explains the tumultuous local politics, and gives us a sense of Tros' stern character, driving ambitions and iron-hard sense of morality.

From this grows a series of character-driven adventures published over the course of the next year. Tros makes friends with Caswallon, the king of the Britons. Caswallon wants to fight Caesar, but must also appease the local chieftains, who are more-or-less politically autonomous—and many of them would rather appease Caesar than fight. Caesar does briefly land an army in Britain, but Tros wrecks the Roman fleet and forces Caesar to retreat. Then, using a ship disguised as a Roman bireme and some forged documents, Tros manages to rescue his father, only to watch him die from the tortures the Romans had inflicted on him.[6]

Outguessing Caesar, Tros attacks and wrecks four more Roman ships and nearly captures Caesar himself. Then it's back to Britain, where they run into a band of Northern pirates. Tros defeats the Northmen and induces them to join forces with him by marrying the daughter of their chief.

Tros isn't much for the softer emotions, but his new wife, Helma, proves to be intelligent, brave and resourceful. Tros gradually and only somewhat reluctantly falls in love with her. In the meantime, he begins to build an extraordinary ship of his own design, a huge vessel bristling with catapults and arrow-firing engines that will allow him to sail around the world.

This causes more trouble. Tros has Caswallon's support, but Roman spies and rebellious chieftains are constant threats. Superstitious locals are a problem as well—people are understandably suspicious of Tros' absurd idea that the world is round.

As his great ship nears completion, both Helma and Caswallon's wife are kidnapped by agents of Caesar. Tros manages a rescue, but Helma is killed by a Roman arrow.

Soon after, Tros' ship, named the *Liafeil*, is completed and launched. To supplement his crew of Northmen and Britons, Tros captures two Roman ships manned by Spaniards and convinces them to join him. Then it's off first to the Spanish port of Gades, then to Rome itself, in an attempt to find a way to draw Caesar's attention away from Britain for good.

Political intrigue eventually goes badly. Events come to a bloody climax in the Roman arena, where Tros and some of his Northmen must fight, one after another, starving lions, three-score Numidian warriors and a phalanx of experienced gladiators.

They win, of course, earning their freedom. In the end, Tros is able to save Britain merely by delivering a message to Caesar, alerting him to the current political situation in Rome. Caesar's attention turns towards home to deal with the machinations of his arch-rival, Pompey. Britain is saved from the Roman yoke, at least for a century or so.

And Tros is free to pursue his dream. "'What shape is the earth? [he asks Caesar] Square? Round?'

"'I would like to know,' said Caesar.

"'I, too. But I *will* know! I will sail around the world!'"

The Tros saga is historical fiction at its best. The characters are completely believable—a set of both likable and dislikable men and women with attitudes and morals that fit the time and place in which they live.

The stories include equal doses of violence, intrigue, espionage and diplomacy, all leavened by an occasional dash of humor that grows naturally out of the situations and characters. And all of this is tied together as much by the shadow of Caesar as by the presence of Tros.

Mundy presents Caesar as an amoral and ruthless egomaniac, eager to conquer Britain in order to win more glory and increase his own power base. But Caesar is also brilliant, courageous and able to command fanatical loyalty among his own troops. He appears personally in the stories on only four or five brief occasions, usually at a climactic moment. But the threat of Caesar hangs over everything that happens, keeping tensions high and influencing nearly every decision the major characters make. He's one of the great villains of literature, as capable as he is dangerous.

Mundy's portrayal of Caesar generated quite a bit of comment from *Adventure*'s readers. Editor Hoffman's efforts to find an intelligent audience paid off here, as readers sent in letters defending Caesar and/or the Roman Empire in general. Mundy himself responded to these letters, defending his own less-generous view of ancient Rome. The result was a sincere and intelligent historical debate, perhaps another reason for considering Mundy's work the high point of the magazine.

Whether Tros made it around the world is a story that, sadly, remained unwritten. When Hoffman left *Adventure*, the editorial slant changed and no further Tros stories saw print until 1935. This later tale was a four-parter involving Tros in more political intrigue, this time revolving around Cleopatra. By the time it's over, Tros has ended up with another wife and is set to continue his circumnavigation of the earth. But Talbot Mundy died in 1940, and Tros' ship was never seen again.

The Tros saga was later collected, at different times, into either one large novel or a series of smaller novels. But they haven't been in print at all since the 1960s. Like Sabatini, Talbot Mundy needs rediscovering.

6. *Weird Tales*: Things That Bump into You in the Night

Weird Tales, like *Adventure*, was a magazine that had to wait for just the right editor to reach its full potential. Also like with *Adventure*, when that editor arrived, the result was the publication of some remarkable literature.

Weird Tales was founded in 1923 by Chicago-based publisher Jacob Clark Henneberger. Henneberger had made a bundle with a magazine called *College Humor* and was ready to try something new. Talking with several well-known Chicago writers, he discovered that many of them wanted to try their hands at stories "of an unconventional type"—stories of fantasy and horror. But no magazine at the time provided a steady market for such tales.

So Henneberger started *Weird Tales* and hired writer Edwin Baird to edit it. At first, things did not go well. Baird's tenure lasted about a year, with the magazine suffering from poor sales from the start. Though some excellent stories did appear, much of what Baird published was mediocre. He simply didn't have a good eye for quality fantasy storytelling.

Henneberger was losing money fast, but he wanted to save *Weird Tales* if he could. He sold the rights to *College Humor* and another magazine he also started in 1923 called *Detective Tales*. Baird left *Weird Tales* to edit *Detective* for its new owner.

That left Henneberger in need of a new editor for *Weird Tales*. He first offered the job to writer H.P. Lovecraft, whose short story "Dagon" had been one of the few highlights of the magazine's first year.

Lovecraft, though, did not want to move to Chicago. Henneberger then turned to Farnsworth Wright, music critic for the *Chicago Herald and Examiner*.

Wright accepted the job and soon began to prove his worth. He had excellent taste in fantasy literature,[1] and, like Albert Hoffman, he built up a cadre of writers he knew he could depend on. Wright did not hesitate to reject a story if he felt it didn't measure up, but he would often work with a writer to bring something with potential up to speed. He enjoyed discovering new talent as well. In 1933 he read a story from the "slush pile" written by Catherine L. Moore. He immediately declared it "C.L. Moore Day" and closed up shop to celebrate his new find.

The story was "Shambleau." If you were to look up the word "creepy" in a dictionary, a perfectly acceptable entry would be: "Just read 'Shambleau.'" It's set in the future — mankind has settled the solar system, and colonies reminiscent of Old West frontier towns have sprung up on Mars. "Shambleau" begins when the outlaw-spaceman Northwest Smith ("whose name is known and respected in every dive and wild outpost on a dozen wild planets") rescues a girl from a bloodthirsty mob. But it turns out that the mob had the right idea. The girl isn't really a girl, but an ancient alien vampire that feeds on the life force of its victims. Smith is seduced by the thing, which emanates a sense of evil so powerful that it arouses an irresistible sense of both repulsion and desire in him. He's saved only by the timely arrival of Yarol, his Venusian partner.

"Shambleau" was a hit with readers, and Moore provided more Northwest Smith stories, as well as equally popular tales of Jirel of Joiry, a medieval swordswoman with a tendency to encounter horrible supernatural dangers.

Another Wright discovery was Clark Ashton Smith, who wrote prose with a poetic rhythm in his tales of dark sorcery and ancient dying civilizations. Smith sold dozens of stories to *Weird Tales*, full of what pulp historian Lee Server called "...the poet's love of rare words and elaborate imagery. His best work has a narcotic, incantatory effect on the reader."[2]

A good example of Smith's work is "The Weird of Avoosl Wuthoqquan,"[3] published in the June 1932 issue. It's a short tale of a moneylender whose greed induces him to follow a pair of ensorcelled emeralds to a gruesome doom. In general terms, the eventual fate of the main character is easy to predict. We know he's going to die, even if we don't know what form his death will take. But Smith's ornate vocabulary and vivid imagery generate a strong sense of growing horror, while the bald, matter-of-fact final sentence gives the story a biting irony.

H.P. Lovecraft continued to be one of *Weird Tales'* most popular contributors, and his tales were published regularly until his death in 1937. His style was very much influenced by Poe. Like Poe — and like his contemporary, Clark Ashton Smith — Lovecraft had a talent for picking the perfect word or phrase to generate the appropriate atmosphere for his stories. "The oldest and strongest emotion of mankind is fear," he once wrote in an essay, "and the oldest and strongest kind of fear is of the unknown." So he created a world of horrible unknowns, lying barely hidden in the shadows around us or in the ground beneath us.

His most important story was "The Call of Cthulu," published in the February 1928 issue. In this story he introduced a mythos that tied many of his tales together. The earth, according to this mythos, had once been ruled by a race of powerful god-like beings that practiced evil magic. These Ancient Ones were eventually expelled from the earth or imprisoned deep underground or under the sea. Mankind rose up to take their place as the nominal rulers of the world.

But the Ancient Ones are still out there, and from time to time one of them attempts to return. When that happens, people die horribly, or unspeakable half-human monstrosities are sired and loosed on the countryside, or innocent men are warped into evil things, or wise men are driven insane. In each individual story, some evil thing may be destroyed or contained, but always with the knowledge that the Ancient Ones are out there and mankind is never quite safe from a collective fate much worse than death.

Lovecraft's work varied in quality, but his strongest stories, such as "The Dunwich Horror" or "The Shadow over Innsmouth," are the stuff of which nightmares are made — guaranteed to keep you awake at night.

Wright was open to all sorts of tales of the fantastic, not just the scary stuff. In 1928 he began publishing a series of science fiction stories by Edmund Hamilton featuring the Interstellar Patrol.

The first story was "Crashing Suns," in which an alien race attempts to ram their dying sun into Earth's sun in order to re-ignite it. This would have the unfortunate side effect of destroying mankind. The plot is foiled by the Interplanetary Patrol, but only after the main characters are captured, manage a violent escape, organize a battle fleet, fight a massive space battle and destroy the alien sun in the nick of time. And all this in a story that runs a mere 20,000 words or so.

During the course of the story, faster-than-light travel is discovered, so the Patrol changes from Interplanetary to Interstellar in later installments. But "Crashing Suns" is typical of Hamilton's science fiction work, both in *Weird Tales* and elsewhere. He never did anything small. It was never just a few lives or even a single planet at risk. It was always the entire solar system or, often, the entire galaxy. There was at least one more

DEC. — 25¢

Weird Tales

MYSTERIOUS   IMAGINATIVE   FANTASTIC

Buccaneers of Venus

The December 1932 issue of *Weird Tales* featured a scene from an interplanetary adventure on its cover, but the real highlight was its inclusion of Robert E. Howard's first Conan the Barbarian story.

attempt to crash another star into the Sun. There was a plot to burn the galaxy away with a fiery nebula, and another plot to black out all light in the galaxy with a giant cloud. Each time it was a scheme by yet another evil alien race. Each time, the Interstellar Patrol saves the day with only seconds to spare.

These regular threats of galactic genocide made for enormous fun. The science in Hamilton's stories never had anything to do with reality, but it had its own internal logic. His plots always jumped right to the point, allowing him to introduce one huge idea after another, generating a narrative current that carried his readers willingly along with him.

Robert E. Howard's first published work was "Spear and Fang," appearing in the July 1925 issue of *Weird Tales*. Howard was just nineteen at the time, but his voracious reading habit had already helped him develop into an effective writer. "Spear and Fang" is a competent tale of a Cro-Magnon man who rescues his lady love from a savage Neanderthal. Howard soon developed into another of Farnsworth Wright's most reliable contributors.

Howard's success as a writer, both within the pages of *Weird Tales* and elsewhere, sprang from his ability to vary the slant and content of his material in order to make it appealing to specific editors or magazines.[4] His prose was always recognizable as his own, but he could turn out a solid boxing tale for *Fight Stories* as proficiently as he could a pirate story for *Golden Fleece*.

In *Weird Tales* he provided intense, violent adventure, soaked equally in blood and the supernatural. Many of his stories for Wright involved the same characters—Puritan swordsman Solomon Kane, introspective barbarian-turned-king Kull, and (his most famous creation) Conan the Barbarian.

Barbarism was a common theme in many of Howard's stories. His main character was often an alien to true civilization and therefore (according to Howard) a more pure and honest human being. The idea was that when a barbarian hacked you to death and stole your gold, he was completely forthright about his intentions; whereas when a civilized man hacked you to death and stole your gold, he created some sort of moral justification for his crime. Civilization did not make us better people, but simply covered everything with a veneer of hypocrisy. Also, in a one-on-one fight, the barbarian could inevitably whip any civilized man.

What good all this does for the poor slob who was hacked to death for his gold is highly debatable, but if you accept Howard's concept for the time it takes to read one of his stories, you'll get along with him just fine.

Howard did not write objective history, nor did he seriously try to advance a specific social theory. He wrote to entertain the reader because he knew that was the only way to make a living as a pulp writer.

Superficially, many of Howard's characters seem similar. Most were physically strong and mind-numbingly brave. They were usually uninhibited by, and often contemptuous of, the rules of civilization. Perhaps most importantly, even when his protagonist was a thief or pirate or mercenary, Howard endowed him with some sort of moral code for which the character would die rather than violate.

But upon closer examination, Howard's characters did have individual personalities. Solomon Kane, for instance, was a 16th century Puritan most often found wandering across darkest Africa, battling both natural and unnatural enemies. Kane, a master swordsman, is brooding and humorless, driven by his faith to seek out evil and avenge the violated innocents of the world. He's introduced in "Red Shadows," published in 1928. Traveling through the French countryside, he comes across a dying girl who had been raped and stabbed when bandits raided her village. She gasps out her tale before dying. Kane rises from her body and:

"A dark scowl had settled on his somber brow. Yet he made no wild, reckless vow, swore no oath by saints or devils.

"'Men will die for this,' he said coldly."

And they did indeed die for it. Kane, who had not known the girl, and in fact did not even learn her name before she died, then spends months methodically tracking down the bandits and killing them. Their leader, Le Loup, is soon the only one left. Kane trails him to Africa, where events are complicated by black magic and vengeful gorillas.

Other Kane stories also stress this curious mixture of compassion and violence. The best Kane story is perhaps "Wings of the Night," from 1932. Kane is back in Africa, where he is attacked by hideous winged men. He kills several, but is severely wounded by their razor talons. People from a nearby village take him in and nurse him back to health. The village is later attacked by the winged men, and the entire population slaughtered. Only Kane, killing several more of the things in savage combat, survives.

The next morning he surveys the carnage "with dull, mad eyes" and immediately begins to plan revenge.[5] Half-insane with grief, he spends weeks preparing an elaborate trap to lure the winged men to their deaths.

But where Kane was someone you would politely try to avoid inviting to a party, Conan the Barbarian liked nothing better than a good time.[6] Conan lived in a prehistoric time that existed between the sinking of Atlantis and the beginning of recorded history. The first Conan tale, published in 1932, was "Phoenix on the Sword," a rewrite of a story that Wright had earlier rejected. Howard changed the characters and added a supernatural element. The result was a strong, violent narrative featuring one of the best sword fights ever put down on paper.

As the story opens, Conan is king of the highly-civilized nation of Aquilonia, having recently led a revolt against a despotic ruler. But his hold on the throne is tenuous, as many people, both nobles and commoners, are unhappy with a foreign barbarian as their king. "Phoenix on the Sword" culminates with a bloody assassination attempt as a horde of killers attacks Conan in his bedchamber. Wounded multiple times, Conan kills both the bulk of the assassins and a supernatural monster that had been "born in no sane or human world."

"Phoenix" was a hit with readers, and Howard sold nearly twenty more Conan stories to Wright over the next few years. They varied in quality — Howard was occasionally off his game — but the best of them are still among the finest fantasy tales ever produced.

Conan's popularity had an interesting side effect. Because he wrote more about this character than any of his others, Howard was able to construct a reasonably complete history for the barbarian. The first two tales featured Conan as king, perhaps in his late thirties or early forties. But the third story jumped back to Conan's youth. "Tower of the Elephant," from the March 1933 issue, showed us a Conan in his late teens, newly arrived in civilization from his native Cimmeria. The plot centers on his impetuous decision to steal a priceless jewel rumored to be kept atop a wizard's tower. Here Conan is not a veteran warrior and responsible king, but a naïve kid who does not think before he acts.

Later Conan stories jumped back and forth through his life. Strung together in internal chronological order, we can see Conan gradually maturing from thief to mercenary to general to king. In his youth, he often survives as much by dumb luck as by the strength of his sword arm. Later on, when as an experienced mercenary he is first given command of an army, he discovers a sense of responsibility and learns to plan ahead. By the time he becomes a king, he's achieved a noticeable degree of wisdom. One of the assassins in "Phoenix on the Sword" is a poet named Rinaldo, who has been openly denouncing Conan. When an advisor suggests hanging the poet, Conan refuses, saying, "I shall die and be forgotten, but Rinaldo's songs will live forever."

This is not to say that Conan ever lost his propensity for violence. The best stories are rousing adventures filled with visceral action sequences, monsters (ranging from venomous spiders to carnivorous apes to hungry dragons), and more than a few malign wizards.

Howard did not depend purely on violent action to move his plots along. He could also generate an atmosphere of horror when he needed one. In "Hour of the Dragon," Conan must follow a procession of priests into an ancient pyramid in order to recover a magic jewel. His successive encounters with a beautiful vampire, bizarre assassins and a newly-reanimated zombie are as chilling as anything Lovecraft wrote.

Howard's single best *Weird Tales* contribution is an outstanding horror story. "Worms of the Earth," from the July 1932 issue, is set in ancient Britain, following that country's conquest by Rome. The title refers to a race of not-quite-human creatures that inhabited Britain before the coming of man. The story's protagonist, Bran Mak Morn, is king of the Picts, a barbarian race battling desperately against the advance of the Roman legions. When a Roman officer named Sulla crucifies a friend of Bran's, the barbarian king becomes obsessed with exacting vengeance. In a sequence dripping with malignant danger, he seeks out the remnants of the pre-human race, now living underground, and forces them to agree to help him. ("They fear you, O king," exclaims Bran's guide. "...who are you that Hell itself quails before you?")

The creatures do help, by destroying a Roman fortress, kidnapping Sulla and killing everyone else. Sulla is brought to Bran, but the things he saw while a prisoner have blasted his sanity, reducing him to a drooling, mindless thing. When Bran kills him, it is an act of mercy, not vengeance.

Outside of *Weird Tales*, Howard did not usually have the option of using monsters and magic to carry his narratives along. But his ability to wrap exciting action set pieces around a good plot allowed him to produce solid stories set everywhere from turn-of-the-century Afghanistan to the Middle East of the Crusades to the American West.

A pulp called *Oriental Tales* (later renamed *The Magic Carpet*) bought a number of Howard stories, two of which highlight his particular strengths.

"The Shadow of the Vulture," from 1934, was set during the 1529 siege of Vienna by the Ottoman Turks. One of the city's defenders is a knight named Gottfried Von Kalmbach, who at first doesn't know that he's been personally targeted for assassination by the Turks because he once wounded their sultan in battle.

Gottfried meets a female soldier named Red Sonya, a Cossack swordswoman who is as skilled and ruthless in battle as she is beautiful.[7] Although she doesn't like Gottfried much at first, she saves his life a couple of times and gradually grows fond of him. Together they manage to ambush the Turks' chief assassin, sending his head to the sultan as a "gift in token of our immeasurable fondness."

Several elements add potency to this story. Howard's characterizations here are notable. Gottfried is something of a happy-go-lucky oaf, but is still believable as a skilled and brave warrior. Sonya is an effective complement to him, combining her courage and loyalty to her companions with the ruthlessness of a professional mercenary. At one point she helps Gottfried obtain information from a captured spy by threatening to kill the spy's son. ("What will you give for the life of your whelp?")

In addition, Howard's vivid description of the siege itself — the slaughter of innocents outside the city walls, the savagery of hand-to-hand combat, the exhaustion of the soldiers after days of non-stop bloodletting — wraps the story in an atmosphere of unbroken menace. From start to finish, "The Shadow of the Vulture" barely gives the reader an opportunity to take a breath.

In "The Sowers of Thunder," published in 1932, the main character is Red Cahal, a medieval Irish king who lost his kingdom when betrayed by the woman he loved. Embittered and fatalistic, he travels to the Holy Land as much for something to do as for any sense of religious devotion. A series of bloody adventures follow, with Cahal playing a key role in trying to stop a horde of Asian horsemen who were overrunning both Christian and Muslim outposts.

During the story, Cahal meets both a carefree traveler named Haroun and a grim soldier named Akbar. Both men turn out to be the same person, a Muslim ruler named Baibars who likes to do his own spy work. Cahal and Baibars come to respect each other, but the Muslim joins forces with the horsemen in order to carve out an empire of his own, making the two enemies. The finale combines yet another great battle scene with an insightful and almost poetically stated commentary on the fleeting glory of kingship.

By the end of the 1930s, things were changing at *Weird Tales*. Clark Ashton Smith quit writing fiction in 1937 to concentrate on other pursuits.[8] Robert E. Howard died a suicide in 1936, while H.P. Lovecraft died of cancer in 1937. Farnsworth Wright, who suffered from Parkinson's Disease, retired after the March 1940 issue and died soon afterwards.

But *Weird Tales* continued, with assistant editor Dorothy McIlwraith taking over from Wright. *Weird Tales* had found a niche audience and, while it rarely generated more than a tiny profit, it continued on through 1954, a run of over three decades.[9] Under both Wright's and McIlwraith's guidance, the genres of fantasy and horror were both continually enriched. Some of Ray Bradbury's early work appeared in *Weird Tales*. Robert Bloch, perhaps the finest 20th century writer of horror, published a lot of his best work there as well.[10] The list of good and great writers filling the pages of "The Unique Magazine" (as it billed itself) is very impressive.[11]

While many *Weird Tales* contributors are in serious need of popular rediscovery, Lovecraft and Howard have fared well. In 1939, pulp writer August Derleth helped start a small publishing firm called Arkham House, named after the fictional New England town where many of Lovecraft's Cthulu tales were set. Derleth helped preserve the work of Lovecraft, whose best stories can still be found in print.

Robert E. Howard was pretty much forgotten by the 1950s when writer L. Sprague de Camp rescued him from obscurity by championing the Conan stories to great commercial success. This in turn led to the rediscovery of some of Howard's other works as well. Since then, Howard's fantasy work has come back into print fairly regularly. Conan has become an industry, with comic books, TV shows, movies, and several dozen novels written by a variety of authors. Though it would not hurt to see an edition of Howard's non-fantasy adventure stories back in print again, much of his best prose is not hard to find.

Another important magazine dedicated to fantasy literature was *Unknown*, which published its first issue in 1939. *Unknown* was edited by John Campbell, who was simultaneously doing extraordinary work as editor of the science fiction pulp *Astounding*. Campbell was looking for something different than the usual *Weird Tales* fare. He felt the tone of that magazine was "old-fashioned" and wrote, "I do not want the unpleasant gods and godlings with penchants for vivisection, and nude and beauteous maidens to be sacrificed."

The opportunity to write fantasy with a different slant (as well as earn better pay) drew *Weird Tales* contributors such as C.L. Moore and Robert Bloch to *Unknown*. Campbell discovered many of the science fiction writers he'd been working with on *Astounding* could produce good fantasy as well.

L. Sprague de Camp, for instance, had contributed several stories to *Astounding*. In 1939 he sold "Lest Darkness Fall" to *Unknown*. A story that could be described as either fantasy or science fiction, it involves a modern man, archeologist Martin Padway, inexplicably transported back in time to the 6th century.

Padway, a strictly rational man, quickly adjusts to the situation. He speaks enough Latin to make himself understood, but needs to find a way to make a living. He decides to distill modern brandy, a drink somewhat stronger than the wine common to the time and therefore bound to be popular. In lieu of the collateral he needs in order to borrow money for operating expenses, he teaches a Roman banker Arabic numerals and double-entry bookkeeping.

Padmay's knowledge of history leaves him painfully aware that Italy is about to be wracked by a devastating war which will destroy the remnants of the Roman Empire and bring about the Dark Ages. Once he's successfully set himself up in business, he beings to work on changing history. He "invents" the printing press, though he must experiment with both ink and paper-making before he discovers something that works. He sets up a public corporation to fund the building of a series of semaphore towers, thereby improving communications. Eventually, he becomes reluctantly involved in politics and military affairs, where his specific knowledge of history and general knowledge of military tactics[12] allow him to quickly end the war and ensure the spread of knowledge.

De Camp constructed his yarn with absolute logic, carefully thinking out the implications of Padway's actions and inventions. He draws a lot of both humor and suspense out of the plot, adding a number of varied and believable supporting characters to give it additional backbone. It's an enjoyable take on the concept of alternate history, full of wit and intelligence.

Perhaps the best stories to appear in *Unknown* were Fritz Leiber's tales about Fafhrd and the Gray Mouser, the first of which appeared in 1940. It was Leiber who coined the term "sword-and-sorcery" to categorize stories like Howard's Conan tales. His own foray into the field involved two protagonists. Fafhrd is a tall, red-haired barbarian with a boisterous personality. The Mouser is short and dresses in gray, a dabbler in magic who tends to be more cynical than his partner. Both are master swordsmen, skilled thieves, treasure hunters and, when the occasion calls for it, heroes. They work so well together that in at least one story they are said to be two aspects of the same personality.

Leiber used unpretentious but intelligent prose to construct strong, witty fantasy tales. Fafhrd and the Mouser were incredibly successful creations, and Leiber would still occasionally recount their adventures half-a-century later.[13] Though he and De Camp had their individual styles, both men shared a talent for combining a sense of adventure with a sense of humor.

Fafhrd and the Mouser's first appearance was in the story "Two Sought Adventure." The partners had recently found a clue to an ancient treasure, supposedly hidden in a tower located in an isolated forest. The clue includes a cryptic warning that the treasure is guarded, though no guardian lives either inside or outside the tower.

Escaping an ambush set by rival treasure seekers, the two near the tower. They take shelter at a farm for the night, where the Mouser enchants the farmer's shy little girl with some sleight-of-hand.

The next morning they approach the tower. The girl warns them not to go, claiming the place is guarded by a giant she's never actually seen. Dismissing her tale as a child's fancy, they continue on.

They encounter their rivals again, leading to a well-described action set piece in which the two heroes stalk their opponents through the thick woods. Later, they enter the tower only to discover the crushed skeletons of several previous invaders.

Here the feel of the story smoothly shifts from adventure to horror. The tower itself is the guardian of its own treasure, coming alive to crush invaders in its doorways and windows. The finale involves the Mouser trying to save the little girl, who has followed them despite her own terror. Simultaneously, Fafhrd recovers a large jewel — discovering almost immediately that the jewel is the tower's "brain," and removing it from its hiding place has driven the building insane.

In retrospect, *Weird Tales* and *Unknown* complemented each other. The former depended on strong emotion, but did not sacrifice intelligence. The latter depended on intelligence and wit, but did not sacrifice emotion. Together they helped develop fantasy and horror into genres that regularly produce strong stories to this day.

7. The Hard-Boiled Detective

Like the Western, the popularity of the detective story carried over smoothly from the dime novels to the pulps. General fiction magazines such as *Argosy* and *Cavalier* printed a fair proportion of detective tales, and, in 1915, *Detective Story Magazine* became the first specialty pulp dedicated to the genre. Soon, whenever you opened a pulp, you were likely to meet a clever policeman, or a brilliant doctor who solved crimes between treating patients, or a professional burglar who has to catch a killer to prove his own innocence.

But though the nature of the protagonists would vary, nearly every such story during the teens and early twenties was stuck in a similar stylistic rut. Influenced on one hand by Sherlock Holmes and on the other by the dime novels, the American detective story plodded along aimlessly. A lot of the stories were good in of themselves, but lacked a true sense of humanity. Violent death served as a plot device, never generating any sense of real emotion. Solutions to mysteries were often contrived, never coming close to the natural cleverness of the best Holmes stories.

But, again like the Western, the sheer volume of new stories meant that someone was bound to eventually do something innovative. The path to innovation for the detective story proved rather tortuous, winding through decades of narrative inertia and a wall of elitist snobbery.

In 1914 noted critic H.L. Mencken became co-editor of a periodical called *The Smart Set*. It was subtitled "A Magazine of Cleverness," and the idea was to provide sophisticated stories for sophisticated readers. But it turned out that there weren't all that many sophisticated readers out there. Circulation was poor, and *The Smart Set* was in perpetual financial trouble.

It's tempting to make fun of Mencken and his magazine. Mencken was a literary snob, contemptuous of the average person's tastes and unable to grasp the idea that genre fiction could be worthwhile. By most accounts, he was also a jerk. To be fair, though, it must be said that Mencken was a good writer and, within his autocratic limits, a good editor. *The Smart Set*, among other accomplishments, helped usher F. Scott Fitzgerald into print.

Regardless of its quality, few people actually read the magazine. Playing to tastes they abhorred, Mencken and co-editor George Jean Nathan started *Parisienne*, "a magazine pandering to the intense popular interest in all things French."[1] *Parisienne* quickly turned a profit. In July 1915, Mencken and Nathan sold it to publisher Eugene F. Crowe for $5,000, using the cash to help finance *The Smart Set*.

A year later they did the same thing, starting up a magazine called *Saucy Stories*, then selling it to Crowe for $10,000.

So far, Mencken and Nathan had demonstrated two things. First, it is occasionally justified to hold the taste of the American public in contempt. Second, *The Smart Set* seemed doomed to remain a financial black hole, sucking up all the money poured into it without returning a cent.

But they still kept trying. In 1920 they created still another pulp, this one promising stories of "Detective, Mystery, Adventure, Romance, and Spiritualism." They seemed to be trying to cover all their remaining bets at once.

This newest venture was called *The Black Mask*. It would soon be responsible for reshaping American literature.

Mencken called *The Black Mask* "a lousy magazine," and at first he was correct. Edited by people with no respect for the sort of stories they published, *The Black Mask* acted simply as a vehicle for making money, gradually narrowing its focus to detective stories because that's what people wanted to read. But despite the lack of quality, it was another success. In November 1920, Mencken and Nathan sold their latest unwanted child to Crowe.

Black Mask began to truly make good in late 1922. By then, George W. Sutton was editor. Sutton knew what the public wanted, but he also recognized and appreciated good writing. Like all good editors, he could satisfy the public while only rarely sacrificing quality. Under his watch, the hard-boiled detective story was born.

Ironically, the first of the hard-boiled detectives appeared in a story just as rotten as most everything else printed in *Black Mask* up to that time. Carroll John Daly's "Two-Gun Terry" (published in the May 15, 1923 issue) featured Terry Mack, a gun-happy vigilante. Daly's prose can generously be described as styleless, and his dialogue as stilted. And Mack proved to be an uninteresting caricature of a thug. But the character was popular with readers, and Daly became a regular contributor to the *Mask*. A later Daly creation, Race Williams, was also an uninteresting thug and just as annoyingly popular.

Sutton recognized the poor quality of Daly's work. In fact, Daly's early stories were bought by an assistant editor while Sutton was on vacation — Sutton freely admitted he would have rejected them. But a Daly story in the *Mask* would increase sales by 25 percent. "Write them," Sutton told Daly. "I won't like them. But I'll buy them and print them."

Fortunately, the bad was accompanied by the good. Another far superior writer began appearing in *Black Mask* simultaneously with Daly. Dashiell Hammett would also write hard-boiled fiction, but with realism and humanity and sharp, concise prose that bites into you when you read it. Daly would eventually fade from the public consciousness,[2] but Hammett was around to stay.

Samuel Dashiell Hammett was born in 1894. After working a variety of jobs in his teens, he took a job with the Pinkerton Detective Agency. Hammett was good at the work, traveling around the country on a variety of assignments.

The First World War interrupted his career. While in the army, he developed tuberculosis. After the war, he returned to the Pinkertons, but ill health and a growing desire to try his hand at writing eventually led him to quit.

At first, Hammett did not draw directly on his experience as a detective, making his initial sales to *The Smart Set*. Under the pen name Peter Collinson, he also began placing stories in *Black Mask*.

It was with his third sale to the *Mask* that he introduced a private detective as protagonist. "Arson Plus" (October 1, 1923) featured an unnamed investigator who worked for the Continental Detective Agency. Though never given a name, the Continental Op[3] was to star in over thirty stories in the *Mask* over the next seven years.

Hammett immediately breathed new life into the genre. The Op stories introduced a badly needed sense of realism, with the protagonist employing authentic investigative techniques. Hammett also had a fine ear for dialogue, giving each individual character his or her own voice. Perhaps most importantly, Hammett's prose was sparse and completely unsentimental. He never wasted a word, never added an unnecessary sentence. He told a story as well as anyone ever did, constructing complex but believable plots in just a few words.

His stories would have been entertaining but forgettable melodrama in the hands of another writer. But Hammett never played to a false emotion. Characters acted and reacted, sometimes sensibly and sometimes foolishly, in ways that the reader would readily accept as genuine.

All this realism — emotion, characterization, investigative techniques— allowed Hammett not only to build complex plots, but also regularly add some of the best and most unexpected plot twists ever devised. These narrative bombs were never carelessly inserted just for the sake of being there, but were always an integral part of the story as a whole. Sometimes the twist would be identifying as a crook someone the reader did not even consider a suspect. Just as often, it would involve something about a particular character's motivation or history — something that Hammett expertly designed to both advance the plot and raise emotional tension to its zenith. In the best stories, such as "The Scorched Face" or "The Girl with Silver Eyes," the twists at or near the denouement can literally take your breath away.

The Op was the centerpiece of all this. Physically, he seemed an unlikely detective. Approaching forty years of age and twenty pounds overweight, he would never be mistaken for Nick Carter. But he was a consummate professional who took pride in his work. In fact, there's little to indicate in the Op stories that he had much of a life outside his work. He likes what he does ("...in the past eighteen years, I've been getting my fun out of chasing crooks and tackling puzzles.... It's the only kind of sport I know anything about") and he's good at it. He is dogged in his pursuit of a case, never allowing his own emotions to interfere with getting the job done.

Another character once describes him as "A monster. A nice monster, an especially nice one to have around when you're in trouble, but a monster just the same, without any human foolishness like love in him..."

This is not to say the Op is amoral. He has chosen to be one of the good guys, and he displays a firm sense of ethics and loyalty. He's someone you respect, though not always someone you like.

The Op stories can roughly be divided into two phases, with the tales appearing prior to 1927 making up the first phase. All the early stories were independent of each other. You can read and enjoy any one of them without prior knowledge of the series.

In 1926 things began to change. By then, Sutton had left the *Mask*. His successor, Philip C. Cody, had been doing an equally superb job. But Hammett was asking for more money. Cody couldn't give him a raise without doing the same for the *Mask*'s other regular contributors — something he did not think the magazine could afford. Hammett quit writing for a time, taking a job in advertising to pay the bills.

But his unhealthy lungs acted up again. Soon, Hammett was bedridden and badly in need of money.

Joseph "Cap" Shaw[4] had taken over as the *Mask*'s editor in late 1926. Anxious to bring Hammett back into the fold, he promised him both a higher word rate and greater creative freedom.

Hammett responded by submitting "The Big Knockover" and "$106,000 Blood Money," two long, interconnected stories that allowed Hammett to begin exploring the character of the Op in more depth. All of Hammett's usual strengths were there, along with the idea that detective work could eventually damage a man's soul. Future Op stories would take this idea further, with the protagonist becoming more and more aware of the danger that his work might be permanently stripping away his humanity.

He was, in fact, presented with evidence of this danger every time he went to work. His boss, the chief of Continental's San Francisco office, is identified in the stories only as the Old Man:

"A tall, plump man in his seventies, this boss of mine, with a white-mustached, baby-pink, grandfatherly face, mild blue eyes behind rimless spectacles and no more warmth in him than a hangman's rope. Fifty years of crook-hunting for the Continental had emptied him of everything except brains and a soft-spoken, gently smiling shell of politeness that was the same whether things went good or bad..."[5]

The symbolism of neither the Op nor the Old Man ever being given a name is obvious. The Old Man doesn't have much in the way of humanity left in him. The Op is heading in the same direction.

Hammett continued to produce longer, interlocking stories that, with a little re-writing, could later be re-published as novels. Four stories running in the November 1927 through February 1928 issues became the first Continental Op novel—*Red Harvest*.

In *Red Harvest*, the Op travels to the city of Personville, commonly known as Poisonville because it is an utterly corrupt place. Several different mobs own the local government and police department, and openly run rackets, such as bootlegging, gambling and loan sharking.

The editor of the local paper hires the Continental Detective Agency to clean up the town. The editor is murdered soon after, but the Op is determined to get the job done, regardless.

His chosen methodology is effective, but ruthless. He investigates the situation, quickly identifying who is who within the Personville rackets. Then, by feeding the various gang leaders scraps of information and occasional lies, he manages to turn them against each other. Soon after the Op has gone to work, the body count in Personville rapidly rises. Mobster A kills Mobster B. Mobster C thinks that Mobster D did the killing and goes after him. And so on.

It was very much a red harvest, with more than a score of violent deaths by the novel's end. The Op is very much aware that he's at least indirectly responsible for most of these deaths. He's also aware that he's enjoying it. "I've got hard skin over what's left of my soul," he comments, "and after twenty years of messing around with crime I can look at any sort of murder without seeing anything in it but my bread and butter, the day's work. But this getting a rear out of planning deaths is not natural to me. It's what this place has done to me."

On the other hand, he's still the good guy, or at least the closest thing to a good guy present in Personville. His objective is not personal gain, but to free the town from the grip of thugs. He's doing a good thing. But to what degree does the end justify the means? It's a hackneyed question, but an important one that Hammett explores without providing a pat answer. He readily acknowledges that moral responsibilities exist, then thrusts his protagonist into a situation where the exact nature of those responsibilities become unclear.

In the end, the mobs in Personville are broken, but the moral question marks surrounding the Op remain. *Red Harvest* is one of the finest crime novels ever written. Its perfectly constructed, Byzantine plot is complemented by moral complexities and intense characterizations.

Hammett was now at his creative high point. Four more interconnected Op stories formed the novel *The Dain Curse*. In late 1929 and early 1930, the *Mask* serialized *The Maltese Falcon*, featuring private eye Sam Spade. Then came four more stories that would make up *The Glass Key*. Each novel is a masterpiece of plot and character.[6]

By 1932, Hammett's career as a writer was effectively over. By then, he had succeeded in wrecking his personal life and thoroughly dousing himself in alcohol. It was as if someone flipped a switch and simply turned off his creativity. Hammett would live another thirty years without producing anything else significant.

Though Hammett was the best of the hard-boiled writers, he certainly wasn't the only one. His contemporaries, many unjustly forgotten today, also produced excellent work. Raoul Whitfield, for instance, contributed stories about a number of different characters to the *Mask*. He wrote quite a bit for other pulps as well, helping to spread the influence of the hard-boiled school.[7]

Frederick Nebel also created several series characters for *The Black*

Mask. These included some wonderful yarns starring a tough big-city police captain named MacBride and a perpetually drunk crime reporter named Kennedy. Other important *Mask* contributors were Paul Cain and Horace McCoy. Earle Stanley Gardner, famous for his Perry Mason novels, created at least five different series characters for the magazine.[8]

Hammett's only true rival in the Best Hard-Boiled Writer category, Raymond Chandler, also broke into print in *The Black Mask*, with "Blackmailers Don't Shoot" in December 1933. Chandler had an ear for sharp dialogue and engaging characterizations, but he wasn't prolific enough to survive writing short stories and quickly switched to novels. His first novel was *The Big Sleep* (1939), featuring the most iconic of hard-boiled private eyes— Philip Marlowe. (Both *The Big Sleep* and *Farewell, My* Lovely [1940] incorporated short stories that had appeared in *The Black Mask*.) Marlowe was as outwardly cynical as the Continental Op, but upon closer examination was still something of a romantic. Chandler saw his private eyes as modern knights-errant, men of honor who follow a strict code of personal ethics. For the Op, catching crooks was a job he took satisfaction in doing well. For Marlowe, it was more of a crusade.

Fans of the genre can argue endlessly over whether Hammett or Chandler was the superior writer. I lean towards Hammett, who was better at tying up complex plot elements into a tight bundle. Chandler's plots were equally Byzantine, but didn't always make complete sense in the end. He got away with this by matching Hammett in skillful characterizations and probably surpassing him in the sharpness of his imagery.

Why did the hard-boiled detective story make such a splash? There are several reasons. It was fresh and vital; it was written by men who knew how to tell a story well; and it injected a badly needed dose of realism into the genre.

Also, its innate cynicism reflected the times. The nastier technical and social byproducts of industrialization — the enormous casualties of the World War, the oppression of workers and the ensuing violent labor strikes, the open corruption in big-city governments— had stripped away feelings of cultural stability.

The hard-boiled hero seemed to thrive on this instability. He knew and accepted this new world as it was—corrupt and undependable. With courage, brains and an automatic pistol, he stood up to whatever was thrown at him.

And he did it with honor. It's possible, perhaps even usual, to read any one hard-boiled story and disagree with some of the ethical decisions of the protagonists. But they *did* have ethics. This is an important point, especially in our age of postmodern moral relativism. Cynicism can be a destructive emotion, but in the best hard-boiled stories it's tempered by the knowledge that there really is such a thing as objective right and wrong. It's nice to read about characters who, despite their often prominent flaws, and despite the sinful nature of the world in general, recognize this and act on it. They could have been successful villains, but they chose to be heroes.

8. *Amazing, Astounding*
Science Fiction

Science fiction wasn't always called science fiction. In the 19th and early 20th Centuries, "scientific romance" was one of the more popular terms. There were a variety of other names for the genre, many also incorporating the word "science" or "scientific."

But when publisher and editor Hugo Gernsback decided to start up a magazine dedicated to such stories, he realized he had to coin a standardized name. His first thought was "scientifiction,"[1] but he eventually settled on science fiction.

Actually, the word "science" was often a misnomer when used to describe most early examples of the genre. Nobody really cared if the more fantastic plot elements might someday be possible. Well, Jules Verne cared—he really did try to create scientifically plausible plots. But a lot of his readers probably just thought the *Nautilus* was really nifty regardless of whether it could truly exist. Certainly his dime novel imitators didn't concern themselves with realism.

But the illusion of scientific reality helped create the suspension of disbelief necessary to make the stories dramatically viable. In a world where impossible things like telephones and radio were becoming everyday items, steam-powered men and time machines didn't seem too unreasonable.

Realistic or not, science fiction remained popular throughout both the dime novel and pulp eras. There were the young inventor tales discussed earlier, as well as H.G. Wells' mainstream novels about time travel and alien invaders. Before long, many general fiction pulps depended almost as much on science fiction as on Westerns or mysteries to fill their pages.

10¢ PER COPY   SATURDAY JAN. 24   BY THE YEAR $4.00

ALL-STORY WEEKLY

The
People
of the
Golden
Atom

by Ray Cummings

A Sequel to

"The Girl *in the*
Golden Atom."

A 1920 All-Story cover provides a typical view of early science fiction. Realism was not a concern — escapist storytelling took precedent over science.

Enter Hugo Gernsback. Born in Luxembourg in 1884, Gernsback had been a science fiction enthusiast since childhood. He came to the U.S. at age 20, where he invented and marketed a home radio set. This led him into publishing when he started a magazine called *Modern Electronics*.[2] Though it was not a fiction magazine, Gernsback soon began to include occasional science fiction stories.[3] Readers liked them, so in 1926 Gernsback founded *Amazing Stories*, the first science fiction specialty pulp.

At first, he depended largely on reprinting work by Verne, Wells, Edgar Rice Burroughs, and other writers of proven popularity, though he gradually began publishing more and more original works. In either case, readers eagerly forked over their dimes and quarters for his magazine. With solid, escapist storytelling, and striking, imaginative covers by artist Frank R. Paul, *Amazing Stories* was a huge commercial success.

Perhaps the most influential single author introduced in *Amazing Stories* was E.E. "Doc" Smith.[4] In 1928, his story "The Skylark of Space" began appearing as a serial.

The narrative begins when good-guy scientist Richard Seaton accidentally discovers a source of ultimate energy and uses it to build an interstellar spaceship called the *Skylark*. Bad-guy scientist Blackie DuQuesne steals the secret and kidnaps Seaton's girlfriend. Soon, Seaton is pursuing DuQuesne through interstellar space. They all manage to get lost and are forced to team up.

They encounter alien races, both good and evil, and develop the habit of getting involved in interplanetary wars. Over the course of the original serial and several sequels, the *Skylark* is continually upgraded, and both Seaton and DuQuesne have their individual intelligences enhanced. Eventually, they're zipping back and forth between galaxies with ease, with DuQuesne plotting conquest and Seaton trying to foil him.

Along with Edmund Hamilton's Interstellar Patrol stories from *Weird Tales*, Smith's Skylark serials were the prototypes of the "space opera"— adventure stories in which faster-than-light travel, death rays, and strange aliens are the norm. Like Hamilton, Smith never did anything small, filling his stories with genocidal wars and exploding suns.

Smith's novels, with his big ideas and straightforward narrative style, are still fun to read today and are at least occasionally reprinted. His characterizations were a bit flat, with the amoral and coldly calculating DuQuesne being the only truly interesting person in the Skylark stories. But he's a prime example of why *Amazing Stories* struck a cord with readers. It was good epic storytelling, with just a hint that the more fantastic elements might someday be possible.

Phillip Francis Nowlan's novelette *Armageddon 2419 A.D.* also appeared in 1928, with its sequel, *The Airlords of Han*, arriving a year later. This was the introduction of Anthony "Buck" Rogers, one of the quintessential space opera protagonists, who would jump from the pulps to radio, comic strips, movie serials and eventually television.

In his original appearance, Rogers was a mining engineer who, in 1927, is rendered unconscious by a strange natural gas while working in a particularly deep mine. He wakes up 492 years later.

Returning to the surface, Rogers (he wouldn't acquire the nickname "Buck" until he became a comic strip character in 1929) soon ends up meeting a woman equipped with a flying belt and a rocket pistol. He helps her fight off a couple of similarly equipped men, then tells her his story.

The girl, Wilma Deering, accepts his tale with remarkable aplomb, then fills him in on current politics. It seems America, along with the rest of Western civilization, has been conquered by a decadent Oriental race called the Han.[5] Surviving Americans have gathered into groups called "gangs," living in rural areas far from the domed Han cities. The men who had been pursuing Wilma were from a gang that collaborated with the Hans.

Rogers joins Wilma's gang and, because of his knowledge of military tactics that had been otherwise forgotten over the centuries, eventually becomes their leader. Alliances with other gangs are formed, and the rest of the yarn is a straightforward war story, with Nowlan having fun inventing tactics used by the two sides based on their respective technologies.

The Americans have pistols and rifles that fire explosive rockets. They've also discovered an anti-gravity metal called inertron, from which they manufacture planes and flying belts. Inertron also provides protection against the Han disintegrator ray.

The Hans have their "dis" ray, along with force fields and giant airships. In a series of campaigns, both sides make use of their assets in various interesting ways. My favorite is an eight-foot-tall bell-shaped suit of inertron, topped off with a rocket gun in a turret, that's worn by some American infantrymen. The Hans have their clever moments as well. When they realize their "dis" rays can't directly damage inertron-shielded aircraft, they learn to play the rays around the enemy planes rather than right at them. This forms vacuums as the air disintegrates, which in turn causes enough turbulence to crash the aircraft.

In the end, Rogers' knowledge of World War I tactics, such as the artillery barrage and bayonet charge, leads the Americans to victory.

Nowlan's story works well enough on this sort of gee-whiz level, but doesn't go any deeper than that. Like E.E. Smith, he had no talent for characterization at all. Rogers is ridiculously casual about being thrust five centuries into the future, and his romance with Wilma could have been cut completely from the story without anyone noticing.

It was another popular story all the same. Readers weren't yet looking for in-depth characterizations. For the first time, science fiction was being regularly mass produced, and gee-whiz super-science was enough to satisfy almost everyone. It wouldn't be long, though, before the genre started to truly grow up.

In 1929, Gernback lost control of *Amazing Stories* to another publisher. He went on to found other science fiction magazines, such as *Science Wonder Stories* and *Scientific Detective Stories*. But to properly trace science fiction as it progressed from adolescence to adulthood, we must leave Gernsback behind and turn to a magazine called *Astounding Stories*.

Other publishers noticed the success of *Amazing Stories* and began to produce their own science fiction pulps. The Clayton magazine chain come out with *Astounding Stories of Super Science*, with the first issue dated January 1930. *Astounding* would have three editors: Harry Bates, F. Orlin Tremaine and John W. Campbell, Jr. Each of these talented men would have their own ideas of what science fiction should be. Under Tremaine and Campbell, *Astounding* would push the genre in important new directions.

Harry Bates, an experienced pulp editor, was there at the beginning, writing in the first issue: "[*Astounding*] is a magazine whose stories will anticipate the super-scientific achievements of To-morrow — whose stories will not only be strictly accurate in their science but will be vividly, dramatically and thrillingly told."

Bates usually got the vivid and thrilling part right, but the science portrayed in *Astounding* was somewhat less than "strictly accurate." He bought stories about underground civilizations, giant man-eating bugs, planets turned into spaceships, and miniature worlds orbiting the nucleus of an atom. Only rarely would a plot element have anything to do with real science, and that seemed to occur only by accident.

But the stories were fun. Despite what he wrote in the premier issue, he was much more concerned with entertaining people than with scientific accuracy. Plot-driven, action-oriented nonsense filled the pages of *Astounding*, to the delight of its readers. It was pure space opera, with more bug-eyed monsters and mad scientists than you could shake an electron at.

Bates combined his eye for good writing with a willingness to pay generously and promptly, setting a word rate[6] that doubled what most other magazines offered their writers. He was thus able to attract popular writers, such as Edmund Hamilton and E.E. Smith, to *Astounding*. Bates wasn't doing much that was innovative — he stuck to story formulas developed in *Amazing Stories* and *Weird Tales*. But these were proven formulas, and Bates used writers who knew how to work well with them.

Astounding sold well, but in 1932 the Clayton magazine chain as a whole was in financial trouble. In an effort to cut costs, *Astounding* went from a monthly to bi-monthly publication schedule, then limped on through the March 1933 issue. When the Clayton chain collapsed, it seemed likely that *Astounding* was gone for good.

Another chain, Street & Smith, bought up some of the Clayton titles. Revived with the October 1933 issue,[7] *Astounding* was now edited by F. Orlin Tremaine. Almost immediately, the magazine began to shift its editorial direction.

Tremaine wanted stories that he categorized as "thought variants" — stories that explored new and hopefully challenging ideas. Stories like "Rebirth," by Thomas Calvert McClary (February 1934), in which a scientist wipes away the memories of everyone on Earth. Or Murray Leinster's "Sideways in Time" (June 1934), in which the protagonists travel not only backwards and forwards in time, but also sideways into alternate realities. Of course, concepts like alternate realities have become old hat to the modern science fiction fan, but in 1934 they were brand new ideas.

Stanley G. Weinbaum placed a number of excellent stories in *Astounding*. If it had not been for his death at age 33 in 1935, Weinbaum would probably have come to be known as one of the great science fiction writers. He was that good.

Weinbaum's first published story appeared in one of *Astounding*'s competitors, *Wonder Stories*, in June 1934. "A Martian Odyssey" is about the first expedition to Mars. One of the astronauts, Jarvis, is separated from his companions and must trek several hundred miles across an alien landscape to rejoin them. Along the way, he meets and befriends an intelligent Martian. Together they encounter several other, more dangerous examples of the local fauna.

What makes the story innovative was Weinbaum's portrayal of the various Martian creatures. Up until then, nearly all aliens had roughly fallen into three categories. There were the ruthless invaders whose inhuman shape symbolized their inhuman intentions. There were funny-looking carnivores, searching for their next meal. And there were occasional allies of the humans, who spoke and acted just like humans despite being shaped like, say, an artichoke.

Weinbaum created aliens who were believably alien, with thought processes or biological instincts that were completely non-human, but still made sense from the alien's perspective. In "A Martian Odyssey," Jarvis tries to communicate with his new Martian companion, but their concepts of spoken language are so different they can't at first find common ground. The Martian — Jarvis thinks his name is Tweel, but he isn't sure — seems to have a different word for "rock" or "stars" every time Jarvis points to one of these. Tweel, though, manages to learn half-a-dozen English words. By using them in clever combinations, he's able to articulate an extraordinary range of ideas during the course of the story.

Traveling together, Jarvis and Tweel encounter an apparently immortal but non-intelligent creature that instinctively builds pyramids out of the silicon bricks it produces as a waste product. Later, Jarvis is nearly trapped by a carnivore that creates illusions to lure in its prey. Finally, they have a run-in with a semi-intelligent species that "looked rather like a barrel trotting along on four legs with four other arms or tentacles." The barrel people seem dedicated to hauling cartfuls of rubbish to a giant grinding wheel before throwing themselves to their deaths under the same wheel. Jarvis never does figure out the reason for this behavior before he and Tweel earn the enmity of the barrel people and suddenly find themselves fighting for their lives.

"A Martian Odyssey" is further strengthened by Weinbaum's ear for dialogue. The story is told in flashback, with Jarvis recounting his journey to his companions after he has rejoined them. He narrates in a natural, conversational style, occasionally interrupted by his friends. It is an interesting and thoughtful bit of story construction, giving the whole tale an additional level of realism.

Weinbaum's stories for *Astounding* showed all the same strengths. His last story was "Proteus Island," about biological experiments gone awry. It was published posthumously in the August 1936 issue.

Another notable *Astounding* contributor was Don A. Stuart, actually the pen name for future editor John Campbell. Campbell wrote standard space operas and straight science articles, but his best stories are those that vividly evoke specific emotions. "Night," from the October 1935 issue, involves a test pilot who, when trying out a new anti-gravity device, is transported billions of years into the future. He finds himself trapped alone on a dead Earth that is only dimly lighted by a dead, blood-red sun. Only the oxygen and heat provided by his flight suit keep him alive.

"I was sitting with a corpse..." recounts the pilot. "The corpse of a dead world in a dead universe, and the quiet didn't have to settle there; it had settled a billion years ago...." He eventually contacts a race of sentient machines— mankind's last creation before the human race perished —

who help him return to his own time. But the whole story drips with loneliness and the inevitability of death.

What saves the story from being completely oppressive are the actions of the time-lost pilot. Despite his situation, he never stops using his brain. He examines the dead, ancient city he finds himself in, makes deductions and eventually takes actions that help him contact the machine race. Though he has no reason to keep trying, he keeps trying all the same. "Night" manages the remarkable task of balancing hope and hopelessness on opposite ends of a narrative see-saw.

Campbell's most famous story was published in August 1938, after he had become editor of *Astounding*. "Who Goes There?" is set at an isolated Arctic research station. The scientists stationed there find an alien creature frozen in the ice and bring it back to the base for study. They presume it's dead, but when it thaws out, it starts moving.

The thing turns out to be a shape-changer, able to assume the identity of any other living creature. More than that, it imitates people (or sled dogs or milk cows) by sort-of digesting the original mass of each victim. It can thus imitate an unlimited number of victims and therefore can slowly take over the station — and eventually the whole world — by replacing people one by one.

So the humans can't destroy the thing until they identify it. They don't know who's human and who's not anymore. Fear and paranoia build quickly, with the story evoking these emotions as intensely as "Night" evokes loneliness.

As in "Night," salvation comes because someone keeps his head and thinks. Eventually, the story's protagonist comes up with a clever blood test to identify those who are no longer human. The alien is destroyed and the world is saved.[8]

Tremaine did not completely set aside *Astounding*'s space opera roots. He published one of E.E. Smith's Skylark stories and also bought several installments of Smith's entertaining Lensman series. But his high standards regarding plot and characterization helped even the space opera reach new heights.

The April 1934 issue included the first part of Jack Williamson's "Legion of Space," one of the most enjoyable of the space operas. Set in the 30th century, it recounted the adventures of John Ulnar, a member of the Legion of Space (an organization of interplanetary law-enforcers), as he battles traitors, aliens and monsters.

What lifts "The Legion of Space" above the pack is first Williamson's expert handling of the action scenes. There's a ray gun battle in the nar-

Jack Williamson's *The Legion of Space*, featured in the April 1934 issue of *Astounding*, was one of the best of the space operas.

row confines of an air duct system. There's a tooth-and-nail fight involving men armed with spears against something "serpent-like, thick as an elephant, covered with hard red armor; it had innumerable limbs, the foremost armed with razor talons." There's a spaceship diving into a dangerous nebula to escape its pursuers. And it's all described in a fast-paced and riveting style.

In addition, Williamson created a compelling group of protagonists, reminiscent of d'Artangan and the Three Musketeers. The hero is John Ulnar, newly graduated from the Legion Academy only to find the fate of the Earth resting on his shoulders. His three companions are all experienced Legionaries. Jay Kalam is quiet and intelligent — a natural leader. Hal Samdu is a strong and skilled fighter — a natural warrior. And Giles Habibula is fat and tends to whine a lot — a natural ... well, never mind.

It's Giles who really makes the story work. By rights, he should have been completely annoying, both to his companions and to the reader. But though he complains a lot, he complains with style. ("I've lost ten mortal pounds, already, scampering through these foul and endless rat-holes.") It also quickly becomes apparent that, despite his grumbling, he is as brave and resourceful as any of the other Legionnaires. He demonstrates talents in picking locks (it's implied he was a criminal before joining the Legion) and in fixing spaceship engines, saving everyone on several occasions.

John Campbell had become Tremaine's assistant in September of 1937. Tremaine, who served as Editorial Director for Street and Smith's entire chain of pulps, stepped down as *Astounding*'s editor in May 1938 and let Campbell take complete charge.

Campbell's influence was already showing by that point. He loved good writing and fresh ideas, but he also wanted the sort of scientific accuracy that Bates had promised when the magazine was founded, but had never delivered.[9] The cover illustration for the February 1938 issue was an indication that this promise would now be kept. It was an astronomically correct view of the sun as seen from Mercury, expertly painted by Howard V. Brown.

Campbell would continue to insist on good science throughout his career. In 1944, a story by Cleve Cartmill, entitled "Deadline," involved defusing an atomic bomb. The description of the bomb was so accurate that Military Intelligence came by to question Campbell, concerned that there had been a leak in the security surrounding the Manhattan Project.

The March 1938 issue featured another title change. *Astounding Stories* was now *Astounding Science Fiction*. Campbell would remain editor until his death thirty-four years later, seeing the magazine through the end

Howard Brown's accurate painting of the sun as seen from Mercury helped mark *Astounding*'s shift to more scientifically sound story ideas.

of the pulp era and still another title change. *Astounding* is still around today, though now it's called *Analog*.

During his tenure, Campbell discovered or provided guidance to some of the most important modern science fiction writers, including Isaac Asimov, L. Sprague de Camp, Clifford Simak, Lester del Ray, Robert Heinlein and A.E. van Vogt. He arguably did more to make science fiction a viable literary genre than any other single person.

Like Tremaine, Campbell liked new concepts — his pet name for them was "mutant" stories. He loved discovering new writers and helping them develop their ideas. Again and again he would lead someone from doing something pretty good into doing something great.

Isaac Asimov is a prime example of this. It was Asimov and Campbell together who worked out the basic concept for Asimov's Foundation stories. These are set in the far future, when a decadent galactic empire is nearing collapse and centuries of barbarism seem likely to follow. Mankind's hope rests with the development of psycho-history. This is a new system of mathematics that is able to predict the future in large-scale terms. It can't predict the actions of individuals, but it can predict the actions of large crowds, nations and entire civilizations.

Setting up shop on a planet called Foundation, scientists hope to use psycho-history to subtly guide mankind, shortening the era of barbarism and bringing back civilization as soon as possible.

The first Foundation story was published in *Astounding*'s May 1942 issue. It was the sort of concept-driven tale that Asimov did best, and the Foundation stories rank among his best work.

Asimov and Campbell also worked out the Three Laws of Robotics.[10] These laws are, first, that no robot could harm a human being; second, that a robot must always obey a human being unless doing so violated the first law; and third, a robot must protect itself if doing so doesn't violate the first two laws.

Asimov wrote a series of stories in which these laws had been programmed into every robot, robots having become important fixtures in human civilization. The stories would usually center on situations where the implementation of these laws resulted in unintended consequences. The first robot story was "Liar," about a robot with telepathic powers who starts lying to the humans it has contact with (telling one woman that a man she likes is attracted to her), all in an effort to spare their feelings. This inevitably leads to a lot of emotional messiness, but the poor robot was just trying to obey the first law.

Other Campbell discoveries include A.E. van Vogt, who, like Stanley Weinbaum, had a knack for creating bizarre but believable aliens. L. Ron

Hubbard had been in the pulp business for years, writing westerns and adventure stories. He tried his hand at science fiction in 1938, contributing excellent prose to *Astounding* before deciding that there was more money to be made by starting a religion.

Lester del Ray was another fine writer, who himself would go on to become an important and influential editor. Jack Williamson continued to improve; his 1938 serial "The Legion of Time" involved two women from alternate futures, each trying to convince the protagonist to help make her future a reality.

So much important science fiction was being published in *Astounding* that it takes an effort to remember that important things happened with the genre elsewhere. Campbell was helping to develop "hard" science fiction — stories where it was important to get the science right. If an astronaut lands on one of Saturn's moons in a hard S-F story, then that moon had better be described with as much accuracy as modern science could provide.

This was an important part of the maturation of the genre, and many S-F stories require this sort of accuracy to work dramatically. But over in the pages of *Planet Stories*, readers were being reminded that hard science wasn't as important as good writing and real human emotion.

Planet Stories was one of a number of science fiction magazines founded in the late 1930s. Here, if an astronaut landed on a moon of Saturn, he was likely to find a breathable atmosphere, fall in love with the beautiful princess he was certain to stumble across, and soon find himself, armed with a sword, battling monsters in order to save his princess from certain death.

In *Planet Stories*, it didn't matter if it was possible. It just had to seem real to the reader. The magazine's most important contribution to the genre was the many Ray Bradbury stories it published during the 1940s. The most important of these was from the Summer 1946 issue. "The Million Year Picnic," about a family fleeing war-ravaged Earth to settle on Mars, was the first story in what would eventually become *The Martian Chronicles*. Written in Bradbury's unique style, which always managed to be simultaneously poetic and conversational, Bradbury's Martian stories are set on a planet that we know could not exist. But it doesn't matter. These stories are often sad and often filled with black humor and biting commentary on technology and the human race. But they are also filled with humanity and hope.

At its best, whether science fiction gets the science right often is beside the point. Getting the emotions right is always more important. That's when science fiction moves beyond saying, "Gee whiz, isn't this cool!" and becomes great literature.

9. Edgar Rice Burroughs: Ape Men, Dinosaurs and Martians

The cover illustration for the February 1927 issue of *Amazing Stories* is one of my favorites. A fun, vibrant painting by Frank R. Paul, it features a German U-boat on the surface of a churning sea, guns blazing away as a trio of monstrous creatures pull themselves onto its deck. Another monster, this one winged, dives down at the sub out of the sky.

At the time, *Amazing* had been around for less than a year, and Gernsback was still relying heavily on reprints of older stories while he waited for the supply of original submissions to catch up with demand. The issue included tales by Verne and Wells. The cover illustrated a scene from "The Land That Time Forgot," written nine years earlier by Edgar Rice Burroughs.

Burroughs was perhaps the single most popular pulp writer. In researching this book, I lost count of the number of critics or pulp historians who referred to him as a "natural-born storyteller." I've given up trying to think of a more original way to phrase it. He really was a natural-born storyteller.

Before turning to writing, Burroughs had failed at everything else. When he made his first sale to the pulps in 1912, he was 37 years old and had already tried his hand at managing a stationery store, as a miner, a salesman and an accountant. Eventually, he found himself in Chicago, barely supporting a wife and two children by placing ads for patent-medicine in pulp magazines.

This gave him an opportunity to read a lot of pulp fiction. Seeing yet another chance to finally make enough money to properly support a family, he wrote a story and submitted it to *All-Story Magazine*. It sold, netting him four hundred dollars.

The story was "Under the Moons of Mars,"[1] which ran as a serial in the February through July 1912 issues.

Burroughs' debut was a sensation, ensuring his career as a writer and strongly influencing the direction of pre–Gernsback science fiction. It relates the adventures of John Carter, a soldier of fortune who finds himself mysteriously transported to the planet Mars.

Carter arrives naked on Mars and is soon captured by a tribe of Martians. These are green-skinned, come equipped with an extra pair of arms, and stand as tall as fifteen feet. Taken prisoner, Carter spends enough time with his captors to learn the language and some of the customs of his new home.

This was a narrative trick that Burroughs would use over and over again throughout his career. His heroes often began a story by encountering a previously unknown civilization. Allowing the hero to spend time as a prisoner was an effective way to provide both him and the reader with all the necessary background information.

Burroughs was also a master of pacing, so these intervals of captivity were never allowed to slow the story down. In John Carter's case, he gets into several to-the-death duels with individual green Martians and has a nasty encounter with the four-armed carnivorous white apes that prowl the Martian landscape.

Mixed in with these action scenes was a description of Martian civilization. Mars is a dying planet, with tribes of nomadic green Martians wandering the dry ocean basins. There's also a fauna of uncanny, unusually dangerous monsters (such as the apes and an eight-legged lion called a banth). Finally, there's a race of human-appearing red Martians, who dwell in cities and are the deadly enemies of the greens.

That's pretty much the key to understanding the Martians—everybody is usually someone else's deadly enemy. The Martians, red or green (and in later stories there were also black, yellow, white and invisible), are unrepentantly warlike. Their technology includes guns with radar sights that have an effective range of two hundred miles. Despite this, they carry swords and spears as well. Hand-to-hand combat remains an important tactic in their constant wars simply because they love it so much.

So, when Carter kills a couple of green Martians, there's no retribution. In fact, he's allowed by custom to keep the weapons and other possessions of the men he killed. Before long, though still a prisoner, he's well-armed. He's also learned that gravity on Mars, much lower than Earth, gives him an advantage in strength and agility over the Martians.

As soon as Burroughs is through establishing background detail, he introduces another character. The beautiful Dejah Thoris, princess of the red nation of Helium, is captured by the green Martians. She's as brave as she is lovely, and John Carter wastes no time falling in love with her. They escape together, but are separated when Carter is captured by still another tribe of green men. He's forced to fight both men and beasts in an arena before escaping yet again.

He eventually tracks Dejah Thoris to the city of Zodanga, deadly enemies to the nation of Helium. Dejah has been forced to agree to marry a Zodangan prince in order to save Helium from an invading army.

Carter rescues her by arranging for Zodanga's capture by green Martians. "And thus," writes Burroughs, "in the midst of a city of wild conflict, filled with the alarms of war; with death and destruction reaping their terrible harvest around her, did Dejah Thoris, Princess of Helium, true daughter of Mars, the God of War, promise herself in marriage to John Carter, Gentleman of Virginia." I love that sentence.

The story doesn't end there. Carter and his princess have ten years of happiness together before he's transported back to Earth as mysteriously as he was to Mars. Separated from the woman he loves, he, like the reader, must wait for a sequel to find out if he'll ever be able to return to her.

"Under the Moons of Mars" is a bizarre, colorful adventure fantasy. Burroughs creates a world that's completely unbelievable, but makes us believe it all the same. In part, this is because the story is so fast-paced that there's no time to notice flaws. But any flaws are minor. John Carter's Mars is internally consistent; a world where a sword fight with a four-armed green giant seems a natural occurrence. Later stories involved invisibility, synthetically created men, giant magnets, brain transplants, and skeleton men from Jupiter. But no matter how fantastic the plot elements, they were perfectly at home on Mars. Burroughs had created the consummate fantasy world, where he could get away with just about anything.

It was a careful combination of barbaric and super-scientific elements that made it all work. Much of Mars is uninhabited — the landscape is dotted with ghost cities abandoned when the oceans receded. This justified the existence of the monstrous wildlife, as well as the nomadic green Martians, riding their eight-legged mounts.

Isolated outposts of human civilization had developed in the meantime, sometimes going in bizarre and often dangerous directions, with the occasional mad scientist throwing a disintegrator ray or invisibility paint into the mix. Add to this the nations like Helium, where red Martian civilization still thrived, and where speedy airships provided an acceptable method for quickly transporting various heroes into far-flung adventures while attempting to rescue their constantly kidnapped princesses.

The first sequel, "The Gods of Mars," was serialized in *All Story* in 1913. This was quickly followed by "The Warlord of Mars." The two serials really make up one long story, with John Carter, now back on Mars, pursuing various villains to both the North and South Poles (and several locations in between) before finally reuniting with Dejah Thoris.

All this proved enormously popular with readers, and Burroughs' Martian stories were widely imitated in the pulps, becoming "the most acceptable form [of scientific romance] for more than twenty years."[2]

As influential as his Martian stories were, they paled before the success of his next creation. "Tarzan of the Apes" was published in its entirety in the October 1912 issue of *All-Story*. You can't get more successful than Tarzan. The ape man has become a permanent part of our culture. Even someone who's never read a Tarzan novel or seen a Tarzan movie recognizes the name and knows his general history.

As he did with "Under the Moons of Mars," Burroughs creates an impossible situation and makes you believe it. The story begins with Lord and Lady Greystoke aboard a ship sailing to one of Britain's African colonies. The ship's crew mutinies against their sadistic captain. Marooned by the crew along the isolated African coast, the Greystokes build a cabin and manage to survive for about a year. But Lady Greystoke dies soon after bearing a child, and her husband is killed by one of the savage apes that live in the area.

Their infant son is adopted by Kala, a she-ape whose own child had been recently killed. So Tarzan — the name means "White Skin" in the primitive language of the apes — is raised as an ape.

Burroughs comes up with a brilliant solution for providing his protagonist with an education beyond learning how to be an ape. While still a child, Tarzan discovers the cabin his parents had built. Inside, he finds several books, including a children's alphabet book and a dictionary. Over the next few years, with patience and a great deal of natural intelligence, Tarzan deduces the purpose of the symbols in the books, then teaches himself to read.

Eventually, a tribe of cannibals migrates into the area. From observing them, Tarzan learns about wearing clothes and using weapons. He had already figured out from the books that he was an M-A-N, not an A-P-E.

When a party of men and women, including the lovely Jane Porter, become stranded nearby, Tarzan helps them. He repeatedly saves them from hungry lions and communicates with them by leaving notes. (Remember, he can read and write English, but has never heard it spoken.)

Various adventures follow, including battles with the cannibals and

SATURDAY   APRIL 8   TEN CENTS

ALL-STORY
WEEKLY

Thuvia,
Maid of Mars
A Sequel to "Warlord of Mars"
by
Edgar Rice Burroughs
Author of the Tarzan Tales

The 1916 issue of *All-Story* featured the fourth of Edgar Rice Burroughs' popular Martian tales. Burroughsian women were kidnapped or otherwise threatened with clockwork regularity.

Tarzan premiered in the October 1912 issue of All-Story. This was one of the first lions he killed in hand-to-hand combat, but his enormous popularity guaranteed it wouldn't be the last.

Jane's kidnapping by an ape. Eventually, Jane and her party are rescued by the French navy. In the confusion, Tarzan is left behind, along with a wounded French officer named D'Arnot.

D'Arnot teaches Tarzan to speak French and English. Together, they return to civilization. Tarzan eventually gets to America, where he proposes to Jane. But though Jane loves him, she has already promised her hand to another man. Ironically, this man is Tarzan's cousin, who currently holds the title of Lord Greystoke.

Tarzan has proof that he is the legitimate heir to the title and its accompanying fortune, but he keeps this a secret so as not to ruin Jane's future husband. Like "Under the Moons of Mars," the first Tarzan story ends with the hero separated from his lady love.

The story's success immediately earned Tarzan a permanent place in the public consciousness. The idea of a human raised by animals was hardly new. Aside from a number of ancient myths, there was Rudyard Kipling's more recent *Jungle Book*. Burroughs was able to build on the concept in several ways. First, "Tarzan of the Apes" was wrapped in a cracking good adventure plot with plenty of violent action. Second, Burroughs presents an intriguing society of apes,[3] tracing Tarzan's mental and physical growth within this society in detail. Finally, he presents an idea similar to what Robert E. Howard would propose two decades later — that a man untainted by the hypocrisies and softness of civilization is superior to his civilized counterpart.

The ape man is the ultimate in wish fulfillment. He's completely self-sufficient. He literally does not know what it feels like to be afraid. He can think or fight his way out of any situation. And beautiful women are always falling in love with him.

What makes Burroughs' success at building a fictional Africa so amazing was his complete ignorance of the real Africa. He knew nothing of African wildlife. In fact, Tarzan fought tigers in the original version of "Tarzan of the Apes" because Burroughs didn't know there weren't any tigers in Africa.[4] So he built his own Africa and created a species of apes from scratch. The result was as much a fantasy world as John Carter's Mars — a perfect fit for Burroughs' style of storytelling.

Despite his failure at so many different careers before turning to writing, Burroughs had a good head for business. He always demanded that he keep the rights to any stories he sold, ensuring future returns from reprints and novels. He also did not tie himself to one magazine. When *All-Story* editor Thomas Norman Metcalf unwisely rejected a sequel to the first Tarzan story, Burroughs sold it to rival *New Story Magazine*.[5] He continued to produce mountains of fiction throughout the pulp era, never losing his popularity with readers.

In "At the Earth's Core," published in *All-Story* in 1914, Burroughs created the underground world of Pellucidar. This is a savage land existing beneath the Earth's crust, with its own sun suspended by gravity at the center of the hollow world. Pellucidar is inhabited by cave men, dinosaurs and an intelligent species of pterodactyls called Mahars that can telepathically control the minds of humans. Later entries in the series added giant ants, reptile men and a visit by Tarzan.

Burroughs wrote a Venus series, and penned quite a few non-series stories was well, such as "Beyond the Farthest Star" and "The Lost Continent." But Tarzan always remained a fan favorite, and he would return to the ape man again and again.

Later Tarzan stories fell into a rigid formula, though they are (with just a couple of clunkers) individually entertaining. Burroughs actually wanted to kill Jane off fairly early in the series, allowing Tarzan unfettered freedom to wander around the jungle. But magazine editors balked at the idea and Jane lived on. Instead, Burroughs simply made Tarzan the world's most inattentive husband, wandering around the jungle for months at a time while Jane waited with apparently infinite patience back home.

During his wandering, the ape man encountered one lost civilization after another. It pretty much got so that he couldn't step behind a bush to answer a call of nature without stumbling over yet another mysterious, undiscovered city. There were the ant men, who used their science to shrink Tarzan down to their size. There was a Roman city, left over from the collapse of the Empire thirteen hundred years earlier. Here Tarzan was thrown into the arena as a gladiator. There was a civilization of knights descended from crusaders that had gotten really, really lost. There was the city of gold, perpetually at war with the city of ivory. There was Opar, inhabited by degenerate descendants of Atlantis, where the men had nearly reverted to apes but the women were still beautiful.

Burroughs usually used the prisoner trick to introduce background information, then tossed Tarzan into the thick of civil war or last minute rescues or battles with lions, crocodiles, giant snakes and the occasional dinosaur. There was often a co-hero, someone who befriends Tarzan and, being unmarried, is available to fall in love with the princess/slave girl/lost heiress who's bound to turn up along the way.

People never got tired of this, and Tarzan became an industry, spanning every aspect of popular entertainment. Burroughs' care in maintaining the rights to his characters meant he could license them to other media for profit, playing an unconscious but important role in the development of modern merchandizing techniques.

One of Burroughs' best works first appeared in three successive issues of *Blue Book Magazine* in 1918. "The Land That Time Forgot" and its two sequels make up a saga involving war, a submarine, sabotage, treachery, a lost world, a bizarre civilization of winged men and lots of dinosaurs. It is, along with Robert Louis Stevenson's *Treasure Island*, the perfect adventure story.

Burroughs' expertise in pacing reaches its zenith here. The story moves at something just over the speed of light, only occasionally slowing down to allow the reader time to take a quick breath before picking up speed once more. For the major characters, it's just one darn thing after another, where an escape from one deadly threat leads you directly to the next deadly threat.

But the prose is never rushed nor the plot cluttered. Everything that happens is part of a logical sequence that makes complete sense in a Burroughsian universe. Just escaped from a hungry allosaur, did you? Well, of *course* you're going to run into a tribe of bloodthirsty cavemen. What else would you expect?

Brief pauses in the action are spaced throughout the saga, allowing necessary expository information to flow in naturally. Burroughs established a steady narrative rhythm, carrying the story along with expertly described action scenes while gradually revealing the mysteries of a strange new continent.

The story begins at the height of the Great War. A passenger liner is torpedoed by a German U-boat in the English Channel. Two passengers, Bowen Tyler (the story's narrator) and Lys la Rue, escape the sinking wreck in a lifeboat. They're soon rescued by an English tug, but then encounter the same submarine a second time.

Rather than submit to capture, the tug's crew board the U-boat and manage to capture it. Because of Tyler's knowledge of submarines (his father owns a shipyard that builds them), he is soon placed in command.

With the help of a traitor, the Germans escape confinement and recapture the sub. With the aid of Miss la Rue, the Allies escape confinement and re-recapture the sub. By the time all this is sorted out, they've gotten lost somewhere in the South Atlantic.

Low on fuel and fresh water, they stumble across a previously undiscovered continent surrounded by unscalable cliffs. They find a subterranean passage that leads them into a volcanically-heated land of thick jungles and some rather diverse wildlife. The sub is immediately attacked by a plesiosaur.

The Allies and Germans decide to set aside their differences until they can get back to civilization. They build a fort and start exploring their new home, hoping to discover some method of escape.

They gradually learn more about the land, called Caspak by the primitive natives. The south end of Caspak is thick with dinosaurs and other dangerous carnivores. As you progress north, along either end of the great central lake, the animals gradually become more evolved. So do the people, who at first are barely more than apes. Successive tribes are more human in appearance and better armed.

It's not until nearly the end of the saga that the full mystery is revealed. Caspak is a world of accelerated evolution, where life arises out of the water at the southern end of the lake. Some of that life develops into primitive apes. Some of the apes—if they avoid getting eaten—change into primitive men during their lifetimes. Some of these men will later progress to the next stage, and so on. Eventually, some few will become "Kro-lu," a completely human race whose women can bear children normally.[6]

Then there's the Wieroo, a race of winged men whose existence is only hinted at early in the tale. They play an important part in the story later on.

Tyler and his band eventually find a source of oil and set up a crude refinery. In the meantime, some natives kidnap Miss La Rue. While Tyler is busy rescuing her, the Germans betray the Allies and sail off in the refueled sub.

Tyler and Lys are separated from the surviving Allies. Tyler puts a written account of their adventures into a thermos and drops it off the cliffs into the ocean below.

The first sequel, "The People That Time Forgot," begins with the discovery of Tyler's thermos. Tyler's best friend, Tom Billings, forms a rescue party and sails to Caspak. Billings flies a seaplane over the cliffs, where he's immediately attacked by a pterodactyl.

His plane crashes. After meeting a pretty Kro-lu girl named Ajor, he experiences numerous adventures, including a really creepy sequence in which he and the girl spend hours stumbling blindly through a pitch-dark series of caves, gradually weakening from hunger and thirst as they search for a way out.

In the end, they find Tyler and Lys living with the Kro-lu. Other members of the rescue party have built a ladder up the cliffs from the far side, giving them an escape route. Tyler and Lys go, but Billings stays behind with Ajor. He loves her, you see, but her father, chief of the Kro-lus, won't let her leave.

"Out of Time's Abyss," the last installment of the saga, tells us what happened to the rest of Tyler's original companions. Several were killed by various large carnivores. One of the others, Bradley, is captured by the Wieroos, who carry him off to their city.

The Wieroos, it turns out, have a problem. They can sire only male children, forcing them to regularly kidnap Kro-lu women to perpetuate their race. Making them even more unpleasant is the structure of their society, which is based on a system of ritual assassination. Wieroos kill each other at least as often as they do their external enemies.

To no one's surprise, Bradley meets a pretty girl. Named Co-Tan, she's a Kro-lu kidnapped for breeding purposes. The two escape, dodging about the city until they find a way out via an underground river used by the Wieroos to dispose of corpses.

Rejoining his companions, Bradley then helps to once again capture the German U-boat, which has returned to Caspak for more fuel. They meet Billings and Ajor, manage to sneak them aboard, then make their getaway to civilization.

It is Burroughs' gradual method of exposition that allows the reader to accept all this. He starts by giving us a lost world full of supposedly extinct fauna. Okay, we can accept that. Then he hints at the biological mystery of the place, only revealing it in its entirety when he has presented enough information to back it up. Fine, we can accept that as well.

All along, he's also hinted at the winged men. Not until the last installment do they put in an appearance. Even then, we at first only receive brief glimpses of them in the dark. By the time one of them takes Bradley into the Wieroo city, we're more than willing to accept them as real also. It's a beautiful example of skillful plot construction and establishing an atmosphere in which the fantastic becomes real.

Burroughs' sense of pacing and structure allowed him to get away with something that spoiled the stories of many lesser writers. He did not hesitate to use coincidence, no matter how unlikely, to move the plot along. If Tarzan, tossed off an ocean liner by an enemy, needs to wash ashore on the African coast at the exact spot where he grew up, that was fine. If Jane, surviving the sinking of another ship, needs to come ashore at the same spot a few weeks later, that's fine as well.[7] In other Tarzan stories, the *Lord of the Apes* encounters different men who are his exact physical doubles, and twice suffers from amnesia at dramatically appropriate moments.

But coincidence in a Burroughs story, no matter how shamelessly used, just becomes another natural part of the narrative flow. In "Tarzan and the Jewels of Opar" (*All-Story*, 1916), an amnesiac Tarzan, three sets of bad guys, Jane, and a friend of Tarzan's, all wandering separately through the trackless jungle, meet each other in a series of perfectly timed fights, captures and escapes. Coincidence is used as a dramatic spur that effectively drives the plot forward.

Many other writers could have constructed a more reasonable and still entertaining plot out of the same situation. Few besides Edgar Rice Burroughs could have kept it so unreasonable and still made it work.

10. Unpleasant Interlude

Anything that man can do well, he can also do badly. Pulp fiction is certainly no exception. And it wasn't just that there were so many badly written stories or poorly edited magazines. That's just harmless incompetence, and it's easy enough in retrospect to concentrate on the more worthwhile prose. But the pulps also reflected some of American society's worst moral failings. It would be improper for any history of the era not to acknowledge this.

There were many glaring examples of casual racism in the pulps. Pulp fiction was produced by writers living in a segregated, racist society. Their stories often reflected this, with non-white characters either absent altogether or portrayed as stereotypes. I'll make no attempt to estimate what percentage of pulp stories contained racist elements. I doubt that's possible, and it's debatable how useful such a number would be. Percentages aside, racism was not at all uncommon.

Edgar Rice Burroughs, for all his extraordinary talent as a storyteller, allowed his bigotries to show through in his portrayal of black Africans in the Tarzan novels. Though he did present individual black characters as good or bad, brave or cowardly, his general attitude was that the white man was of the superior race. The relationship between whites and blacks was either hostile or that of a father watching over children.

Black and Hispanic Americans, as was common in other media of the time, were often used as clowns to provide comic relief. Orientals were often part of the Yellow Peril, involved in a secret plot to undermine or conquer white civilization. This latter stereotype was first popularized by Sax Rohmer's Fu Manchu stories,[1] and carried over into several pulp magazines featuring Oriental master criminals. Philip Nowlan's Buck Rogers stories used this idea as well.

I am not lamenting a lack of political correctness. There's nothing inherently wrong with a writer using a Chinese villain. But when a character is a villain (or a clown) purely because of his ethnicity, the modern reader can't help but wince.

Often, as in Burroughs' case, the writers were reflecting their own racism. Sometimes it might have been of more innocent intent, reflecting the conventions of the time without thinking about the harm it caused. One of the many unfortunate aspects of a segregated society is that even good people can say hurtful things without having the slightest idea they are hurtful.

In the end, it is fair to remember that racist attitudes were reflections of the times, and I think it's okay to still read and enjoy Burroughs or Nowlan. Someone else, though, might think differently regarding any one particular story. It's a subject that's fodder for an interesting debate. To what degree can we forgive these attitudes within the work of an otherwise talented writer? There's no answer to that question that could ever satisfy everyone, which means we need to keep asking it. Modern politically correct thought often stifles such discussions, making it that much more important to have them anyway.

The Weird Menace pulps are especially difficult to take. The first of these was *Dime Mystery Stories*, which began publishing Weird Menace stories in 1933. Its success spawned a number of imitators.

Weird Menace tales tended to be badly constructed horror stories involving psychopathic and often deformed killers who threatened beautiful, scantily-clad women. They were the antecedents of modern slasher movies, with the same lack of style, skill or intelligence.[2] Women in these stories suffer every conceivable form of degradation. They are regularly stalked, kidnapped, and threatened with torture and rape.

A high level of violence is not unusual in fiction. Violence is a legitimate part of drama. Placing characters in danger is equally legitimate. A writer can have his women characters kidnapped on a regular basis with a perfectly clear conscience. In fact, many pulp stories would cease to exist without this plot device.

If a writer can handle the subject with real emotion, he can even place a woman in danger of rape or torture. All of this can serve as justifiable fodder for storytelling.

The Weird Menace tales, though, did not handle these situations with anything resembling real emotion. What made them so offensive was the idea that the portrayal of a woman in danger of sexual violation was itself sexually titillating. This was the direct and only appeal of these magazines.

Women weren't placed in danger to generate suspense or terror. Weird Menace pulps based their entire existence on the idea that the image of a woman being tortured or raped was a turn-on.

To say that this was disrespectful to women would probably be the world's greatest understatement. Unfortunately, these magazines were successful, selling well for most of the 1930s before a campaign by New York mayor LaGuardia to clean up the newsstands scared publishers away from the genre.

Sadly, some of the better quality magazines used Weird Menace tactics from time to time. *Weird Tales* would occasionally use cover illustrations depicting, for instance, one nearly naked woman whipping another. At least one regular contributor to *Weird Tales*, Seabury Quinn, would purposely include such scenes in his stories to increase the chance of them being chosen as the subject for the cover.

The Spider, one of the single-character pulps that will be discussed in the next chapter (and an otherwise worthwhile magazine), often placed the Spider's luckless girlfriend, Nita Van Sloan, in the hands of lecherous thugs. Once again, the slant of the prose wasn't meant to generate concern for the character. Rather, it was to arouse the men and boys reading the story.

One has to recognize the individuality of tastes. Many perfectly reasonable people might honestly find some of the stories I've been praising as offensive as I find the Weird Menace pieces. But for most readers, when someone starts treating women as pieces of meat that must suffer to give men pleasure, even in strictly a fictional context, then a moral line in the sand has definitely been crossed.

11. Shadows, Spiders and Flying Aces: The Single-Character Pulps

There were many recurring characters in the pulps, such as Tarzan, Conan the Barbarian and the Continental Op—characters whose popularity with readers brought them back regularly for additional adventures. Another example of this was Zorro, the masked outlaw who fought against a tyrannical government in Spanish California.

Created by Johnston McCully, Zorro first appeared in the serial "The Curse of Capistrano," published in *All-Story Weekly* in 1919. The story was adapted into a film starring Douglas Fairbanks in 1920, then republished as a novel in 1924. This success inspired McCully to write dozens more Zorro adventures over the next several decades.

The masked man was a great character, a master swordsman who used his wits as much as his blade, outsmarting his frustrated enemies again and again. McCully's original serial is fast-paced and full of humor. Many of the later stories lack the same level of charm and spontaneity as the original, but are still worthwhile.

Considering the success of so many individual characters, it's amazing that it took publishers so long to start printing magazines concentrating on specific heroes. The dime novels, after all, had done this for years. But the first single-character pulp didn't appear until 1931.

This was *The Shadow*. Its success opened the floodgates, and single-character pulps would become a common sight at newsstands for nearly two decades.

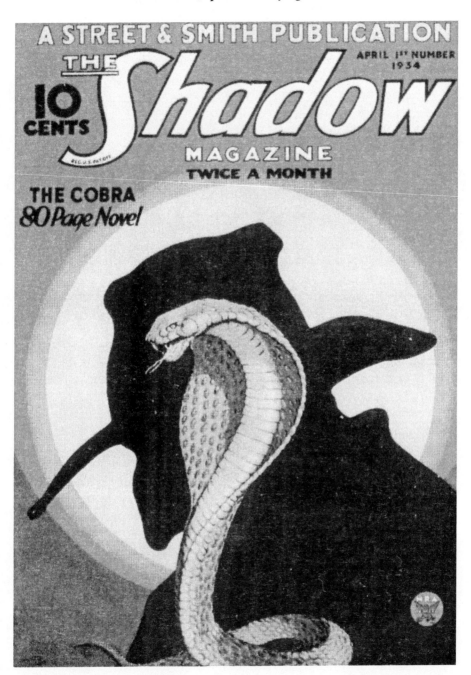

Artist George Rozen provided atmospheric and often eerie covers for many issues of *The Shadow*.

The Shadow got his start on radio. In 1930, publishing firm Street & Smith tried out this new medium to advertise one of its magazines. They sponsored a weekly show called *Detective Story Hour*, which dramatized stories from the popular pulp *Detective Story Magazine*. The show's narrator was a mysterious character called the Shadow.

As an advertising gimmick, the show worked well — just not in the way Street & Smith expected. People were asking newsstand operators not for *Detective Story*, but for the magazine featuring the Shadow.

Street & Smith's general manager, Henry William Ralston, quickly decided there actually needed to *be* a magazine featuring the Shadow. Ralston instructed editor-in-chief Frank Blackwell to find a writer.

Blackwell brought in Walter Gibson, who had written many articles on professional magicians and magic tricks, as well as stories for true crime magazines. Gibson proved to be the perfect choice, creating a mythic character whose exploits would be published regularly for eighteen years. There would be 325 issues of *The Shadow*, most of them featuring a novel-length adventure. Gibson would write about 280 of these.[1] He was an incredibly fast writer, turning out up to 15,000 words a day on a manual typewriter, often stopping at day's end only when his fingertips began to bleed.

At first, all Gibson had to work with was the name and a creepy voice. From this, he created a mysterious figure armed with a pair of .45 automatics and garbed in a black cloak — someone able to blend into the shadows around him and thus seem to appear or disappear at will. He was dedicated to fighting crime and seemed to have unlimited funds and resources with which to do the job. No one knew who he really was, not even the many agents he recruited to assist him.

The premiere story, from April 1931, was "The Living Shadow." It begins with a young man, Harry Vincent, standing atop a bridge in New York City. Broke and broken-hearted, he contemplates suicide. But the Shadow appears and offers him a choice. "I will improve [your life]," he says. "I shall make it useful. But I shall risk it, too.... This is my promise: life with enjoyment, with danger, with excitement.... Life, above all, with honor."

Vincent accepts, becoming an agent of the Shadow. Immediately he's hip deep in a case involving secret codes and stolen jewels.

This first story tells us nothing about the Shadow's background or true identity. We discover he has remarkable physical and mental prowess, and is a master of disguise. But the air of mystery around him remains thick.

It wasn't until 1937, in "The Shadow Unmasks," that readers learned who he really was. The Shadow had been using several identities, the most common being wealthy Lamont Cranston. But he was only borrowing this name and face while the real Cranston traveled in Europe and Asia. The Shadow was actually Kent Allard, a flying ace from the Great War. Allard had disappeared after the war, supposedly having crashed while flying over a Guatemalan jungle. Somewhere in that jungle he found great wealth. Secretly returning to civilization, he began his private campaign against crime.

His agents were an important part of this campaign. Aside from Harry Vincent, there was Clyde Burke, a newspaper reporter, and Cliff Marsland, whose ties to the underworld made him a valuable undercover man. There were at least a dozen others.

The Shadow himself had a wide range of skills. He was an expert with firearms and in unarmed combat. He could disguise himself as just about anyone. He often used sleight-of-hand or other magician's tricks to good effect, especially when escaping from frequent death traps. He used suction cups to climb the sides of buildings. He wore a ring mounted with a flaming red opal, which he could use to hypnotize people. He was a master strategist, keeping his agents constantly working to follow or investigate suspects.

The success of the Shadow soon convinced Street & Smith to change the publication schedule from monthly to twice a month. That meant Gibson had to provide twenty-four novel-length stories a year, rather than twelve. He not only did this, but usually managed to stay about six months ahead of schedule.

Still, to cover their bets, Street & Smith commissioned another writer, Theodore Tinsey, to writer four stories a year. Regardless of who the actual writer was, the byline in each issue would read "from the Private Annals of the Shadow, as told to Maxwell Grant." Grant was a house name used to maintain a sense of continuity to the series despite multiple authors. The same trick was often used in later single-character pulps.

Tinsey wrote some pretty good stories, but Gibson was generally superior in developing tight plots.[2] Gibson's stories were very straightforward, well-paced and never wandered off unnecessarily.

Gibson used several standard plots repeatedly, setting the Shadow against gangsters in one story, then spies or anarchists in the next. There were quite a few master criminals and a number of super-scientific devices that had fallen into the wrong hands. The plots were formulaic, but Gibson varied the details enough to make them seem fresh almost every time. His background in magic, for instance, allowed him to come up with an incredible variety of death traps and an equal number of clever ways to escape from them.

A typically strong Shadow story is "Double Z," from the June 1932 issue. It begins when a newspaper reporter locates a judge who has been in hiding for a year. The judge had been in constant fear for his life since learning the identity of a master criminal known only as Double Z. Double Z had been responsible for a series of murders designed to increase his own power over the criminal underworld. The reporter calls his editor, but he's shot before he can pass on Double Z's true name.

Clyde Burke, a reporter on the same paper, passes on this information to the Shadow. An investigation begins.

Another agent, Cliff Marsland, soon manages to hook up with a gangster working for Double Z. When the gangster receives an order to kill one of his boss' enemies, Cliff comes along. Cliff sends a message to the Shadow, but through bad luck its delivery is delayed.

Cliff tries to stop the murder on his own. He fails and is himself nearly killed. The Shadow arrives just in time to save him. The gangster falls to his death trying to escape over a rooftop, leaving Cliff's undercover status as a criminal intact.

The investigation to identify Double Z continues. Cliff and Harry Vincent, following different trails, both arrive at the lair of Chinese criminal Loy Rook, another Double Z confederate. Loy captures them, using them as bait to lure the Shadow into a room that can be flooded with poison gas.

But the Shadow detects and eludes Loy Rook's death trap. In a wild gun battle, Loy Rook and several gangsters are killed. Harry and Cliff are rescued.

By now, Double Z is running out of men. Finally, the Shadow gathers enough clues to identify and confront him. Double Z turns out to be one of his own victims— having earlier faked his own death to divert suspicion. The story concludes with the crack of a pistol, when the villain makes the final, fatal mistake of trying to shoot it out with the Shadow.

Fueled by an unending stream of plot twists and death traps, *The Shadow Magazine* continued until Street & Smith cancelled its entire line of pulps in 1949. Towards the end, sales had dropped off and the magazine had gone to a quarterly schedule. Gibson had moved on by then, and some of the later stories, written by Bruce Elliot, were of low quality.

But at its best, *The Shadow* had been a high point in the history of the pulps. A truly mythic figure, he personified justice and honor and courage. He used his skills not to help himself, but to help others. And with the assistance of Walter Gibson, the Shadow did it all with style.

The success of *The Shadow* soon had Street & Smith preparing another single-character pulp. Initially, they planned to feature a character very similar to the Shadow. But to their credit, general manager Henry Ralston and *Shadow* editor John Nanovic opted to do something a little different. Working together, they came up with a 30-page summery for "Doc Savage, Supreme Adventurer."

Nanovic hired pulp veteran Lester Dent to write Doc Savage's adventures. The result was another hit, with *Doc Savage Magazine* soon selling 200,000 copies a month. Using the house name Kenneth Robeson, Dent would write 161 of the 181 adventures.

The first story was "The Man of Bronze," published in March 1933. The title referred to Doc, whose skin was permanently tanned a deep bronze. His hair, too, was bronze, just of a slightly different shade. He was over six feet tall, incredibly muscular, and had "weird, commanding eyes, like nothing so much as pools of flake gold."

If any fictional character could rival Tarzan as a surrogate for wish fulfillment, it is Doctor Clark Savage, Jr. Aside from his physical prowess and enormous strength, he's also a mental giant. He's a brilliant surgeon and an expert in chemistry, biology, engineering, and just about everything else. He's constantly inventing really cool stuff, including submarines, machine guns that fire mercy bullets, oxygen pills that allow you to breath underwater, and rocket-powered dirigibles. All this costs a lot of money, but that's no problem. A race of ancient Mayans hidden deep in the Central American jungles, grateful to Doc after he once helped them out, keep him well supplied with gold.

Doc's home and headquarters is on the 86th floor of a Manhattan skyscraper, guarded by all sorts of traps and alarms. A warehouse along the Hudson River houses his many planes, boats, subs and other vehicles. He has a Fortress of Solitude, a secret structure located somewhere above the Arctic Circle, where he stores many of his more potentially dangerous inventions. He also uses the Fortress for occasional periods of intense study, where he brings himself up to date on all recent scientific advances, and adds a few advances of his own.

Just as the Shadow has his agents, Doc Savage has his assistants. Ham, Monk, Renny, Long Tom, and Johnny are all brilliant men in their own right, each an expert in a different field. All are completely devoted to Doc, willing to follow him anywhere and always ready to fight at his side.

There were many additional agents scattered around the world, used to gather information or assist in any other way needed. Doc Savage had a unique method of recruiting these men. Whenever he captured a criminal, he took him to a special clinic located in upstate New York. Doc would perform brain surgery, after which the crook had lost all memory of his sordid past and had become a law-abiding citizen. Often they went on Doc's payroll.[3]

Like most pulp heroes, Doc Savage had to be prepared to deal with anything from dinosaurs to death rays to giants with bad attitudes.

Doc and his friends dedicated their wealth and talents to helping others. Sometimes this was straightforward. Doc would pass a nearly blind woman begging on the street. Diagnosing her condition at a glance, he would give her the name of a specialist who could cure her. Doc's name on a note was sufficient to ensure that there would be no fee for the specialist's services.

Most of the time, though, Doc's instinct to help people would bring him into conflict with powerful criminals and demented would-be world conquerors. Lester Dent wrote rapid, slam-bang prose perfectly suited to this formula. He piled cliffhanger atop cliffhanger, filling each story with a torrent of captures, escapes, fist fights, gun fights, and chases. Any one story usually began with Doc in New York City, but before long he'd be zipping off to a South Sea island or the jungles of Africa or a secret underwater city. There were monsters, lost civilizations, death rays, and robots.

"Land of Terror," from the April 1933 issue, was the second Doc Savage adventure published. It begins when chemist Jerome Coffern, in fear of his life after an assassination attempt, contacts Doc for help. But Coffern is murdered before the two men can meet. The thugs who kill him use a mysterious gray gas to disintegrate the body.

Doc and his men investigate. Soon they learn that a criminal known only as Kar has obtained a supply of the Smoke of Eternity, which can dissolve almost anything. Coffern had been killed because he knew too much about the gas, and possibly about Kar's true identity.

There occurs a quick succession of violent encounters with Kar's minions. Monk is kidnapped and hidden aboard a submersible barge, but is soon rescued. An attempt to use the gas to rob a bank is foiled. Finally, Kar's supply of the gas is destroyed.

But Kar still remains on the loose and unidentified. Doc has learned that the mineral needed to manufacture the gas is located only on a remote Pacific island. Doc and his men fly there, hoping to head off Kar's probable attempt to get the mineral. They are accompanied by Oliver Bittman, a friend of Doc's late father, who has also become involved in the case.

Arriving at the island by plane, they are immediately attacked by a pterodactyl and forced to bail out. The island, it turns out, is inhabited by prehistoric creatures. For awhile, the adventurers are kept busy just staying one jump ahead of hungry tyrannosaurs. But Kar's men have also arrived, and Doc's companions are captured. Fortunately, Doc has finally deduced that Bittman is Kar. Doc rescues the others, and Kar/Bittman meets his end in the jaws of a giant carnosaur.

Dent had accomplished something similar to what Edgar Rice Burroughs had done. He had constructed a fictional universe in which the most fantastic events were made to seem reasonable. When Doc was on a case, he conducted an intelligent, logical investigation. The clues he found might lead him to an island full of dinosaurs or to the discovery of a water-breathing people descended from ancient Egyptians, but they'd be fair clues that made perfect sense in the context of the story.

During the 1940s, the series began to lose steam. The super-scientific elements were gradually toned down. By the time *Doc Savage* was cancelled in 1949, Doc had become little more than a smarter-than-average detective. But during its heyday in the 1930s, *Doc Savage* was one of the most consistently entertaining pulps on the market.

In 1933, Harry Steeger, head of Popular Publications, was looking for a way to revive sales of *Battle Aces*, a pulp specializing in World War I aviation tales. Aware of the growing popularity of single-character magazines, Steeger decided to try this concept within *Battle Aces'* wartime setting.

He brought in writer Robert J. Hogan, who was himself a flyer and war veteran.[4] Hogan was experienced in producing aviation stories, but to keep a series about a combat flyer interesting in the long term, something more than airplanes and dogfights would be needed.

Steeger and Hogan came up with a two-fold solution. First, the hero would not just be an ace pilot, but a spy. In fact, he'd be the top spy in Allied service during the Great War, undertaking only the most dangerous and vital assignments.

Second, he would encounter a succession of lethal, uncanny adversaries— mad scientists, giant bats, zombie pilots, Viking warriors and leopards that leapt from plane to plane in mid-flight. These menaces would constantly threaten to wipe out entire divisions, devastate civilian populations, rip holes in the Allied lines, ruin morale, and bring about total defeat. The hero would not just be stealing military plans or rescuing downed flyers; he'd be saving hundreds of thousands of Allied lives and preventing German victory on a monthly basis.

The first issue of *G-8 and His Battle Aces* was published in October 1933. G-8 is a typical formula pulp hero— a master of disguise and expert fighter pilot. When the series opens, his exploits have already made him famous across the battlegrounds of France.[5] But with "The Bat Staffel," his life starts to get a bit weird.

German scientist Herr Doktor Kreuger has invented giant flying planes in the shape of bats. Armored and nearly impervious to machine gun fire, these planes will be used to spread poison gas across Allied territory just before the German army launches a new offensive. G-8 learns of this plot and, infiltrating German lines, manages to put a stop to it. The giant bats are destroyed and the gas released not on the Allies, but into a secret underground lair housing a hundred thousand German troops.

One threat to Allied victory has been averted, but a master spy's work is never done. A month later, Doktor Kreuger is back, turning captured Allied pilots into suicide bombers with purple faces.

And so it went. Kreuger appeared as G-8's nemesis twenty-seven times, and other villains also made repeat appearances. Most of G-8's adversaries came and went more quickly, but always with the threat of killing thousands in a variety of horrible ways.

As was typical in the successful single-character pulps, the master spy's commercial success was a result of linking him with just the right author. Hogan wrote all 110 issues of G-8, signing his own name to each issue. His knowledge of aviation helped add verisimilitude to the action sequences, and his prose was snappy and direct.

Hogan employed a formula perhaps even more rigid than those used by Walter Gibson and Lester Dent. The latest German threat would be introduced quickly, often in the first paragraph. G-8's ability as a pilot and disguise artist helps him move quickly from location to location, on both sides of the Front, as he investigates and fights back. Fist fights, gun fights, escapes and dogfights continuously punctuate the story.

It was a formula that left little room for indepth characterization, and Hogan did not attempt to add any. G-8 is described in broad terms—he's stalwart, resourceful and clever. His companions, the "Battle Aces," are also defined by a few key attributes. Nippy Weston is small and wiry. He's an expert in magic and sleight-of-hand. Bull Martin is large and muscular, a former All-American fullback. Like G-8, both are ace pilots. Together, the trio exists purely to carry the plot along as swiftly as possible.

G-8 also employs the services of an English butler named Battle. Battle is dumber than a turnip, misunderstanding almost everything said or done in his presence. But he's an expert make-up artist and essential in helping with G-8's disguises. Battle's malapropisms and general idiocy were supposed to provide comic relief, but, unfortunately, he was just annoying. Hogan, skilled at plot construction and action sequences, had no talent for comedy.

One interesting character element did occasionally pop up in a G-8 story. Hogan often portrayed the average German soldier with a fair amount of sympathy. This was expressed in little episodes mixed in with the larger plot. G-8 might pause to give comfort to a dying enemy or help a terrified 16-year-old draftee get to safety. Simplistic characterizations prevented these moments from carrying any real emotional impact, but

When they weren't using giant robot bats or invisible planes, the Germans often employed the undead in their efforts to win the First World War. The January 1938 cover of *G-8 and His Battle Aces* depicts the master spy at work on a (for him) typical day.

it's interesting to note that Hogan managed to keep a reminder of the tragedy of real war hovering in the background of his otherwise fantastic yarns.

Still, the main purpose of a G-8 story was always to provide an hour or two of vicarious excitement. In "The Vampire Staffel," from February 1934, G-8 investigates after several German planes release hordes of locust over Allied lines. Soon, Allied troops are dropping dead from some new plague, their skin bleached white as the disease thickens the blood to the point where it can't circulate.

G-8 learns that an Egyptian named Amen Sikh is responsible for spreading the plague. The master spy, disguised as an elderly clockmaker, sneaks behind enemy lines in an attempt to obtain the antidote. Discovered, he's captured and taken to Amen Sikh's fortress deep in the Black Forest.

One clobbered guard/gun battle/escape later, and G-8 is back in France. With him is a German scientist named Ernstein, who has been working with the Egyptian. Ernstein knows how to make the antidote. He also reveals that Amen Sikh is planning on releasing the plague on the Germans as well as the Allies—part of a scheme to eventually conquer the world.

Complicating matters further is the fact that the only supply of the antidote's key ingredient is inside Amen Sikh's fortress.

The Germans and Allies decide to team up against this common threat. With German help, G-8 returns to the fortress. He's captured yet again and locked in a room full of plague-carrying locust. Another escape follows. Weakening rapidly as the plague begins to take hold, G-8 manages to steal the needed ingredient and fly to a German airfield before he collapses. He's given the antidote in the nick of time, while German and Allied bombers destroy Amen Sikh's base.

Everyone goes back to killing each other by more conventional means—at least until next month, when G-8 would battle "The Skeleton Patrol." There were over a hundred issues of such unabashed, enjoyable silliness before G-8's career finally ended.

If one were to judge by the pulps of the Popular Publications chain, peacetime New York is nearly as dangerous a place to be as the front lines during the Great War. G-8 had saved us again and again from the horrific creations of German scientists, but who would save us from the criminals and anarchists bringing death and terror on a similarly massive scale to the streets of Manhattan? This month might bring the destruction of the Empire State Building. Next month, someone would release the bubonic plague onto the city. The month after would see swarms of rabid bats attacking a panicking populace.

The police, typically, would be helpless. The National Guard would be pinned down outside the city by a heavily-armed horde of insane hoboes. Men in bulletproof iron suits would be looting banks. Bombs, bullets, flame throwers, poison gas, poisoned food supplies, poisonous insects, clouds of acid, madmen such as Judge Torture and the Emperor of Vermin, leprosy, insanity drugs and giant Neanderthals are but a few of the unstoppable threats that baºe the authorities and kill thousands of innocents.

There are but two options open to the frightened New Yorker — move to Duluth or trust the Spider to save us all once again.

The first issue of *The Spider* was cover dated October 1933, the same month G-8 premiered. Created by Harry Steeger, the Spider was at first little more than a clone of the Shadow. He was a rich guy, Richard Wentworth, who had dedicated himself to fighting crime. Like the Shadow, he adopted a creepy persona intended to frighten criminals. In this case, Wentworth disguised himself as a fanged, long-haired hunchback.

The first two issues were nothing special. But in December 1933, Norvell Page became the magazine's regular writer. Using the house name Grant Stockbridge, Page would write 91 of the 119 Spider stories.

Page immediately began to throw one enormous threat after another at poor Richard Wentworth. His plots only barely made sense — if they made sense at all. But his stories are so full of energy and breathless conflict that the details of the plot almost don't matter.

It was Page's characterization of the Spider that gave the stories enough dramatic backbone to make them work. Richard Wentworth could have had anything he wanted. He was a millionaire in love with the beautiful heiress Nita van Sloan, who loved him just as intensely. He wanted nothing more than to spend the rest of his life with her.

But he couldn't. Not while the innocent suffered. As long as he had the skills and resources to help those in need, giving that help would always be the first priority in his life.

So he became the Spider, a vigilante willing to stand up against a steady stream of mass murderers. Working outside the law, wanted by the police and feared by the populace, he fights on with unstinting courage.

Nothing stops him. And I mean *nothing*. If he's shot in the lung, he stuffs his fist in the wound and keeps going. If he's captured and chained to a wall by his ankle, he begins to search for something with which to cut off his foot so he can keep going. If he's trapped in a burning building, surrounded by the police and temporarily blinded by gas, he'll quickly but methodically find a way to escape. If he hears a little girl crying from behind a locked door while he's escaping from the burning building, he'll pause to rescue her first.

Page put so much raw emotion into each story he wrote that he simply bludgeoned past problems of melodrama and incoherent story construction. The Spider yarns literally scream aloud, "I am my brother's keeper and I will give my life if necessary to keep my brother safe!"

Though the odds were always against him, the Spider at least did not have to fight alone. Nita knew of his secret identity and actively assisted him, often offing a number of bad guys on her own during any one adventure. Wentworth's servants, Jackson and Ram Singh, fought at his side. The elderly Professor Brownlee provided the Spider with all sorts of useful gadgets, such as the lightweight but nearly unbreakable rope called the Spider's Web.

Being an ally of the Spider was as dangerous as being the Spider himself. Nita was kidnapped or wounded nearly as often as was Wentworth. Jackson and Ram Singh suffered countless bullet or stab wounds. And poor Professor Brownlee was eventually murdered.

In "The Spider and the Slaves of Hell," from July 1939, Nita is recovering from crippling injuries received in the previous month's story. Her convalescence, however, will not go undisturbed. Wentworth's home is dynamited into rubble in the first chapter. This is the opening move by a villain called the Butcher, who soon after begins destroying crowded public and commercial buildings. The Butcher's purpose is two-fold. First, the explosions cover the escape of his minions after they've looted a place. Second, he plans to extort money in exchange for sparing future buildings. On top of all this, the Butcher has equipped his men with guns that fire exploding bullets.

Wentworth disguises himself as a thug as he tries to learn the Butcher's identity. He's captured and tossed into a cell occupied by man-eating dogs. Escaping, he learns of a plan to destroy a department store.

He rushes to the store, where he manages to scare the shoppers into evacuating. A gun battle with the Butcher's men ensues. The police also start shooting, and the Spider is badly wounded. Stumbling from the store, he leads the police on a chase back to the location where he'd been held prisoner. Then he hides in a truck that's driving out of the city.

The Butcher evades the police and continues blowing up buildings. Wentworth, meanwhile, recovers from his wound at a country hospital. Returning to the city,[6] he adopts yet another identity in order to infiltrate the Butcher's gang.

Following more chases and gunfights, Wentworth finds himself a prisoner of the Butcher yet again, with heavy metal balls chained to his limbs. Despite this, he escapes, kills several bad guys and arranges the evacuation of another doomed building. Then, with the balls still chained to his arms and legs, he climbs the sheer wall of the building to rescue Nita, who's being held captive on the roof. The story ends with the inevitably anticlimactic identification and death of the Butcher.

The series had flaws even beyond the illogical plots. The motives of the villains often were uncertain or too mundane to justify their complex schemes. The level of violence invited at least occasional tastelessness. One villain, Judge Torture, delighted in turning people into letters of the alphabet while keeping them alive as long as possible. That's more information than we probably need. And Page often gave in to the temptation of combining torture and the threat of rape with sexual titillation.

But Page's better sensibilities usually came to the fore. Nearly all the hero pulps built on the theme that the highest possible calling was helping one's fellow man. *The Spider*, at its best, left us no doubt that this was true. We really are our brothers' keepers. Richard Wentworth used to remind us of this on a monthly basis.

There were many other pulp heroes. Vigilantes such as Secret Agent X, the Avenger, and the Phantom Detective[7] brought countless criminals to justice. Government agent Operator #5 and military pilot Dusty Ayres led desperate fights against foreign invaders. Tarzan clones such as Ka-Zar swung from tree to tree through trackless jungles. There were even a few pulps that featured villains.

By the end of the 1940s, though, the pulps were fading away. The hero pulps were especially hard hit. Comic books provided younger readers with the flashy, four-color adventures of a new breed of superheroes, drawing them away from Doc Savage and the Shadow. Also, many of the single-character magazines had been around for years by this point and were simply running out of creative energy.

The last attempt to resurrect the genre came in 1949, when Popular Publications tried out *Captain Zero*. The magazine featured a hero who, as a result of government experiments with radiation, turned invisible at midnight and reappeared at sunrise.

Written by pulp veteran G.T. Fleming-Roberts, *Captain Zero* is quite good. The plot of the premiere story is similar to Dashiell Hammett's *Red Harvest*, with the protagonist trying to clean up a town controlled by several rival gangs. It offers solid, well-constructed storytelling, realistic in every way other than a main character who turns invisible.

And even that aspect was treated with relative realism. The problems of invisibility dog the hero constantly, from footprints in thick rugs to the fact that he can't drive a car without the sight of an apparently driverless vehicle attracting attention. Captain Zero—his real name is Lee Allyn— has bad eyesight and must wear contact lenses that occasionally reflect light and give him away.

Allyn is presented as just a regular guy trying to use his power to do good, but subject to normal fears when facing danger. He's competent but prone to mistakes and bouts of pure terror. Even the fact of his invisibility understandably scares him. "The first time it had happened," we are told, "he had almost lost his mind." He more or less gets used to it, but always in the back of his mind is the worry that next time he won't reappear when the sun rises.

The magazine was an attempt to draw adult readers back to the hero pulps, but it didn't catch on and lasted only three issues. Hero pulps were dead, and the rest of the industry was dying.

12. The Death of the Pulps

The pulps were killed by a combination of factors. As previously mentioned, comic books began providing a more graphic and easily accessible source of fantasy adventure and wish fulfillment. The late 1930s saw paperback books introduced to the marketplace. They steadily grew in popularity throughout the next decade, providing a competing source for affordable fiction. World War II brought paper shortages, forcing publishers to cut back on print runs and often causing the cancellations of even profitable magazines.

In 1949, Street & Smith cancelled its entire pulp line, salvaging only *Astounding Science Fiction* as a digest-sized magazine. Other publishers also left the field or simply went out of business. By the mid–1950s, pulp magazines had ceased to exist.

Perhaps it was time for them to go. They had served a purpose while they lasted, drawing themes and story content out of the perpetual societal and technological upheavals brought about by industrialization. Genres such as westerns, mysteries and science fiction had developed into true literature largely within the pulps. The single-character magazines, along with newspaper comic strips, had directly spawned the comic book superhero, itself a vibrant addition to American popular fiction.

New fiction still floods the marketplace, with digest magazines and paperback adventure series replacing the pulps in intent if not in sheer variety. Much of this fiction is good. Some of it is great. Nearly all of it builds on work that first appeared on pages of cheap paper, selling dreams of adventure for ten cents a pop.

Part II

Adventure Comic Strips; or, War, Death, Horror, and Fine Art

In the late 19th century the newspaper was the only regular and reasonably prompt outlet for news, gossip and baseball scores. Big cities often had half-a-dozen major papers, while even small towns might often support two or three. New York City had *The New York Times*, *The New York Observer*, *The Evening Post*, *The Sun*, *The New York Tribune*, *The New York World*, *The Morning Journal*, *The Herald*, and several others. Competition for readers was fierce, and publishers tried anything and everything to increase circulation. They reported scandals, rushed to scoop one another, and made up news when they couldn't find anything appropriately sensational. Sometimes, making up news could generate the real thing. Sensationalized reports of events in Cuba were a factor in the start of the Spanish-American War.[1]

By the last decade of the century, printing technology had improved enough to make the use of color viable for newspapers. Joseph Pulitzer, owner of *The New York World*, bought a four-color press[2] in 1893, announcing that it would be used to reproduce famous paintings. Other papers followed suit. Color supplements and illustrations soon became a major selling point for newspapers.

In the meantime, the cartoon was slowly developing as an outlet both for simple comedy and for social and political satire. Several elements of

HE WAS CHASING THE DUCK.

Little Mickey Dugan—Hey, dere, Sloppy, yez kin git arrested an' pulled up by de society fer doin' dat. It's agins le law fer minors wot ain't of age.

An early example of R.F. Outcault's *Hogan's Alley*. The feature paved the way for the true comic strip.

the modern comic strip began to pop up now and then. The occasional dialogue-conveying word balloon appeared. In 1827, a Swiss artist named Rodolphe Topffer developed what he called picture stories, with sequential images telling a specific tale.

Color printing and cartooning met one another in 1895, when *The New York World* began publishing *Hogan's Alley*.

Hogan's Alley is often credited with being the first comic strip. That's not strictly true, since it used just a single panel rather than a series of images. But it featured a regular cast, headed by a young bald boy in a yellow shirt, and a regular setting. Printed every Sunday, it was a huge commercial success. With that success, a new American art form was born.

13. The Early Years

Sunday comics soon became a staple of the industry. Pulitzer's chief rival, William Randolph Hearst, began his own color comics section in the *New York Journal*. Other papers quickly followed suit. Hearst hired *Hogan's Alley* creator, R. F. Outcault, away from Pulitzer. Pulitzer hired another artist to continue to do the feature for the *World*. The ensuing court case ended with Pulitzer owning *Hogan's Alley*, but also with Outcault allowed to draw the main character—the Yellow Kid—for Hearst.[1] Two competing versions of the Yellow Kid were soon appearing—the origin of the term "Yellow Journalism."

Additional comic features appeared, and the comic strip exploded onto the cultural landscape. Much of the visual vocabulary of comics was established in those first few years. Word balloons became the standard way of presenting dialogue. Rudolph Dirks' *Katzenjammer Kids* used simple lines to represent movement or explosions—something that's become so standard it's difficult to remember that someone had to be the first to think of it. Dirks was also one of the first artists to use sweat beads to convey fear or worry. Dirks, Winsor McCay and others played with the arrangement of panels, constantly improving their strips in terms of visual artistry, effectiveness of gags and basic storytelling.

More innovations followed. In 1907, "Bud" Fisher created *Mutt and Jeff* for the *San Francisco Chronicle*. This was a daily strip, running six days a week in black and white. It wasn't the first daily, but Fisher used storylines that continued from day to day. This internal continuity, first attempted in a failed strip called *A. Piker Clerk* a few years earlier, became another comics tradition.

By 1912, a daily as well as Sunday comic page was a typical and necessary part of nearly all successful newspapers. Popular features were by

An example of Rudolph Dirks' *Katzenjammer Kids* from 1907. Dirks was one of the comic strip's early innovators, helping to introduce motion lines and sweat beads into the art form's visual vocabulary.

then being syndicated nationally. With the comic strip's own unique visual language now fixed in the public consciousness, artists began to discover more and varied storytelling opportunities within the medium.

For the first two decades the humor strip dominated the art form. Yet

An example of Winsor McCay's *Little Nemo in Slumberland* from 1907. McCay played with the shape and arrangement of individual panels to help create truly beautiful imagery.

even this single genre showcased some extraordinary work in a variety of visual styles. It wasn't long before creative energies began to push the comic strip in entirely new directions.

Winsor McCay's *Little Nemo in Slumberland*, a Sunday strip that first appeared in 1905, was a wonderful example of visual fantasy. Each week, McCay let us enter the dreams of his main character, a little boy named Nemo. It was a premise that allowed McCay to do pretty much anything he wanted. Nemo's adventures involved walking beds, mushroom forests, chariots drawn by oversized rabbits, and trips to the Moon and Mars in a giant zeppelin. McCay's work was visually stunning, using peculiar images, shifting colors, distorted perspective and thoughtful panel arrangement in perfect synergy. There were continuing storylines, but there was no requirement for these to unfold in a logical manner. Instead, McCay used fantasy to explore themes of hope, fear, loneliness, disillusionment and wonder.

It was possible for *Little Nemo* to exist in 1905 because at that time many Sunday strips received an entire page to themselves. That meant artists like McCay had a poster-sized area every week within which to work. They could add whatever level of detail they needed, use however much dialogue was appropriate. Without fear of having to share a page with four or five other strips, they could arrange individual panels to the best effect.

This would hold equally true for the artists who would soon create adventure strips. It was the guarantee of a full or half page — the simple fact of giving a creator the room to properly create — that would eventually infuse the medium with complex plots and characterizations.

14. Wash Tubbs: An Unlikely Adventurer

The first successful adventure strip started life as just another humor strip. In 1923, a young artist named Roy Crane met with Charles Landon, art director for the Newspaper Enterprise Association. The NEA was a comics syndicate in the business of selling features to interested newspapers.[1]

Crane and Landon kicked around ideas for a new strip and came up with *Washington Tubbs II*, a feature about a short, bespectacled goof who works in a grocery store and thinks of himself as a suave lady's man. The strip, with the title shortened to *Wash Tubbs*, began in 1924.

Crane was an excellent artist. He drew lively, animated characters, using both body language and facial expressions to convey mood, whether it be glee, fear, boredom or anger. Though capable of complete realism, he adopted a slightly exaggerated, cartooney approach to character design. This was appropriate to a humor strip, but would ironically continue to serve him well after *Wash Tubbs* turned into something completely different.

For a few months the new strip followed Wash as he competed with a rival for the attentions of a stuck-up girl. Though the gags were reasonably funny and the art work notable, there was nothing new or special about it. But Crane's skill as both writer and artist would soon begin to make a difference.

A fresh storyline gradually unfolds, involving a series of apparent break-ins at the store where Wash works. Soon the mystery expands to include a blank piece of paper that a thug named Caliento Tamalio seems willing to kill for. Wash ends up in possession of the paper, eventually discovering that it's really a map, drawn in invisible ink that reappears when heated, leading to a treasure buried on a South Pacific island.

Wash, dreaming of riches and pretty girls, takes a job aboard a ship sailing for Australia, intent on recovering the treasure. Pursued by Tamalio, Wash ends up stranded on an island, captured by cannibals. At first he's meant to be the main course at the next big feast, but he gets into the king's good graces by repairing an automobile that had been recovered from a shipwreck. In the end, Wash makes it back to the U.S. with a small fortune in pearls.

Though played mostly for laughs, the storyline contained a notable element of danger as well, especially when Wash encountered the knife-wielding Tamalio. Suspense was maintained nicely from day to day, hinting at better things to come.

Crane was developing strengths as an artist that added to his already strong figure work. He had an eye for detail, paying close attention to background and to the overall layout of each panel.[2] He was an innovator in the use of lettering, using bold type and exclamation points to enhance the emotions already expressed so well by his character design. "The very style of lettering," wrote comics historian Richard Marschall, "suggested a mood; their display revealed a voice; even their size conveyed actual emotion."[3] As with Winsor McCay — as with any successful comics artist — Crane's strengths complemented each other, adding up to more than the sum of their parts.

It was Crane who pioneered the use of onomatopoeic sound effects in comics, adding "bam," "pow," and "wham" to what had previously been an almost entirely visual vocabulary. Crane had fun with this, tossing in an occasional "ker-splash" or "lickety-wop" along with what would become the more standard effects. Words as well as images became vehicles for carrying along his increasingly fast-paced storylines.

Following Wash's initial adventure, the strip reverted to a dependence on gags for a time. But Wash had acquired a taste for travel and adventure. He also tended to lose fortunes as often as he found them. Though humor was always an important part of the strip, by 1928 it was no longer the primary focus.

A storyline beginning that year involved yet another treasure map. Wash had by now partnered up with Gozy Gallup, a tall, gangly fellow from Wash's hometown. They had acquired a map leading to the buried loot of Blackbeard the pirate. Hiring a ship, they set out after this prize.

The ship's captain, Bull Dawson, double crosses them after they reach the island.[4] Wash and Gozy are forced into hiding, watching helplessly while Bull and his heavily-armed men search for the treasure. Events come to a bloody conclusion when a rival set of bad guys arrive, attacking Bull's faction. In the confusion, Wash and Gozy make their escape on Bull's ship, taking the treasure with them.

There are few traditional gags here. The scenario depends entirely on generating excitement and suspense. At one point, Bull beats the snot out of Wash and Gozy — a beating that lasts from one day's strip into the next. The final battle between the opposing gangs runs through a week of strips, beginning with a gun battle and ending with a nasty fist fight between Bull and the rival gang leader.

Wash Tubbs had come a long way from jokes about getting a date for Saturday night, and it was here that Crane's exaggerated character design and expressive layouts really began to pay off. This was violent stuff, graphically presented. The art was just realistic enough to make it all dramatically viable. At the same time, it was just cartooney enough to keep the violent imagery from becoming tasteless or offensive. Crane would often include action sequences — anything from bar fights to full-scale war — that would run for days or sometimes weeks. But no matter how high the body count, his visual style always made it seem like good, clean fun.

By modern standards, Crane's style fails badly in his visual portrayal of blacks. Drawn with huge white lips, black characters in *Wash Tubbs* today recall offensive stereotypes. I believe, though, that this was a side effect of Crane's character design and not representative of any racist intent in his work. In a storyline that ran soon after their encounter with Bull Dawson, Wash and Gozy are lost in the Sahara, pursued by an armed band of Arabs. An escaped black slave named Bola, experienced in warfare and desert travel, takes command and leads them to safety. Bola is presented as clear-headed, intelligent and brave. The white protagonists willingly follow his lead and treat him as an equal.

Crane's writing, as well as visual style, also helped balance violent action with escapist fun. Crane liked to make puns of names. An Arab sheik is named Hudson Bey. Much of the action is set in small European

A strip from 1933 shows Roy Crane at his graphic best. Wash Tubbs and Easy, shanghaied aboard a whaling ship, encounter more than they bargained for.

countries with names like Kandelabra and Sneezia. Crane counterpointed the silly names with a constant sense of real danger and excitement. Kandelabra suffers a bloody revolution. Sneezia goes to war with neighboring Belchia. Storylines in general and action sequences in particular unfold with strict logic. It was all part of Crane's deft thematic balancing act.

Crane varied his plots, mixing together wars, political intrigue, kidnappings, murder mysteries, whaling voyages, smugglers, gold prospecting and gangsters. He sometimes repeated ideas, like seeking hidden treasure or stranding his protagonists on a remote island, but he always gave the situation a fresh twist. He also experimented with different supporting characters, stumbling over one particular fellow who would eventually take over the strip.

It was in strife-torn Kandelabra that Wash met the future star of the feature. Captain Easy was a soldier of fortune, a square-jawed brawler who had fled an unhappy past to become a mercenary. Gozy had by this time retired from adventuring, and Easy became Wash's new partner. He quickly grew popular with readers, convincing Crane to bring him back after briefly writing him out of the strip in 1931.

Together, Wash and Easy survive Kandelabra's revolution. They visit Wash's hometown, where Wash is falsely accused of murder and Easy does some detective work to clear him. Soon after, they find themselves stranded on a Pacific island, battling headhunters. Then there's a stint as commanders of the army of Cucumbria, an isolated southeast Asian country. Later, Wash has several adventures alone or with another partner, then Easy returns just in time for the pair to get tossed into a French colonial prison in South America, accused of being revolutionaries.

Crane's increasing skill at characterization made the unlikely partnership believable. Wash always remained an excitable nerd, with a dan-

Captain Easy appeared in the strip in 1928; he and Wash immediately found trouble together. Roy Crane's combination of realism and slightly "cartoony" character design kept the strip exciting and entertaining.

A strip from 1932. Wash provided comic relief, but could more or less hold his own in a fight when he had too.

gerous tendency to fall in love with every pretty woman he meets. But he's loyal and sticks with his friends in a fight, even if he's sometimes ineffective in that fight. Performing still another balancing act, Crane portrays Wash as just capable enough to keep around without sacrificing his goofy charm or role as comic relief. In one story he'll be suckered by con artists playing on his innate naivety. In another he'll remove a bullet from Easy's leg with a pocket knife, saving the delirious mercenary's life.

Wash Tubbs eventually began appearing in the Sunday papers, at first in gag strips independent of the continuity and events of the daily feature. In 1933, Crane replaced Sunday's *Wash Tubbs* with *Captain Easy, Soldier-of-Fortune,* chronicling Easy's adventures before he met Wash.[5]

Crane's boisterous visuals, in four colors on a full Sunday page, looked magnificent. The mid and late 1930s were a high point for Crane, a time when it seemed he could do no wrong as a storyteller.

In 1937 the NEA began a trend that would eventually nearly eradicate the adventure strip from popular culture. In a campaign to cram more strips into fewer pages (and therefore increase profits), artists were required to design their pages using a specific template of identically-sized panels. This would allow the strips to be printed on either full, half, or third pages. Freedom to vary panel size and arrangement was gone. Features like *Captain Easy,* in which the overall layout of Sunday strips was a major part of its visual appeal and dramatic effectiveness, suffered badly.

Even worse, NEA artists were required to include optional panels that could be dropped — once again in a drive to fit each strip into as small a space as possible. Humor strips could get around this by including a short introductory joke that could be dropped without harming the main gag. Adventure strips did not have this alternative. By forcing the inclusion of panels that did not directly influence the plot, the policy had a ruinous effect on the storytelling process. For a disciplined writer like Crane, this proved enormously frustrating.

One of the first *Captain Easy* Sunday strips from 1933. Crane was a master of page design, arranging panels to highlight his boisterous visuals while still telling the story effectively.

World War II forced another change, this one in the strip's thematic focus. The immediate realities of war could not be ignored, even in fiction, so Easy began to battle Nazis. Make believe countries and villains with absurd names faded from the strip. Inevitably, *Captain Easy* took on a grimmer demeanor.

Crane, always a professional, continued to do excellent work despite changes and unwelcome restrictions. But by 1943 he had enough. He left the NEA and *Captain Easy* behind, moving to rival syndicate King Features. Here he created *Buz Sawyer*, retaining ownership and creative control of the new feature.[6]

Buz Sawyer was, from the start, a more realistic strip than *Easy* in terms of both storylines and character design. Buz was a Navy pilot, later a CIA agent, who fought the Axis during the war and was an active Cold Warrior afterwards. Adventures were set in real places such as Hong Kong or Vietnam. Thematic differences aside, Crane's artistry and storytelling skills remained undiminished. But the glory days of the Sunday *Captain Easy* could never be recaptured. Sunday strips, was well as dailies, continued to shrink in size. After leaving *Easy*, Crane never again attempted to tell a story in the Sunday comics. *Buz Sawyer*'s continuity was kept within the dailies, with Sunday being given over to gags featuring Buz's sidekick Roscoe Sweeney. The adventure strip had begun its slow fade into oblivion.

Crane died in 1979. *Buz Sawyer* was continued by other artists until 1989.

15. Dick Tracy: Cops in the Comics

Wash and Easy traveled to far-off, exotic lands in search of adventure, but at least one comic strip hero found all the danger he could handle pretty much right outside his front door.

By the early 1930s, an unending stream of mobsters and bandits seemed to be overrunning a society already devastated by the Depression. Organized crime was growing and was sometimes openly controlling big city governments. Thugs like John Dillinger and Clyde Barrow slipped through the fingers of the police again and again.

People desperately wanted reassurance that their society was still basically stable — that laws were enforced and criminals brought to justice. In fiction, one response to this need was pulp magazines like *The Shadow* and *The Spider*. Once adventure comic strips began to grow in popularity, it was perhaps inevitable that they too would begin to reflect the same real-life concerns.

Chester Gould was working as an artist for the newspaper *Chicago American* when he began to submit his work to the Chicago Tribune–NY News Syndicate, one of the more successful comic strip distributors. He sent in political cartoons and ideas for humor strips, but it was a proposal for a strip called *Plainclothes Tracy* that finally earned a response.

Tracy would be an adventure strip, with a big-city cop as the protagonist. The storylines would follow Tracy as he investigated crimes, gathered evidence and methodically tracked down the guilty.

Joseph Patterson, head of the Tribune-News Syndicate, suggested changing the title to *Dick Tracy*[1] and adding an origin story. Tracy would

A Sunday *Dick Tracy* strip from 1951. Chester Gould wasn't much on anatomical accuracy, but his expressionistic style vividly conveyed both emotion and the flow of the action.

join the force after his girlfriend's father is murdered, soon proving himself to be a skilled detective.

Dick Tracy was an immediate commercial success. Gould was a superb writer, creating energetic, well-paced storylines. As an artist, though, he seemed to possess glaring weaknesses, at least superficially. His figure work

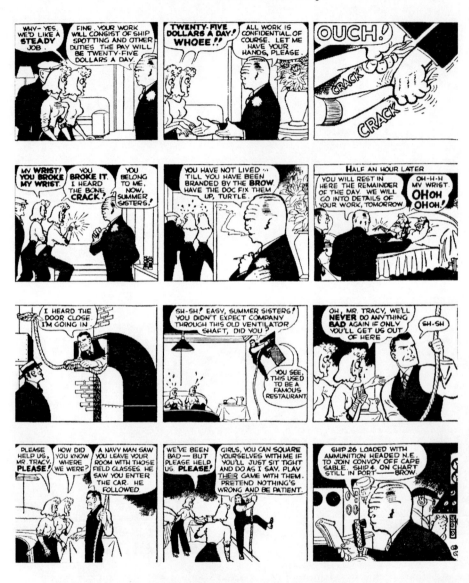

A Sunday strip from June 1944. The Brow was one of many villains whose physical deformity symbolized his moral depravity.

was poor, and his perspective often weak. But Gould's greatest strength was an ability to turn his faults into virtues. He was a master of composition, using a shifting point of view, extreme close-ups and astute character placement to make *Tracy* a visual delight. Gould was an expressionist, relinquishing strict realism for a style more fitting to his abilities. His figures and sense of perspective looked just right within the world he created, allowing him to skillfully convey emotion and story content.

"Nobody drew dead people like [Chester Gould]," wrote mystery author Max Allan Collins, who scripted *Tracy* himself after Gould retired.[2] This sounds gruesome, but it's true. Part of the strip's effectiveness was Gould's ability to impart a real sense of pain and loss suffered by victims of violent crime. Images were not gory or tasteless, but the emotions communicated were real. When characters were hurt, the reader felt sympathy pains. When characters died, the reader felt a genuine sense of loss. That was perhaps *Dick Tracy*'s greatest appeal.

Dick Tracy's world was one of clearly defined good and evil. By 1940, even the character design has begun to reflect this. A series of grotesque villains started to appear — the Blank, Flattop, Prune Face, the Brow. In each case, the criminal's horrible visage was symbolic of his evil nature. They were bank robbers or hit men, con artists or (during the 1940s) Nazi spies. It almost didn't matter what their exact crimes were — they were all representative of the worst aspects of human nature.

Facing off against them was honest, loyal Dick Tracy and his fellow cops. The detective was a determined professional, unerringly following leads until he finally cornered his prey. It was far from a smooth or easy job. Tracy was shot, beaten, kidnapped, and tortured with regularity. His girlfriend and eventual wife, Tess Trueheart, was often endangered, as was Tracy's adopted son Junior.

But Tracy never gave up. For him, police work was more of a moral calling than a job. It was his responsibility to protect the innocent and preserve society. He never stopped and never compromised. He certainly never plea-bargained. In this regard, Tracy was the comics counterpart to the Spider, determined to fulfill his duty regardless of the personal cost.

Gould wrapped his morality plays[3] in strong, violent plots that followed a rational progression. The villains were smart as well as vicious, making them effective adversaries. Tracy, though, matched them in intelligence, usually making equal use of his brains and his gun before he closed a case. He employed modern crimefighting techniques such as fingerprints and ballistics tests, as well as fanciful ones such as the famous two-way wrist radio.

A typical Tracy storyline ran for four months in 1944, encompassing both the daily and Sunday strips. The villain is the Brow, a Nazi spy whose oversized forehead is sculpted with large, overlapping ridges. Also involved in the case are the Summer sisters, May and June, who are introduced when they try to pick Tracy's pocket.

Chester Gould appreciated the dramatic impact of occasionally killing off sympathetic charcters. The Summer sisters had survived quite a lot, but still met a grim fate on July 31, 1944.

The Summer sisters are not hardened criminals. They had originally come to the city to break into show biz, but were soon broke and hungry. Gould's visual design of these characters typifies his expressionist slant. The girls are personifications of naivety, projecting an aura of helplessness and innocence even when they're breaking the law.

Through bad luck, the sisters become involved with the Brow. The Nazi forces them to help spy on a Navy base, breaking their wrists in order to establish his dominance over them. May and June prove surprisingly spunky, though, when they kill a couple of Nazi henchmen and injure the Brow before escaping. During this sequence, their expressions and demeanor shift subtly from helplessness to grim determination.

The Brow evades the police by hiding in a pool and breathing through a hose. Later he forces a car carrying the sisters into a lake. In a series of macabre images, the two girls futilely attempt to escape from the sinking car. Both of them drown.

Tracy trails the Brow out of the city to a country theater set up in a barn. Throwing the broken end of a lightning rod like a javelin, the Brow wounds the detective and escapes again.

Wounded himself, the Brow passes out. He's taken in by a lonely female hermit named Gravel Gertie. Gertie treats his wounds and soon convinces herself that she's in love with him. She tries but fails to hide him from the police. Tracy, despite his wounded shoulder, beats the Brow into unconsciousness.

But it's not over yet. After everyone is taken to headquarters, Gertie snatches a gun from a cop and tosses it to the Brow. Tracy throws an inkwell at him, knocking the Brow out of an eighth floor window to be impaled on a flagpole.

Few villains ever made return appearances in *Dick Tracy*, since few were taken alive. Tracy's world was a grim one, and justice was both swift and deadly.

Gould wrote and drew *Dick Tracy* until 1977. The strip retained its law-and-order focus throughout Gould's run, becoming even more strident in this social point of view during the 1960s. About the same time, the strip became more fanciful, with Tracy taking an interplanetary voyage and encountering a civilization of moon people. This was a serious dramatic misstep — science fiction and Dick Tracy did not mix well at all.

For the most part, though, Gould remained a solid storyteller. The strip's prestige meant it retained full or half pages on Sundays in many papers well into the 1970s. Even when shrunk down, it was less affected than strips like *Captain Easy*, as Gould's Sunday compositions had employed a standard panel size and arrangement right from the start.

Dick Tracy fared reasonably well after Gould left, with several sets of writers and artists providing strong stories. It continues today, as the detective still tracks down bizarre villains with traditional determination. But he's just not the man he once was, exhibiting only a fraction of the dramatic power he wielded in the 1940s. In part, this may be because even the best fictional characters need a break after seven decades. Mostly, it's the curse of the shrinking comic strip, limiting the opportunity for effective graphic storytelling. Tracy could take a lightning rod through his shoulder without blinking an eye, but even he can't truly survive being crammed into one-sixth of a Sunday page, chopped apart and reassembled with no thought at all given to artistry.

16. From the Jungle to the Round Table

By the late 1920s, syndicates were actively looking for new adventure strips. The pulps provided an obvious source of ready-made heroes, and in 1929 Buck Rogers jumped from *Amazing Stories* to the comics page.[1] In 1938 the Shadow began a short but respectable four-year run as a strip.

Tarzan's popularity in the pulps and movies made him a natural choice for a comics hero. He received a test run of sorts in 1929, with advertising artist Hal Foster producing an excellent daily comics adaptation of the first Tarzan novel.

The success of this run led to a regular Sunday strip, distributed by United Features Syndicate,[2] using original stories. Foster, though, was unwilling to permanently leave advertising work. Instead, United Features gave the job to staff artist Rex Maxon.

The strip began on March 15, 1931. Unfortunately, Maxon was exactly the wrong artist for the job, providing unimaginative storylines and awkwardly drawn characters. Edgar Rice Burroughs did not hesitate to voice his concern — Tarzan belonged to him, and he wasn't about to let anyone else diminish the highly-marketable ape man.

Later that year, Hal Foster was finally persuaded to take over the Sunday feature. (Maxon continued to do a daily Tarzan strip until 1947.) Foster quickly began a fast-paced, violent storyline involving the Foreign Legion, Arab bandits, a besieged fort, captures, escapes and rescues. Unlike Maxon, Foster's artwork precisely complemented the subject material. He gave the jungle setting a raw, primitive look, with thick foliage, hanging vines and jutting tree branches adding to the feeling of wildness. His figure work was realistic, endowing both human characters and animals with

From October 23, 1932: When the supply of man-eating lions ran low, Tarzan could always turn to fighting dinosaurs. Hal Foster endowed the strip with a sense of primitive savagery.

grace and vitality. He forsook word balloons, carefully positioning narration and dialogue to further facilitate the visual flow of the story.

Foster usually illustrated storylines provided by other writers, though there's often no record of who those writers were. Plots were pretty basic, mirroring the formula Burroughs had developed in the pulps. In a sequence from 1932, Tarzan and a friend have found the secret elephant's graveyard. Attacked by dinosaurs and pterodactyls, they take refuge inside the ribcage of an elephant's skeleton. Escaping, they navigate a subterranean grotto, emerging in a swamp inhabited by still more dinosaurs. After a running battle with one of the prehistoric beasts, they travel through another series of underground caves. They arrive in an isolated area surrounded by impassable cliffs, where they encounter a lost Egyptian civilization. Soon Tarzan is embroiled in a struggle between the Pharaoh and a faction of power-hungry priests. Eventually, the plans of the priests are foiled and the high priest fed to crocodiles. But the Pharaoh's sister is kidnapped by bandits and Tarzan is off to rescue her...

Foster's wonderfully choreographed action sequences gave vivid life to these formulaic adventures. Again and again he provided images that drew the reader inescapably into the story: Tarzan and his friend crouched beneath a huge ribcage, dodging the jabbing beaks of pterodactyls; Tarzan leaping from tree top to tree top, a hairs-breadth ahead of an angry dinosaur; an army of chariots charging through the gates of a city; Tarzan and a band of apes charging a line of spearmen; a gigantic idol toppling onto its terrified worshipers; an angry mob battling soldiers amidst the ruins of a temple.

Like Burroughs, Foster was a natural-born storyteller. Where Burroughs used prose as his tool, Foster used his visual artistry, combining dynamic figure work with carefully composed backgrounds to generate a phenomenal level of excitement.

Foster gradually grew dissatisfied with the strip. Initially reluctant to enter comics, he had become convinced of the storytelling potential of the medium. He wanted more creative freedom and more opportunity for character development. To this end, he created a strip called *Derek, Son of Thane*, a medieval saga set in Arthurian England. He offered the strip to United Features, but the syndicate wasn't interested. Rival syndicate King Features, though, *was* interested. In 1937, Foster left both United and Tarzan behind.

We'll rejoin Foster later, but for the moment remain loyal to the ape man. Foster's replacement was Burne Hogarth, a superb artist in his own right who didn't miss a beat when he took over.

From September 26, 1937: Burne Hogarth took over the strip from Hal Foster without missing a beat. His strong, dynamic art carries the action smoothly from panel to panel.

Hogarth came aboard in the middle of a storyline involving the defense of a jungle city against a mercenary army equipped with modern weapons. Already leading a band of human fighters, Tarzan supplements his force by recruiting apes, a pride of lions and a herd of elephants. He wages a savage hit-and-run campaign against the mercenaries. Events climax when Tarzan's "army" attacks a convoy of trucks and tanks. Elephants shove armored vehicles off cliffs, while apes and lions wipe out the foot soldiers.

Like Foster, Hogarth drew realistic, dynamic figures that actually seemed to move across the page. His backgrounds—jungle foliage, rocks, water—were as alive as his figures. Every perfectly composed panel exudes danger and suspense. It didn't matter how absurd the idea of elephants fighting tanks might be when considered objectively. Hogarth's art was completely subjective, and he made it seem real.

Hogarth stayed with the strip almost continuously until 1950.[3] He worked from scripts written by others, but didn't hesitate to rewrite them when necessary. He understood the medium as well as anyone, seamlessly melding together story and vibrant imagery. We watch as the ape man battles countless foes. Tarzan lures a rampaging dinosaur into a trap, impaling it on a giant spear. He escapes from one city torn apart by volcanic eruptions only to be caught in a neighboring city deluged by a tidal wave. Clad in a diving suit, the Lord of the Apes fights an octopus on the ocean floor. He duels with a hulking swordsman atop a narrow rocky arch stretching over a deep chasm. He encounters Amazons, Vikings and Nazis. The word "breathtaking" is something of a cliché, but Hogarth's artistry can literally make you gasp for air.

By now, you can probably guess what finally went wrong. In the 1940s, King Features began requiring panels that could be arranged into either full or half-page layouts. Hogarth's compositional skills allowed him to maintain high quality despite this restriction, but the end was near. Both the narrative flow and the visual impact of the strip began to suffer. Quality was being inexorably supplanted by quantity.

By the time Hal Foster's new strip was published in February 1937,[4] the name had changed to *Prince Valiant*, but the basic premise, involving Arthurian legend, had remained the same. The first episode followed an exiled Scandinavian king and his few loyal followers as he fled his homeland. Sailing to England, they're attacked by "half-savage Britons" and fight their way inland. Eventually, they make peace with the Britons, settling on an island surrounded by near-impassible swamps.

It wasn't until the end of the third Sunday strip that the reader finally

From March 16, 1941: Hogarth at his graphic best — an exciting, tense action sequence with literally breathtaking visuals.

SYNOPSIS:
CORNERED UNDER THE EAVES BY THE REMAIN-ING OUTLAW, VAL IS A TARGET FOR A FLIGHT OF SCREAMING ARROWS—IT SEEMS BUT A MATTER OF TIME BEFORE ONE BRINGS HIM CRASHING TO THE COURTYARD BELOW.

REMOVING HIS CLOTHING, THE YOUNG PRINCE TIES HIS GAR-MENTS IN A BUNDLE WHICH HE USES AS A SHIELD.

UNABLE TO REACH HIM FROM ABOVE OR BELOW, THE OUTLAW PLANS VAL'S DOOM CAREFULLY. HE REMOVES ALL THE WEAPONS FROM THE TOP FLOOR

LOCKING THE DOORS SO VAL CAN-NOT ESCAPE, HE LIGHTS THE SIGNAL BRAZIER.

WHEN IT IS BLAZING HOTLY HE LOWERS IT TO VAL'S POSITION.

QUICKLY VAL LOWERS HIMSELF TO THE WINDOW BELOW AND SWINGS IN.

BUT HIS ENEMY HAS PLANNED CAREFULLY—THE WAY TO FREEDOM IS BLOCKED.

From January 29, 1938: A young Prince Valiant quickly finds high adventure. Fos-ter effectively used panel shape and arrangement to describe the flow of the action.

met the title character. The first few episodes make up a well-constructed prologue; Foster took the time to properly set up his premise, but did so without a delay in introducing the spirit of adventure that would infuse the feature.

The king's son, Prince Valiant, is still a boy, perhaps in his early teens. Reckless and eager to explore, he soon has a dangerous encounter with a dinosaur-like creature called a marsh lizard. Other short adventures follow before he meets a witch, who prophesizes, "You will have high adventure, but nowhere do I see happiness and contentment."

Despite this warning, the impetuous youth leaves the swamps to "seek adventure." He has no trouble finding what he seeks, and soon ends up in Camelot as the squire of Sir Gawain.

The premise allowed Foster greater opportunity for character development than he had with *Tarzan*. The ape man's personality and motivations were set in stone. Prince Valiant, on the other hand, begins his career as a hero while still a youngster. Reading through Foster's work in collected reprints, it's possible to trace how carefully he plotted out Val's maturation into a knight and leader of men. At first, he's impetuous and quick-tempered (qualities he would always have, to some extant). But he's also courageous and clever, and able to think under pressure. He learns to control his temper. An early romance ends tragically and he learns about heartbreak and loss. Finally, about two years into the strip's run, Val plays a key role in helping King Arthur fight off a Saxon invasion. After a fierce battle, "...amid the wreckage of that terrible field, [Arthur] makes Prince Valiant a knight of the Round Table!"

Though Foster didn't stint on using narration and dialogue, it was his magnificent visuals that carried the bulk of the story. His artwork had gradually grown more disciplined during his years on *Tarzan*. By the time he began *Prince Valiant*, the rawness that had been so appropriate for the ape man was gone, but his improved style was more fitting to the stories he now wanted to tell. Both his figure work and his backgrounds had jumped up a notch from an already high level of realism. He also made increasingly effective use of color, light and shadow.

Foster used differing panel sizes and arrangements more often on *Valiant* than he had on *Tarzan*. A particular Sunday might use nine identically-sized panels arranged three by three. Another week might see a third or half page given to a panoramic view of a castle or battlefield. As Roy Crane did with *Captain Easy*, Foster used the overall layout of each Sunday page in synergy with the composition of the individual panels. The dramatic and emotional effect of this often was astonishing. It was effective in terms of basic storytelling as well. Storylines followed logical progressions. The tactics of large-scale battles were clearly and concisely explained. Character motivation was clearly delineated.

Foster's setting was mythological — a sixth century England that reflected Arthurian legends as developed by Medieval troubadours. Anachronisms abounded — knights in full plate armor, jousting tournaments,

Compare this *Tarzan* strip from 1933, with its primitive look that effectively complemented its subject...

...with this *Prince Valiant* strip from 1942. Foster's figure work and backgrounds had grown more technically accurate, infusing *Prince Valiant* with a sense of realism that added to its dramatic impact.

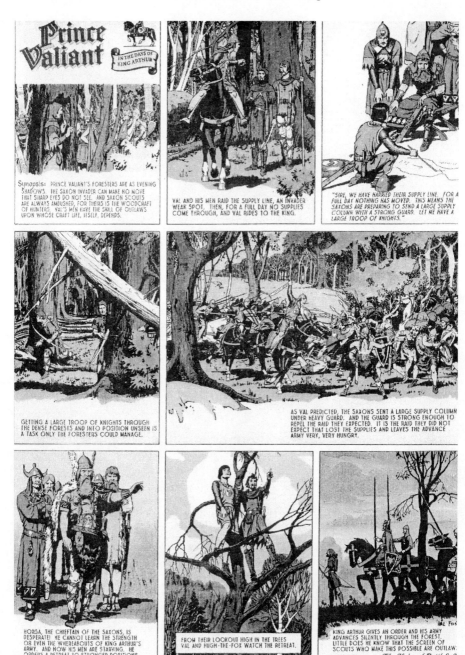

From August 25, 1946: Hal Foster maintained the same high quality of art and storytelling throughout his 34-year run on *Prince Valiant*.

saddles with stirrups, and medieval-era castles. But Foster was a meticulous researcher, portraying weapons, armor and castles with precise detail. His image of Camelot might be nearly a millennium out of place, but it still looked right.

This combination of accuracy and anachronism, seasoned with an occasional element of pure fantasy, allowed Foster to create a believable alternate history — a world in which the nobility of the Round Table coexisted with the ugliness of the real world.

Val never did lose his wanderlust, allowing Foster to introduce a wide variety of settings over the years. Val led an army against Hun invaders on the European mainland. He traveled on a Viking longship to Africa. He visited Asia and the Americas. He crossed deserts and trackless forests. He helped his father win back his rightful throne.

Eventually, he met his future wife, Aleta, Queen of the Misty Isles.[5] Their courtship proved tumultuous, with a feverish and only half-sane Val at one point kidnapping the poor girl. But true love wins out in the end. They marry, and their children end up demonstrating that the urge to seek adventure is genetic.

Foster retired in 1971. He was succeeded by John Collen Murphy, who continued to provide a high-quality combination of story and art. Like *Dick Tracy*, *Prince Valiant*'s prestige often allowed it to retain at least a half-page size into the 1970s. Also like *Tracy*, its prestige and honorable history only took it so far, and editors gradually began to shrink it down. *Prince Valiant* is today still a strong, well-illustrated strip, but it only hints at the magnificence it once had.

17. Milt Caniff: Fighter Pilots, Pretty Girls and the Dragon Lady

Joseph Patterson, head of the Chicago Tribune–NY News Syndicate, had a good eye for talent. It was Patterson who recognized Chester Gould's potential. And it was Patterson who, in 1934, helped artist Milt Caniff get started on what is arguably the greatest of all adventure strips.

Caniff was already doing a strip called *Dickie Dare*. The title character was a young boy who daydreamed about helping legendary and historical figures like Robin Hood and General Custer.[1] The strip was aimed at children, but Caniff always remembered that it was grownups, not kids, who actually bought newspapers. He began to market an idea for a more mature strip. This soon brought him to Patterson's attention.

Caniff's proposed strip was in some ways similar to *Dickie Dare*. The main character would be a young boy, accompanied by an older man who would act as protector and father figure. The setting would be China and other points East, where the pair would encounter bandits, smugglers and other assorted villains. Patterson liked the idea, and it was apparently he who came up with the name *Terry and the Pirates*.[2]

Terry premiered as a daily strip in October 1934. A Sunday strip, at first with a separate continuity, appeared a few months later.[3] It all began with young Terry Lee arriving in China, accompanied by his guardian, a rough-and-tumble fellow named Pat Ryan. Terry, an orphan, has a map to the mine discovered by his grandfather some years earlier.

They hire a boat to sail upriver to the mine. Bandits, learning of the map, follow. A gun-and-fist-fight in an abandoned temple finishes off this

An early *Terry* strip from 1934. Caniff's style was a little cartoony at this point, but still made for strong, direct storytelling.

set of bad guys, but it turns out the mine is being used as a hideout by a second, larger bandit gang. Captures and escapes follow quickly. In the end, a supporting character sacrifices his life so Terry and friends can escape. The mine is blown up and flooded.

It was a good, solid start for the feature. Caniff understood story construction, building an exciting yarn populated with interesting characters. Terry was smart and brave, but Caniff left most of the heroics to the older Pat, thereby keeping the action believable. Aside from these two, a third regular character was Connie (short for George Webster Confucius), their Chinese interpreter. Big-eared, buck-toothed and given to saying stupid things in mangled English, Connie was at first pure stereotype, whose only role was as comic relief.

It wasn't long, though, before Caniff apparently realized that it made no sense for Pat and Terry to keep Connie around if he wasn't actually useful. Before the first adventure was over, Connie had shifted from cowardly and stupid to brave and resourceful. He would remain a regular character throughout the 1930s, still providing comic relief but also acting as a loyal and dependable friend.

Visually, Caniff's initial character designs were perhaps too reminiscent of the "semi-caricatural style"[4] he had used in *Dickie Dare*, failing to properly complement the violent action and realistic dialogue in *Terry*. Making up for this was his remarkable compositional skills; he filled panels with rich background detail, and paid careful attention to the placement of characters and props. Caniff admitted to being influenced by motion pictures, and he made good use of a constantly shifting point of view. He skillfully combined long shots, close ups and cuts back and forth between simultaneously occurring events.[5] The result was smooth, concise storytelling that was never in any danger of growing dull.

In 1935, an artist named Noel "Bud" Sickles began to assist Caniff. Remaining a creative part of the strip for much of the late 1930s and early 1940s, Sickles provided just what Caniff needed to achieve visual perfection. With Sickles' help, Caniff's figure work became smoother and more realistic. Caniff began to make greater use of light and shadow, employing patches of black to heighten dramatic effectiveness and, on Sunday, to highlight colors.

Caniff continued to complement his art with strong plots. Terry and Pat dealt with smugglers, con artists, kidnappers and the occasional outbreak of cholera. The feature was often heavy with dialogue to provide exposition or establish motivations, with word balloons carefully inserted into the overall compositions. Dialogue became an integral part of the strip, never slowing the story or breaking the visual smoothness of the narrative.

This allowed Caniff to construct relatively complex plots, and flesh out both regular and supporting characters. He had a firm understanding of human nature, recognizing both our capacity for good and our tendency towards evil. Character traits, as much as fist fights, drove the stories. Any one person's bravery or cowardice, nobility or selfishness, might be the pivot upon which everything turns.

Many of the supporting characters were good-looking women,[6] but all of them were more than just window dressing or damsels in distress. Normandie Drake is a spoiled rich girl who gradually matures into a kind-hearted woman. Burma is a sort-of criminal who can never quite ignore her feelings of compassion for those in need. April Kane is a strong-willed, motor-mouthed teenager. Rouge seems like a nice person at first, but turns out to be a cold-blooded Axis spy.

Caniff's most famous female creation is the Dragon Lady, an amoral Eurasian bandit leader who turned up again and again throughout the strip's run.[7] Smart and ruthless, she always hovers in a gray area between heroism and villainy. There's no doubt she'd unhesitatingly kill someone to further her own ends, but occasional glimpses of something deeper — a small act of kindness when she thinks no one else is looking — made her a fascinating and convincing character.

The Dragon Lady featured prominently in a storyline from 1934. Her bandit gang had been waging guerilla warfare against the invading Japanese.[8] Along with Terry and Pat, she and her men are besieged in a small valley by a rival bandit gang that's working for the invaders. The defenders are bombed and shelled constantly. They run low on food and ammunition.

Caniff's style grew more realistic, allowing him to inject complex plots and characterizations into the strip. Like other comic strip legends, he was a master of page design. This Sunday page from 1939 is heavy with dialogue, but each panel is designed to include the wordage without slowing down the story.

Pat comes up with a plan to lure some of the enemy into an ambush. They capture several men, but the Dragon Lady refuses to allow the prisoners into the shelters when the shelling resumes. Pat, in turn, refuses to abandon the helpless men, leading them to the best cover he can find. The latest barrage lifts. Pat and the Dragon Lady clash again over whether to feed the prisoners.

Meanwhile, the enemy bandit leader, named Klang, lures a hungry sentry from his post with the smell of cooking food. The sentry is killed, and Klang's men secretly enter the valley, capturing nearly everyone. Some quick thinking and daring action by Connie allows Pat to pull off a last minute rescue. Klang's men are themselves captured, and Klang himself tumbles off a cliff after a nasty fist fight with Pat.

The story offered a logical plot and plenty of action, including several full-scale set-tos between the rival bandit gangs. But it was the characterizations that really spiced things up. The tension between Pat and the Dragon Lady is balanced by their attraction to each other. Terry is stricken with young April Kane, who's also trapped in the valley during the siege. Terry's rival for April's affections is Deeth Crispin, a British boy Terry wants to hate, but who keeps proving himself to be brave and honorable. This constant influx of real emotion added enormously to the level of suspense.

Caniff's skill at characterization was best demonstrated in a brilliant 1941 storyline. Terry, separated from Pat, hooks up with a couple of old friends. Dude Hennick is a pilot flying supplies into a camp for war refugees. Raven Sherman is a rich American who spends her time and money running the camp.

The two are reluctantly falling in love with each other—a process interrupted when black marketeers steal most of the camp's medical supplies. Most of the crooks are caught or killed during a wild chase over a remote mountain road, but their leader captues Raven. Thrown from a moving truck, she's badly injured.

Terry and Dude desperately try to carry her back to civilization, but they don't make it. The strip for Friday, October 17, 1941, was one long panel, without dialogue, showing Dude and Terry standing over Raven's grave.

Raven was a great character, strong-willed and independent. She was good-hearted, but sometimes too mistrustful of others and not always easy to like. All the same, she had gotten under the skin of many readers—her death generated a strong emotional reaction. Every October until his death in 1988, Caniff would receive letters from fans on the anniversary of Raven's passing.

This strip, from October 17, 1941, is a tribute to Caniff's skill as a writer and artist. Raven Sherman's death generated a strong and sincere outpouring of emotion from the strip's fans.

Terry aged normally as years passed, and by 1942 he was old enough to join the army and train as a fighter pilot. Pat faded from the strip, and ace pilot Flip Corkin became Terry's new mentor. After the war, Terry stayed in China and in the Army as an intelligence officer, working under-cover as a pilot for a small commercial airline service. Stories and art work both remained strong.

In 1946, Caniff was lured away from *Terry* by the promise of total creative control over a new strip.[9] *Steve Canyon*, distributed by King Features, began in early 1947.

Like Terry, Steve was a pilot and war veteran, now running his own small air service in Asia—though he would rejoin the Air Force during the Korean War and become a career military man. Through the rest of the '40s and '50s, Caniff continued to provide superb art, strong plots and lots of pretty girls.

Eventually, Caniff began to run out of storytelling steam. During the 1960s he gradually allowed his assistants to create more and more of the art. Later, he began to concentrate stories on Steve's home life (the character got married in 1970), hardly the fodder for stimulating adventure. Extended dream sequences placed Steve in Valley Forge during the Revolution or back in high school. The excitement and emotion of the early years were gone. The strip ended with Caniff's death in 1988, but by then it was running in very few papers.[10]

18. Assigning Blame

We've touched on just a few of the best adventure strips. Alex Raymond did extraordinary graphics for a Sunday *Flash Gordon* feature. Later, he created a strong feature titled *Rip Kirby*. Harold Gray regularly tossed the spunky Little Orphan Annie into the hands of kidnappers and gangsters. Superman jumped from comic books to the newspapers, featuring in stories that often dealt directly with social issues like poverty or war profiteering.[1] The comics section, especially on Sunday, was a marvelous gateway into a variety of robust, colorful worlds.

The comic strip is an art form that, when done well, fully engages the reader. Unlike prose or radio drama, visuals are provided for us. But these are static images that still require both artistic skill on the part of the creator *and* imagination on the part of the reader to make them come alive. It's the reader as much as the artist who makes the characters move and fills in the gaps between panels. Unlike the relatively lazy mediums of movies and television, comics obligate us to become active participants in the storytelling process. This is something that applies equally to radio drama, and we will return to the idea later.

During their heyday, comic strips influenced writers, illustrators, fine artists and filmmakers. Comic *books* came into being initially as a format for reprinting popular strips. This changed in 1938, when the introduction of Superman pushed comic books into concentrating on original material.

Even so, comic books lifted their visual language directly from newspaper strips. Over the years, comic books have hit numerous creative highs and lows, today remaining the closest thing to a replacement for the adventure strip.

But it's not the same as having a weekly or *daily* dose of storytelling brought right to your doorstep. The regular flow of gradually unfolding plot twists, characterizations and cliffhangers, presented in a seamless melding of words and images, has its own unique and valuable appeal.

Why did something so wonderful virtually disappear? In some part, it was no one's fault. Economic factors and wartime paper shortages made comics a more expensive proposition for newspapers. Something really did have to go.

What went was quality. And it's here that blame can justly be assigned. It's the fault of syndicates, who forced artists to shrink their strips— not out of unavoidable necessity, but out of pure greed. More features per page meant more money. Whether this was a viable artistic option didn't matter at all.

It's the fault of local editors for ignoring the quality of the product they bought. They were in a position to refuse to purchase second-rate material and should have done so. Economics would have forced some painful decisions. The number of pages in most Sunday sections would have had to shrink. An editor would have had to choose between a full-page *Captain Easy* or a full-page *Tarzan*. But one great strip is clearly preferable to three or four mediocre ones.

Mostly, it's the fault of the average reader. People could have — and *should* have — objected to the deterioration of the comics pages. Some few people did, but most just accepted what they were given. There is a natural laziness nestled inside most of us. We want to be entertained, but we don't want to expend that little bit of extra mental effort that makes entertainment ultimately more enjoyable and relaxing. Thus, without even thinking about it, our culture complacently left something vital and important behind.

So today we open the Sunday paper to read tiny strips crammed sometimes six to a page in ugly, thoughtless layouts, and we don't even remember anymore what we're missing.

Part III
Radio Drama and Adventure; or, Just Shut Up and Listen

Guglielmo Marconi's first demonstration of "wireless telegraphy" took place in 1895. Nine years later, Sir John A. Fleming's invention of the vacuum electron tube made it possible to transmit words and music. By 1913, long-range radio reception proved practical.

It was a nifty new toy for modern society to play with, though at first no one new exactly what to play. Many saw radio merely as a convenient tool for ships and areas where telegraph wires could not easily be strung. Prior to World War I, a few experimental stations began transmitting short poetry readings and bits of music, but few homes had receivers.

The world war brought about both improvements in the technology and military restrictions regarding its use. After the war, radio began to grow. Companies such as the American Marconi Company (which later merged with RCA) and Westinghouse began to manufacture receivers that were affordable on a middle-class budget.[1] More experimental stations popped up. The first federally licensed station, KDKA in Pittsburgh, began transmitting in 1920. Within six years, nearly six hundred stations were in business across the country. Air time was filled with a mish-mash of music, lectures, news, sports and whatever else broadcasters thought might draw an audience.

Of course, these stations had to pay their expenses. Many early stations transmitted directly out of department stores or hotels, acting as an outlet to promote the specific business that owned them. Westinghouse opened its own station in November 1920, purely to give people a reason to buy radios. All this would gradually evolve into a system in which sponsorship of specific shows was sold to individual businesses.

The rapid commercialization of the new medium worried some. "I believe the quickest way to kill broadcasting," argued Secretary of Commerce Herbert Hoover, "would be to use it for direct advertising." But nobody had any better ideas. In a capitalist society, if something doesn't turn a profit, it doesn't survive.

The next natural step was linking radio stations together in order to broadcast standardized programming, something that would increase revenues by making regional and national advertising possible. AT&T toyed with this idea, developing a plan to use its phone lines to transmit signals from station to station. Instead, they leased their lines to radio veteran and entrepreneur David Sarnoff, who then founded the National Broadcasting Company. On November 15, 1926, NBC aired its first program — a four-hour mixture of music and comedy, giving birth to the variety show. Soon, NBC was operating two separate networks, called Red and Blue. The Blue Network would become ABC in 1943.

Before long, the fledgling network soon had competition. William Paley, owner of the Congress Cigar Company, saw cigar sales jump after he sponsored a musical show in Philadelphia. He bought a chain of sixteen stations and, in September 1927, started CBS.

By the late 1920s, much of the early experimentation with content had faded away. The novelty of radio had worn off, and programming became more standardized. Music, sports and politics had all proven popular and would remain a mainstay of radio to this day. The first huge national success, though, was the CBS comedy *Amos and Andy*. Created by Freeman Gosden and Charles Correll, who also played the title characters, the show, at its peak, drew 40 million listeners.[2] Movie theaters took to stopping films in order to play the show over speakers. *Amos and Andy* quickly demonstrated that radio could grab hold of a national audience.

The networks built on this success, and comedy became another radio mainstay, producing geniuses such as Jack Benny, Fred Allen, Bob and Ray, and Jim and Marion Jordan (better known as Fibber McGee and Molly). The situation comedy and variety show formats, later transferred largely intact to television, were developed. Soap operas got their start on radio as well. Finally, by the early 1930s, adventure and mystery shows had also carved out their own niche.

19. Thundering Hoofbeats and Silver Bullets

The Lone Ranger was as corny as a show can get. The plots were formulaic, and the heroic, faultless hero left no room for character development. By rights, it should have run perhaps a year or two before it grew tiresome. Instead, it lasted over two decades, spawning novels, movie serials, and comic books before eventually jumping to television.

The Lone Ranger was created and produced by people who turned its potential faults into virtues, making it a joy to hear. With good acting, brilliant sound effects, perfectly chosen theme music and a heartfelt moral backbone, it rarely failed to entertain either the children it was intended for or the adults who simply didn't care who the target audience was supposed to be.

The show didn't come from the networks, but rather was created at an independent station that had left CBS to strike out on its own. In 1929, businessmen George Trendle and John H. King bought WXYZ in Detroit, then a CBS affiliate. Three years later, Trendle (who had been actively managing the station) broke with the network, convinced that he could make more money with locally produced and sponsored programs.

At first, this move seemed unwise — the station was losing $4000 a month by the end of 1932. Trendle decided that a new show was needed to draw in more listeners.

It would be a drama, something that could use inexpensive local actors. It would be aimed at kids, who were less critical of content than adults. Eventually, Trendle decided on a western.

From then on, creating the show was a group effort. Years later, those involved often disagreed on who first suggested what.[1] Trendle, director

Jim Jewell, and several others had a brainstorming session. They decided the show's protagonist would be a loner; perhaps a former Texas Ranger. Perhaps the "Lone Ranger."

With the basic idea worked out, the next step was finding someone to write the scripts. Jim Jewell decided to contact Fran Striker, a writer from Buffalo who had sold scripts to WXYZ in the past. It was here that the Lone Ranger was guaranteed immortality. In a situation that paralleled Walter Gibson and the Shadow, Striker would prove to be the perfect scribe for the Lone Ranger. He would define who the Ranger truly was, endowing him with mythic appeal.

Striker had been working as a free-lance writer for several years. He would write scripts, then sell different stations the rights to produce them locally. His first Ranger script was actually a rewrite of a western series he'd created called *Covered Wagon Days*.

It may have been an old plot, but Striker still began to individualize the Ranger, giving him silver bullets and a horse named Silver. Other attributes were forced on him by Trendle, who wanted to keep the show wholesome enough for the children at which it was aimed. The Ranger always had to speak in grammatically correct English. No slang was allowed. He would not drink or smoke. He would, in fact, never enter a saloon, even if disguised as a bad guy. He would almost never kill, but (as a later writers' guideline put it) aim "to maim as painlessly as possible." He would be, Trendle declared, "the embodiment of granted prayer." Striker didn't see these requirements as restrictions. Instead, he made them an integral part of both the character and the overall feel of the show.

The first broadcast came in late January or early February 1933.[2] A recording doesn't exist, but the script does. In that initial outing, the Ranger was a boisterous, outspoken fellow. After rounding up the crooks, he rode off, shouting, "Come along, Silver! That's the boy! ... Hi-Yi! (hearty laugh).... Now cut loose, and awa-a-a-y!"

Trendle immediately nixed the laugh, deciding the Ranger should be a stable and serious man. Striker changed the closing signature to "Hi-Yo, Silver, away!"

Other elements were falling into place. *The William Tell Overture* had been chosen as the opening theme music. This rousing melody proved to be a faultless mood-setter. Often playing for over a minute before the opening narration cut in, it conjured a vivid image of Silver galloping across the southwestern plains, enticing the listener into an Old West that never actually existed. Other bits of classical music (Tchaikovsky, Shubert and others) provided musical bridges during the course of individual episodes.

The music took care of mood, but there was still a problem with basic story construction. After ten episodes, Striker realized that the Ranger spent far too much time talking to himself—an awkward way of letting the audience know what was going on. The Lone Ranger needed a partner, if only to provide a method for smoother exposition. So Tonto, faithful Indian companion, rode into the show.[3]

Dramatic realism required Tonto to be more than just a sounding board. Striker made him an expert tracker, and fluent in Spanish and a number of Indian languages.[4] Though it was always clear that the Ranger was in charge, the two men otherwise treated each other as equals. It was a partnership based on trust and mutual loyalty—a dynamic that quickly became one of the show's strengths.

Several actors played the Lone Ranger over the first few months. Then, in May 1933, Earl Graser won the job, giving the Ranger an authoritative but easygoing voice. John Todd played Tonto, and a skilled group of actors furnished a variety of voices for the supporting characters. An equally skilled group of sound effects men created hoofbeats (using bathroom plungers on sand), as well as providing the sounds of gun shots, carriage wheels, train whistles, rain storms, and whatever other noises might be needed.

Audiences loved it, and Trendle had the hit he was looking for. The same month Graser took over the lead, the show offered the first of many premiums. This one was a pop gun to be given to the first 300 kids who wrote in. WXYZ was deluged with 24,905 responses.

From the beginning, Trendle had arranged for stations outside Detroit to broadcast *The Lone Ranger*, including WGN in Chicago and WOR in New York. This became the basis for yet another network—the Mutual Broadcasting System. By 1936, Mutual was coast to coast, with *The Lone Ranger* as its cornerstone. Later, the Ranger jumped to NBC's Blue Network, staying there when the Blue became ABC. Regardless of which network it called home, *The Lone Ranger* retained its popularity through the 1940s, with each episode originating from WXYZ in Detroit.

In 1941, Earl Graser died in an automobile accident. Brace Beemer, who had been the show's announcer and had played the Ranger in public appearances, took over the part.[5] To ease the transition, Fran Sriker wrote a series of episodes in which the Ranger was badly wounded, often lying unconscious in a cave as Tonto cared for him. For several weeks it was up to Tonto to carry on alone, working to prevent a range war and protecting his friend from killers. When the Ranger finally recovered, it was now Beemer's deeper voice crying out, "Hi-Yo, Silver, away!"

Fred Foy was the new announcer, and soon became as much the voice of the show as the Ranger himself. Foy's crystal-clear, emotional delivery is so much fun to listen to he could probably have just read the phone book and made it entertaining. His opening narration ("Nowhere in the pages of history can one find a greater champion of justice! Return with us now to those thrilling days of yesteryear! Out of the past, come the thundering hoofbeats of the great horse Silver! The Lone Ranger rides again!") is one of the best known bits of pop culture in the world. He provided third-person narration at intervals throughout each episode—concise exposition that became as natural a part of the narrative as the actors speaking their lines.

Striker continued as the primary writer for the entire run. Jim Jewell called him "the greatest hack writer who ever lived." At one point, Striker provided scripts for *The Lone Ranger*, *Challenge of the Yukon* and *The Green Hornet* simultaneously, as well as writing Lone Ranger comic books and novels. His output reached 60,000 words a week.

Like the pulp writers, Striker handled this by relying on strict formulas. The Ranger encountered pretty standard threats— outlaws, hidden caches of gold, Indian uprisings, and the occasional natural disaster. Some stories had the Ranger encountering historical figures, such as Buffalo Bill or Wild Bill Hickok. Backed by the skilled professionals at WXYZ, and the strong moral center formed by the main characters, these formula plots were brought to exuberant life.

During the 1940s, multi-part stories became more common. There was a four-parter from 1947 involving the construction of the Union Pacific Railroad. Another four-parter took the Ranger to San Francisco, where he encountered an opium ring and an outbreak of plague. An unusual six-part arc from 1943 pitted the Ranger against a mad scientist who used electricity as the basis for deadly booby-traps.

The longest story arc ran for about twenty weeks in 1941–42. A secret organization known as the Legion of the Black Arrow planned to destabilize the West through acts of terror, a prelude to eventually breaking off the frontier from the United States and forming a dictatorship. For months the Ranger and Tonto opposed the Legion as it tried to blow up bridges and wipe out isolated bands of settlers. Each time the Ranger caught a man he thought was the leader, that man would be murdered by someone still higher up. Where the Ranger had previously worked to save relatively few lives at a time, now the entire nation was at risk.

It was during the Legion story arc that the Ranger's origin, hinted at for years, was fleshed out. We learn that he was the last survivor of a band of Texas Rangers that had been ambushed by outlaws. Found by Tonto and nursed back to health, he had chosen to allow the outlaws to think he was dead. He wore a mask to hide his identity, using the proceeds from a secret silver mine to pay his expenses and provide him with silver bullets.[6]

A six-part arc from 1942 introduced a new supporting character. We learn that the Ranger's older brother, Dan Reid, had been one of the men killed in that original ambush. Later, Dan's wife and baby disappear after their wagon train is attacked by Indians. Years afterwards, the Ranger finds his nephew, also named Dan, living with an old lady named Grandma Frizby. She had rescued Dan from the wagon train after the boy's mother was killed. Dan became a fairly regular member of the cast, traveling with his uncle when not attending boarding school.

Over the years the Ranger stuck his finger into a lot of pies. A four-part story from 1947 revealed that he even played a role in the eventual discovery of atomic energy.

Scientists in Washington believe that an as-yet-undiscovered chemical element exists that can unleash unbelievable amounts of energy. Minerals from a meteor that crashed in California decades before might contain the secret of this element. The government had twice tried to ship the mineral to Washington for study, but both times foreign agents had stolen the shipment.

Messages are sent to certain locations in the West, asking the Lone Ranger to contact a particular government official. When the Ranger does so, he's asked to guard the next shipment. A letter from a government man contains the identity of the Ranger's contact, but the letter is stolen by a couple of crooks working for the foreign spies. The Ranger captures the crooks and recovers the letter, but not before it's partially burned. Part of the instructions regarding how to contact the government agent are lost.

A third, unidentified man knocks out Tonto and rescues the captured outlaws. The Ranger and Tonto ride west, determined to protect the mineral shipment.

They contact the driver and guard of the stagecoach that's carrying the shipment. There's also two passengers, a man named Martin and a woman named Mary Demming. In addition, another man is seen following the stage at a distance.

The Ranger suspects Martin might by the government agent. He knows the agent will be carrying a silver bullet, but does not know where. It might be on his gun belt, or his watch chain, or elsewhere. A requirement for secrecy prevents the Ranger from just asking Martin, so he and Tonto decide to fake a stage robbery to provide an excuse for searching him.

During the "robbery" attempt, the two men who had earlier stolen the letter attack the stage. The Ranger and Tonto drive them off, then follow their trail to a cave. Returning to the stage, they find that the driver and guard have been killed. Martin is knocked out and Mary Demming tied up. The mineral shipment is gone.

Martin and Mary confirm that the same two outlaws, joined by the man who had been trailing the stage, had doubled back and stolen the shipment. The Ranger returns to the cave hideout, disguising himself as an outlaw to try and gain the confidence of the gang and learn the whereabouts of the stolen shipment.

But the Ranger has been fooled. Martin and Mary are part of the spy ring. They lied about the third man, who is, in fact, the government agent. Martin hopes the agent and the Ranger, each thinking the other an enemy, might kill one another.

The two men do meet at the cave, but they talk and figure out what's going on. Martin's gang attacks, coming at them from two directions (the cave is actually a tunnel). A desperate gun fight ensues. Tonto, who has been waiting nearby, arrives in time to turn the tide of battle. But the government man is killed, telling the Ranger to take his ring (which is mounted with a miniature silver bullet) before he dies.[7]

Most of the gang had been killed or captured, and the mineral shipment recovered. Martin and Mary escape and travel ahead to the next town, reporting that the Ranger had robbed the stage and stolen a gold shipment. The sheriff leads out a posse, capturing the Ranger and leaving him tied up as he chases Tonto and the "stolen gold." One of the deputies drops his eyeglasses, which the Ranger recovers and uses to focus the sunlight, burning away the ropes that bind him. He discovers that the ring has a secret compartment containing a paper that gives him the password he needs to identify himself to a government contact. After the Ranger establishes his bonafides, Martin and Mary are arrested. The shipment reaches Washington safely, one day to help mankind harness the power of the sun.

One element of this story arc demonstrates that even well-written shows take occasional missteps: the Ranger's plan to fake a stage robbery is just plain dumb. Otherwise, the meteor saga highlights the strengths of both *The Lone Ranger* in particular, and radio drama in general.

The plot offers several twists and turns involving the identities of different characters, but tidy and straightforward storytelling makes it all clear to the listener in the end. The friendship between Tonto and the Ranger, as well as their dependence on one another, is nicely emphasized at several points in the tale.

The gun fight in the cave — the most exciting part of the story — is a perfect example of what made radio such an effective storytelling medium. Using the usual exemplary sound effects, the fight is presented as a series of shots and ricochets, with the various characters shouting out orders or warnings. Each person listening would imagine something a little different, but each would be able to follow clearly the general action.

Radio had become the modern analogue to the oral storyteller. Like comic strips, it forces the audience to do some of the work — in this case, to provide the visuals. In doing so, radio activates and stimulates the imagination. It forces you to pay attention and rewards you with a level of emotional engagement that few other mediums outside of oral storytelling can match. We're in that cave along with the Lone Ranger — with each of us contributing our own private theater of the mind to flesh out the sounds we hear.

WXYZ developed several other successful shows. *The Green Hornet* (1936–1952) was, in a way, a sequel to *The Lone Ranger*. The main character, Britt Reid, was the son of Dan Reid, the Ranger's nephew. Britt was publisher of a big-city newspaper called the *Daily Sentinel*. He was also secretly the Green Hornet, a supposed criminal who actually helped catch crooks. Over the years, he and his assistant Kato nabbed mobsters, counterfeiters and extortionists.

Challenge of the Yukon (1938–1955) was essentially a western transferred to a colder climate. Canadian Mountie Sgt. William Preston, with his dog Yukon King, trailed bad guys across the trackless waste of the frozen north.

Both shows featured the same adroit actors and technicians who worked on *The Lone Ranger*. It's the Ranger, though, who made it into modern mythology alongside Tarzan. When Fred Foy asks us to return to the days of yesteryear, we really do.

20. As Inevitable as a Guilty Conscience: The Shadow on Radio

"The Bride of Death," "Ghosts Can Kill," "The Leopard Strikes," "The Case of the Three Frightened Policeman," "Death Is a Colored Dream," "Doom and the Limping Man," "Etched with Acid," "The House Where Madness Dwelt"; if it had accomplished nothing else, the Shadow's return to radio in 1937 deserves credit for coming up with the coolest episode titles. The show *did* live up to its atmospheric titles, though. Well-plotted and well-acted, *The Shadow* is, along with *The Lone Ranger*, one of the best remembered programs from radio's Golden Age.

While the Shadow's popularity as a pulp hero grew during the early 1930s, on radio he remained a narrator, taking no active part as a character in the stories being broadcast. *Detective Story Hour* ran through July 1931. A few months later, the Shadow returned to host mystery dramas as part of a variety show called *The Blue Coal Revue*. At the same time, in what must have been a truly horrible idea, he narrated *Love Story Hour*.[1]

In 1932 the Shadow received his own show, which ran intermittently on both CBS and NBC for the next three years. Throughout this early run he usually remained the narrator of self-contained stories that featured no continuing characters. Effectively voiced by Frank Readick, who developed a creepy, sneering laugh as the Shadow's vocal signature, he remained a popular radio fixture.

Consequently, the sponsor, Blue Coal, was happy with things as they were. But publishers Street & Smith wanted to change the format and present the Shadow as the active crime-fighter he was in the pulps. When the

The Shadow started on radio, jumped to the pulps, then jumped back to radio. He also took a side trip into the comics. He's perhaps the best example of how these mediums were cross-pollinating one another.

two camps were unable to resolve their differences, the Shadow's voice went silent.

Eventually, a compromise was reached. Blue Coal would sponsor the show with the new format, while Street & Smith agreed to return to the old Shadow-as-narrator format if this change wasn't successful.

Writer Ed Bierstadt wrote the premiere episode, which was broadcast on September 26, 1937.[2] To research the character, Bierstadt read many of the pulps and met with Walter Gibson. An early draft of the script included Harry Vincent as the Shadow's assistant. But radio is a very different medium from the pulps, and major changes soon were made.

A new character, "the lovely Margo Lane," replaced Vincent. This provided a clear difference in the voices of the protagonists and gave the Shadow a romantic interest.

With the need to tell complete stories in half an hour, much of the Shadow's pulp mythology was dropped or simplified. Aside from Margo, he had no agents. Where the pulp Shadow just borrowed Lamont Cranston's identity (one of many he used), the radio Shadow really *was* Cranston.

The most important change came in replacing the billowing cloak and blazing automatics with incredible mental powers. As the opening narration explained, Cranston had "the power to cloud men's minds so they cannot see him." He could, in effect, turn invisible.

In a way, it's too bad the pulp Shadow never got the chance to see how he'd do on radio. But the radio Shadow turned out to be such a good idea there's really no room for complaints. "How could there be a more perfect radio character," wrote Shadow expert Anthony Tollin, "than an invisible man as ethereal and unseen as the radio waves themselves?"[3]

Producer Clark Andrews hired 22-year-old Orson Welles to play the Shadow. Welles, as we will later see, had already become a busy and respected radio actor. He was busy on Broadway as well, with his Mercury Theater troupe preparing a modern-dress version of *Julius Caesar*.

Because of his hectic schedule, Welles was not required to attend rehearsals. Showing up every Sunday for the live broadcast, he'd read the part cold. An amazing actor, Welles could sight-read, scanning a few lines ahead as he spoke, to guide his performance. A Mercury Theater actress, Agnes Moorehead, played Margo Lane.

The first episode, "The Death House Rescue," got the show off to a strong start. An innocent man is on Death Row, scheduled to be executed soon. The Shadow, making use of both his invisibility and a talent for mental telepathy, visits the man in his cell and plucks from his memory a clue leading to the real killers. The crime-fighter then uses this clue to goad the killers into giving themselves away. The innocent man is freed.

Throughout the 1937–38 season and a syndicated summer series, Welles and Moorehead continued to give solid performances as Cranston and Margo.[4] They were backed by talented supporting actors, high production values and excellent scripts.

The plots featured a variety of criminals, mobsters and mad scientists. In "Death from the Deep," the Shadow encountered a modern pirate using a submarine. "Power of the Mind" and "Message from the Hills" involved telepathic communication. The "White God" was a mad scientist who tore planes from the sky with a magnetic beam; while the "Firebug" was a psychotic arsonist. The best episodes generated an aura of real spookiness within its detective show framework, with the Shadow using his strange abilities, deductive reasoning and psychological warfare to bring criminals to justice.

The new format was a hit and would have a seventeen-year run. Blue Coal would remain the sponsor until 1949.

In mid–1938, Welles left the show to concentrate on *The Mercury Theater on the Air* at CBS. Bill Johnstone, who had played the wrongly accused man in "The Death House Rescue," took over as Cranston. Soon after, Marjorie Anderson replaced Moorehead as Margo Lane. Johnstone's characterization was more authoritative than Welles', and was well-suited to the strong scripts that the staff of writers continued to supply.

In "Death Keeps a Deadline" (November 1, 1942), a thug named Rabbit Eddie Burke tries to mug Cranston and Margo. Cranston recognizes Rabbit, who's well-known in the underworld as a coward unable to make himself shoot a gun. Rabbit is easily overpowered and spends a year in prison.

When he gets out, he's obsessed with taking revenge on Cranston, but still lacks the guts to do anything about it. Rabbit's friend, the gangster Tony Morello, sympathizes with him, then tells him he's looking sick. Morello arranges a doctor's examination, and Rabbit is told he has only six months to live.

Without having to fear the electric chair, Rabbit finds the "courage" to kill. For months, Morello uses him as a hitman to do in both criminal rivals and policemen. Morello has an alibi for each killing, frustrating the cops. No one suspects the cowardly Rabbit.

Word reaches Cranston that Rabbit is supposedly dying. The Shadow visits the doctor and learns that the diagnosis was a lie. The whole thing was a set-up by Morello to turn Rabbit into an easily-controlled assassin.

Except that Rabbit is no longer easily controlled. He kills Morello when the gangster objects to his plan to finally take revenge on Cranston. Kidnapping Margo, Rabbit phones Cranston to taunt him with the knowledge that the girl is about to die.

Cranston hears a water pump in the background during the call. Checking with the water commissioner, he learns the location of a broken main. As the Shadow, he finds Rabbit and Margo in an apartment near the main. The Shadow tells Rabbit about Morello's trick. Suddenly terrified again of the electric chair, Rabbit kills himself.

Bill Johnstone left the show in 1943. Bret Morrison took over for most of the remaining run. (John Archer played the role for a year in 1944–45.) Margo was played by a number of actresses. By the 1950s, the overall quality of the scripts had dropped. Cranston's mental powers (other than his invisibility) had disappeared. Villains and other characters became more mundane. The spooky aura so important to the Shadow was lost to overfamiliarity.

Still, there was the occasional gem. "The Vengeance of Angela Nolan" (June 27, 1954) involves another attempt to take revenge on Cranston, who had helped send Angela's brother Angel to the electric chair.

The episode starts with a strong, emotional scene as Cranston and the daughter of the man Angel killed sit in the police commissioner's office, waiting for the moment of Angel's death. Soon after, the girl is murdered by Angela's henchman. With ruthless efficiency, Angela frames Cranston for both that killing and the murder Angel had committed.

It proves hard to keep a guy who can turn invisible locked up. Cranston escapes from the police. Together, the Shadow and Margo gaslight Angela, driving her to confess. Cranston's name is cleared.

Right until the end, *The Shadow* often remained a prime example of how good actors and writers could make magnificent use of radio's unique storytelling attributes. Just as radio convinced people that the Lone Ranger had once galloped across the West, it also convinced them that a man could turn invisible.

On October 30, 1938, radio would convince a few million listeners that the world had been invaded by Martians.

21. Orson Welles: Master Storyteller

Orson Welles got into radio in part to make money — it helped fund his theatrical work — and in part because he recognized its tremendous dramatic potential. Welles, only 22 years old when cast as Lamont Cranston, was a true prodigy. He would be an innovator not just in radio, but in theater and film as well.

He was already an experienced actor at age nineteen, debuting that year (1934) on Broadway in the part of Tybalt in *Romeo and Juliet*. Soon he was directing as well as acting, and in 1937 he and producer John Houston formed the Mercury Theater.

Welles' radio career began almost simultaneously with his New York stage debut. While his theater work was critically and often commercially successful, it was expensive to produce. Radio, especially for an actor who needed little or no rehearsal, could provide a steady source of extra income. By 1936, Welles had taken part in several hundred broadcasts, often hiring an ambulance to carry him from Broadway to CBS to NBC to Mutual, siren blaring as it sped through the streets in defiance of traffic laws. He'd arrive at a studio just before a broadcast, be handed a script and told who his character was, then go on the air. When one show ended, he sped off to do another.

A few months before he began doing *The Shadow*, Welles got a chance to write and direct his own radio production. His growing reputation had earned him a promise from the Mutual network of complete creative control over a seven-part adaptation of *Les Miserables*.

Using his fellow Mercury Theater troupers for his cast,[1] Welles developed or perfected techniques that allowed him to faithfully transfer Victor

Hugo's classic novel to another medium. Portions of the books were used verbatim as narration. Montages of dialogue, accompanied by appropriate sound effects, were employed to condense large sections of the story into a manageable time frame. Extended dialogue between characters was also taken directly from the book, with care to keep the tone conversational and dramatically believable. Everything — dialogue, sound effects and music — was completely integrated into a dramatically viable whole. The result was a riveting piece of drama that ranks among Welles' best work in any medium.

The techniques used on *Les Miserables* would serve Welles and the Mercury Theater well a year later, when *The Mercury Theater on the Air* began its run.

One of radio's advantages was that it was inexpensive. You could set a story in the kitchen, on a remote desert island or on the Moon using the same small budget. Because of this, the networks could experiment, allowing new shows to run without a sponsor, sometimes for months. The hope, of course, was that the show would become popular enough to attract a sponsor. In the meantime, the writers and directors of "sustained" (unsponsored) shows were free to indulge themselves creatively.

The Mercury Theater came to CBS without a sponsor and, at first, with very low ratings. The premise of the show would be an adaptation of a classic novel each week. Welles intended to start with *Treasure Island*, but changed his mind three days before the first show was set to air. Instead, the troupe would present Bram Stoker's *Dracula*. John Houseman, the program's producer and writer, spent seventeen straight hours with Welles in a restaurant hacking out a script.

Dracula was broadcast on July 11, 1938. The need to fit the story into an hour required a lot of condensation, but Welles and Houston did the job intelligently. Though several characters were dropped, the overall plot remained remarkably intact. The novel had been written in the form of letters and diary entries, providing a convenient framework for narrating the action on radio. Key scenes were transferred faithfully to the air waves, reconstructing the plot so as to tell the tale quickly while preserving the aura of horror that permeates Stoker's original work.

The script was backed up by a superb cast. Welles played both Dracula and Dr. Seward, one of the vampire hunters. Agnes Moorehead was Mina Harker, and Martin Gabel was Dr. Van Helsing. Ray Collins played the Russian captain of the ship that brings Dracula to England, narrating a gripping sequence in which the vampire kills off the crew one by one. Welles paid the same careful attention to sound effects, music and comprehensive dramatic integrity as he had on *Les Miserables*. Bernard Herrmann, one of the most brilliant composers of the 20th century, wrote and conducted the music.[2]

The second week finally brought *Treasure Island*. Subsequent weeks featured, among others, *A Tale of Two Cities*, *The Man Who Was Thursday*, *Julius Caesar*, and *The Count of Monte Christo*. Soon, Howard Koch was brought in to take over the writing chores from the overworked Houseman.[3] Ratings remained low, but the quality of each show stayed high.

One reason the ratings were low was the competition. Starting in September, the *Mercury Theater* was broadcast Sunday nights at 8 pm. Playing on NBC at the same time was the enormously popular Edgar Bergen/Charlie McCarthy Show, which generated ratings nearly ten times higher. But the Mercury players soldiered on — marching along with Dickens, Shakespeare and Jules Verne for company.

As Halloween approached, Welles decided to do something spooky. He chose *War of the Worlds*, overruling objections that the novel was too dated and unbelievable. Welles told Koch to build the script around news bulletins, updating the Martian invasion to the present day. The idea wasn't to fool anyone, but to give the story verisimilitude. At first, Koch had trouble with the script, but it gradually came together.

The first half of the broadcast began with a simulated dance music show, interrupted with increasing frequency by news reports of a meteor landing in New Jersey. The meteor, of course, was actually a vehicle carrying the Martians. Soon, in huge tripodal fighting machines, the Martians are marching towards New York, sowing death with heat rays and poison gas.

The first half ended with the destruction of New York. A reporter atop the CBS building succumbs to the gas, and the lone voice of a ham radio operator is heard asking, "Isn't there anyone on the air? Isn't there anyone..."

The second half employed first person narration, as Orson Welles' character wanders about the deserted countryside and city streets until the Martians die from exposure to Earth's bacteria. It wasn't until the show ended at 9 pm that the cast and crew found out they had panicked a nation.

In a way, it was all Edgar Bergen's fault. About ten minutes into his show that night, he introduced a singer that many of his listeners didn't care for. People began to spin their radio dials, searching for something else to listen to for a few minutes.

On CBS, they found a live news report coming in from the site of a meteor crash in Grovers Mill, New Jersey. This sounded interesting — they paused to listen as the incredulous reporter described the hideous creature that crawled from a cylinder in the crater. Horrified, they continued to listen as the creature's heat ray struck out, instantly killing scores of people. The army was called in, only to be wiped out. The Martians advanced on New York. There were reports of more cylinders landing all around the world.

It was definitely time to panic. Men hustled their families into automobiles and fled from the cities. They frantically phoned friends and relatives. Police stations and government offices, as well as the CBS switchboard, were deluged with calls.

As stated earlier, there was no deliberate attempt to fool people. The play, after all, was about a *Martian* invasion. So why did so many people fall for it?

Many of them tuned in late, missing the introduction and opening narration that clearly identified the broadcast as a play. The fear of war in Europe and Asia was strong, leading many people to conclude that the "Martians" were perhaps a German secret weapon. Add to all this the realism and expertise of the faked newscasts. Frank Readick played the reporter at the scene of the initial encounter with the Martians. To prepare for the role, he repeatedly listened to a recording of the live report from the *Hindenburg* disaster, then worked to imitate that same desperate tone. Other actors proved equally convincing, and the sound effects were of the usual high quality. In order to further simulate realism, no background music was used during the invasion sequences.

Also, the play's first half was perfectly paced. It started out slow, with Herrmann and the studio musicians taking the part of "Ramon Raquallo and his orchestra." As director, Welles stretched the musical interludes out, with at first only occasional, fairly innocuous interruptions describing explosions observed on Mars. As the play progressed, the news bulletins began to come more quickly, culminating in the Martian attack.

By now, the pacing of the show had picked up to faster-than-reality. Events that would have taken hours or days were compressed into minutes. The army rushes to Grovers Mill. They encounter the Martian fighting machines and are defeated. The Martians advance on New York City. An Air Force strike fails. A line of artillery is destroyed by poison gas. New York falls. Civilization collapses. All in about thirty-five minutes. So expertly was this done that the time compression isn't obvious unless you stop to think about it.

None of the Mercury players were aware of the chaos they were causing while on the air. After the show ended, Welles and Houseman spent an uncomfortable night wondering if they were going to be arrested or if their careers were in ruins. In the end, though, *The War of the Worlds* proved to be the ultimate career boost. No one had been hurt, and many commentators saw the broadcast as a useful example of how unprepared the nation was for war. Ratings for future episodes shot up, and the show gained Campbell Soups as a sponsor. With the new title *The Campbell Playhouse*, Welles and the Mercury Theater continued to air adaptations of the classics (and, at Campbell's insistence, movie adaptations as well) on a weekly basis for another two years.[4] Though they did occasionally fail, the majority of their broadcasts remained both classy and entertaining.

The March 17, 1940, adaptation of *Huckleberry Finn* is a particular delight and deserves special mention. The backbone of Twain's novel is the relationship between Huck and the escaped slave Jim. In an hour-long broadcast, it would be difficult to present the friendship and loyalty that grew between the two protagonists with the same depth and care.

Instead, the radio play was constructed to emphasize Twain's mastery of the English language. The script, like the book, is structured around Huck's narration. Former Little Rascal Jackie Cooper played Huck, while Welles took the part of one of a pair of con men who join Huck and Jim on their river journey. But Welles also played himself, in a sort of competition with Huck over who gets to read narrative and descriptive passages taken verbatim from the novel.

The single best-written bit of prose in American literature is the beginning of Chapter 19 of *Huck Finn*, describing a sunrise on the Mississippi River with such loving, vivid detail that it makes your heart ache to hear it. When this point is reached in the play, Huck begins to read the passage. Welles interrupts him, politely suggesting — and then more strongly insisting — that Huck is tired and that he (Welles) should take over. Huck reluctantly cedes the narration for the course of the passage before convincing Welles to let him take over again.

The story remains intact, and the friendship between Huck and Jim is still there, but the purpose of the play is to act as a funny, sincere expression of love for literature in general, and Mark Twain's beautiful, biting prose in particular. It was the high point of the Mercury Theater's radio work, even more so than *The War of the Worlds*.

Welles left *The Campbell Playhouse* in late 1940 to concentrate on filmmaking. But he remained regularly connected with radio for the remainder of its reign over popular culture. The Mercury Theater returned for a run of half-hour shows in the summer of 1946.[5] An excellent syndi-cated series with Welles playing Harry Lime, his character from the movie *The Third Man*, was recorded in 1951–52. Welles guest starred on many shows. He loved radio and, along with the Mercury players, regularly demonstrated just how perfect a storytelling medium radio was.

22. Faster Than a Speeding Bullet: Superman

All the new outlets for storytelling created by industrialization brought an explosion of fictional characters who, to various degrees, became entrenched in our culture. Nick Carter, the dime novel Buffalo Bill and Jesse James, Tarzan, the Shadow, Sam Spade, the Lone Ranger, Dick Tracy — all played a part in reflecting and sometimes influencing who we are. Perhaps the single most influential and popular character in modern fiction, though, is Superman.

The Man of Steel was almost single-handedly responsible for establishing comic books as a viable commercial industry. From there, he immediately spilled out into newspaper strips, a prose novel, animated cartoons, a variety of merchandise, and (of course) radio.

His appeal is multi-faceted. Like Tarzan and Doc Savage, he's wish-fulfillment by proxy, gifted with extraordinary powers and self-confidence. In the comics, his colorful costume made him visually unique.[1] His double life as mild-mannered Clark Kent was a secret in which readers could share and delight. Most importantly, he was a hero, using his powers to help the powerless. Though born on another planet, he came to represent the best aspects of humanity.

During the first few years of his existence, Superman's origin and powers remained in a state of flux, with details often changing from story to story. Things settled down by the mid–1940s, and a complex but self-consistent mythology was established around the Kryptonian. Most of the myths came from the comic books and daily strips. A few details were taken from an entertaining 1942 novel written by George Lowther. Quite a few elements of Superman's story first appeared on radio.

The Adventures of Superman came to radio on February 12, 1940, at first as a transcribed (pre-recorded) syndicated series produced at WOR in New York. Ratings were high enough to earn it a spot on the Mutual network by 1942.

Like *The Lone Ranger, Superman* was aimed at children but done well enough to win a fair proportion of adult listeners. Done as a serial, the show broadcast three times (later five times) a week, with storylines running for an average of about three weeks, and individual 15-minute episodes often ending with cliffhangers.

The first few episodes recounted the destruction of Krypton, with the lone survivor, a baby, sent to Earth in a rocket ship. In order to plunge Superman into action as quickly as possible, the radio Superman grew to adulthood during the space journey.[2] Adopting the secret identity of Clark Kent, he goes to work as a reporter for the *Daily Planet*.

The radio series added several important elements to the Superman mythos. Lois Lane had been a character since *Action Comics* #1, but now *Daily Planet* editor Perry White and cub reporter Jimmy Olson joined the cast. Kryptonite, the one element that can harm Superman, was introduced in a 1943 storyline. White, Olson and kryptonite all became a regular part of Superman's comic book universe as well.

Playing the lead was Clayton "Bud" Collyer, who used a tenor voice for Clark and shifted to a baritone for Superman. Usually the shift came in mid-sentence — "This looks like a job for ... SUPERMAN!"— providing an audio cue that alerted audiences to his frequent costume changes. His shout "Up, up, and away!" accompanied by a marvelous gush-of-wind sound effect,[3] took listeners into flight alongside him.

Joan Alexander played Lois Lane for most of the series. Julian Noa acted the part of the gruff, quick-tempered Perry White, and Jackie Kelk was young, eager Jimmy Olson. Kelk once wrote, "We all had great fun on the show,"[4] and this comes through in their performances. The best episodes have a palpable sense of fun generated by more than simply good scripts and production values. We have a good time listening, in large part because the cast had such a good time performing. With the help of writers who treated the show's premise with respect, the actors built a dynamic of friendship, trust and loyalty among the characters they played.

In 1943, Jackson Beck joined *Superman* as announcer. Like Fred Foy on *The Lone Ranger*, Beck became the irreplaceable voice of the show, able to jump in at any time to provide narration without interrupting the dramatic rhythm. It was Beck who read the famous opening narration each week ("Faster than a speeding bullet! More powerful than a locomotive!

Able to reach tall buildings in a single bound!"), adeptly leading us into the latest chapter of Superman's adventurous life.

Though supposedly "mild-mannered" (a demeanor that helped preserve his secret identity), the radio version of Clark Kent was a brave and intelligent reporter, doggedly investigating stories and helping expose crime and corruption. *The Adventures of Superman* was, in fact, as much a mystery show as a fantasy. Superman would show up when needed to save Lois, shore up a bridge or divert a Nazi torpedo, but it was Clark who did the legwork and deductive reasoning.

The criminals were not usually superpowered villains, but racketeers, bank robbers and corrupt politicians. Though it might seem that these minor-league bad guys were wasted on a hero who could juggle planets, clever plots with fairly planted clues made it work.[5]

In addition, the construction of individual episodes helped build and maintain suspense. The serial format, when done well, is one of the most effective methods of storytelling. Each chapter carries the plot along just a little, ending with a new, vital piece of information introduced, or with a character in danger.

One storyline running for about three weeks in late 1945 involves a murderess named Dixie Lamarr, who's wanted for killing a federal agent. Dixie's confidant, Dr. Bly, realizes that she is an almost exact physical double for Lois Lane.

Luring Lois, Jimmy and Jimmy's friend Dick Grayson to the amusement park where they're hiding out, Bly and his henchmen kidnap the trio. Clark Kent, aided by Batman,[6] arrives at the park to search for them. Batman falls through a trap door, but Superman rescues him, along with Jimmy and Dick, from a tank of freezing water. Soon after, a drugged Lois turns up, along with evidence that she killed the federal agent.

Clark and Batman continue to investigate. Clark eventually deduces that Lois must have a double. A search of police records uncovers Dixie's existence. Batman and Robin find her, but Batman is shot and wounded by Dr. Bly's thugs. Robin gets away and brings help in the form of Superman, who disposes of the crooks and captures Dixie. Lois is exonerated.

Another storyline concerned a circus strongman who robbed banks dressed in a Superman costume, then escaped on a cable towed by a cloud-camouflaged zeppelin. A plot to drive Lois and Jimmy insane and use them to kill Perry White involved small radio receivers hidden in their wristwatches, making them think a nearby cat was talking to them. All potentially silly stuff, but it worked due to the skill of actors and writers who played each story straight, without irony or parody.

The emphasis on mystery gave the fantasy premise an aura of believ-ability, but the writers never forgot that the show *was* still a fantasy. Super-man received ample opportunities to be super, and occasionally he'd go up against an opponent powerful enough to endanger even him.

In 1946, Superman and Jimmy ended up on the moon for awhile, with the Man of Steel battling giant birds and saving an underground city of moon people from a horde of ants. In 1948, Superman traveled to another planet to fight that world's tyrannical ruler.

Usually when Superman was himself at risk, kryptonite was involved. The most famous storyline from the series came in late 1945, right after Lois was cleared of murder. A Nazi scientist figures out how to dissolve kryptonite and inject it into the bloodstream of a fanatical confederate. This created "the Atom Man," a supervillian who could shoot atomic radi-ation from his fingertips, and whose mere proximity to Superman would weaken the hero. The two fought it out in the sky over Metropolis, with Jackson Beck breathlessly providing a blow-by-blow account. It was one of radio's most exciting moments.

A couple of years later, a corrupt politician uses kryptonite to cap-ture Superman and hold him prisoner while trying to starve him to death.[7] For several weeks, Batman and Robin search for the missing hero.[8] When Superman manages to get away from his captors, prolonged exposure to kryptonite has given him amnesia. He ends up playing for a minor-league baseball team, hitting home runs every time he bats and striking out 27 in a row when he pitches.

Sometimes a strong dose of reality blended with the fantasy. Like many of the early comic stories, *The Adventures of Superman* often dealt quite strongly with social issues. Corruption in the city government was not an uncommon theme, usually concentrating on how such corruption hurts the poor. Several storylines dealt with racial prejudice, with Klu Klux Klan–like organizations attacking synagogues and burning crosses. For a children's show produced in the 1940s, this was a bold move, and it's very much to the credit of the cast and crew that these stories were told. Amer-ican society at the time was still pretty casually racist, and suggestions of social equality made many people uncomfortable. Superman, though, treated racial equality and religious freedom as a given, portraying vio-lent bigots with open contempt. Interestingly, I've found no mention of any radio stations, including Southern stations, refusing to air these episodes. It seems that *Superman*'s status as a kid's fantasy allowed it to sneak in subject matter that many adult shows were unwilling to touch.

Superman continued as a serial until mid–1949. Then it jumped to

ABC for a couple of years with self-contained half-hour episodes.⁹ These were often condensed versions of previous multi-part stories—a little too rushed sometimes, but, in general, still done well. The last episode was broadcast on March 1, 1951. Superman lives on in other mediums—*Action Comics* is the longest-running comic book in the industry's history—but he was gone from radio forever. Television proved deadlier than kryptonite.

23. Frights for Smart People: Horror on Radio

The pulps were innovative in helping create or perfect entire new genres of fiction: hard-boiled mysteries, intelligent science fiction, character-driven westerns, and so on. Radio drama (and comic strips) proved equally innovative, but in a different way. Drawing on already established genres, they used new technologies to create new *methods* of telling stories.

Certainly this was true in the genre of horror. Between the gothic writers of the 19th century and the more recent works of Robert Howard and Clark Ashton Smith, horror fiction at its best had come to combine a keen grasp of human nature with honestly earned scares. When radio came along, it built on the prose writers had already accomplished, using the unique strengths of the medium to earn its own share of honest frights.

Radio horror shows were almost always anthology series; it's difficult to have continuing characters when the stories being told often require everyone's death at the end. Most series used a host to provide a common link between episodes. *The Witch's Tale* (1931–38) featured Nancy, the Old Witch, a part originally played by Adalaide Fitz-Allen. When Fitz-Allen died at the age of 79, 13-year-old Miriam Wolfe took over the role. Such is the advantage of radio.

The Mysterious Traveler (1943–52) was played by Maurice Tarplin, whose unnamed character told his spooky tales to fellow passengers on a train. A mix of crime stories, horror and science fiction, *The Mysterious Traveler* varied in quality, but managed to present its fair share of good episodes.

Its best episode, "Behind the Locked Door," involves an archeologist named Professor Stevens and his assistant Martin. The two, searching an isolated Southwestern mountain range for Indian artifacts, find a cave entrance that had been deliberately blocked up with large stones at some time in the past. Hoping to find a tomb, they blast the cave open. What they find instead are the remains of a large wagon train. Examining the wagons and the numerous skeletons, they deduce that the train had been forced into the cave while fleeing an Indian attack. The Indians had then sealed the entrance. Now, over a century later, the cave has been opened again.

The two scientists and their guide explore the cave and enter a vast, honeycombed maze of caverns. Lighting their way with flashlights, they discover an underground river, with large piles of fish bones piled along the shore.

The guide, convinced they are being watched, runs off. When the two scientists find him, he's been clawed to death.

Professor Stevens grasps the horrifying truth. What if some of the members of the wagon train, trapped in the caverns, had found the river? With this supply of food and water, they might have lived. Perhaps some of their descendants, raised in the pitch dark, still lived.

They'd be blind, reasons the professor, with their other senses magnified. He won't even guess as to what they might look like.

Lost, the two men wander the caverns for hours. The flashlights give out. Professor Stevens is attacked and killed. Martin is attacked soon after, but regains consciousness with "a heavy, calloused hand" washing his face.

He can't see his savior in the dark. When he tries to move away, the creature prevents him. Desperate, he jumps into the river. The creature jumps after him. Martin passes out again. When he wakes a second time, he and the creature are on a sand bar on the Colorado River.

Martin takes the creature to a cabin he owns. His girlfriend Cathy finds him there. He tells her what happened, but she thinks he's hallucinating. She opens the door to the bedroom, where he's keeping the blind, now helpless creature, intending to prove to him it isn't there. Then she screams.

What did the creature look like? The Traveler suggests we ask Cathy, though she tends to become hysterical whenever the subject is broached. He'd tell us himself, but here's our stop. It's time to get off the train.

"Behind the Locked Door" is an absolutely terrifying story, perfect for radio. Set almost entirely in the dark, it depends on sound and adroit plot construction to maintain a growing sense of menace. The twist at the end leaves us hanging — the only possible effective ending. Any solid hint as to what the wagon train descendents looked like would inevitably have been an anticlimax. It's a sublime example of how radio could take old ideas—in this case, scaring the pants off of people—and make them as fresh and dramatically effective as they ever were.

Inner Sanctum's host was simply named Raymond, played both by Raymond Edward Johnson and Paul McGarth. Even more memorable than Raymond's macabre narration was the sound of a squeaking door that bookended each episode, letting us into Raymond's sanctum to hear his latest tale. It was yet another great audio mood-setter, on par with *The William Tell Overture* or the gush of wind as Superman took flight.[1]

Boris Karloff was a frequent guest star on *Inner Sanctum*. A great actor with a distinctive voice, Karloff did much of his best work on radio. In "The Wailing Wall," from 1945, he plays a man who murders his shrewish wife, sealing her body within a wall of their house. Soon after, he hears a wail coming from inside that same wall. Convinced the sound is being made by his dead wife, he does not dare leave the house or allow anyone else in. For 40 years he lives as a hermit. Only as a broken, half-starved old man does he learn that the wail is just the wind blowing through a crack in the wall.

"Birdsong for a Murderer," from 1949, is another atmospheric outing. Karloff stars again, introducing himself as "Carl Warner. I'm not a young man anymore, but I don't mind that. I wasn't very happy when I was young, and now at least I'm not unhappy." Those lines, calmly delivered by Karloff, instantly establish mood and character for a story of blackmail, murder and warped loyalty, with yet another bizarre twist at the end.

Lights Out ran on and off from 1934 to 1947. Though originally created by Wyllis Cooper, it's best remembered for some famous tales written by Arch Oboler, one of radio's finest scribes.

Sometimes Oboler went for pure shock. In "Revolt of the Worms," scientifically enlarged worms engulf and smother their creator. "Chicken Heart" involves a heart kept alive and made to grow until it gets out of control and eventually covers the entire world.[2] The steady thump-thump of the heart is another classic sound effect.

Oboler could build up horrors more subtly when need be. "The Coffin in Studio B" follows a pair of actors and a director as they rehearse an upcoming *Lights Out* show. They are interrupted by a man who insists on selling a coffin to one of the actors. They get rid of him only when his reluctant customer picks a sample out of the salesman's catalog. The show goes on the air and, during a murder scene, one actor accidentally kills the other. The salesman returns to deliver the now much-needed coffin.

Much of this story simply involves the characters rehearsing the murder scene, discussing line readings and sound effects. This establishes a normal, natural atmosphere that plays nicely against the initial visit by the coffin salesman and the tragic death at the climax. Oboler had an ear for dialogue, and, like all the best horror writers, an understanding of authentic emotions and motivations.

After a brief career writing screenplays in Hollywood, *Lights Out* creator Wyllis Cooper returned to radio in 1947 to pen yet another horror show. *Quiet, Please* ran for two years, presenting excellent tales of horror that top even *Lights Out* in quality. Cooper's scripts often were masterpieces, simultaneously advancing both plot and characterizations straight into a usually fiendish twist at the climax. "My Son John" is narrated by a lonely man who tries to bring his son back from the dead. He succeeds, sort of, and must deal with the consequences. The protagonist in "Good Ghost" begins the story by matter-of-factly describing his own murder.

Cooper's best script is "The Thing on the Fourable Floor," broadcast on August 9, 1948. Set on and around an oil derrick, the story casts one of the roughnecks working there in the role of protagonist. One evening, he and a geologist examine core samples from over a mile down. To their surprise, they find a gold ring and a finger. The finger is made of stone.

The geologist grows jumpy, on several occasions convinced he sees something moving on the "fourable floor"—the platform located high up on the derrick. Porky, the roughneck, falls asleep, only to awaken and find the geologist dead with a broken neck.

The next day another man is killed when a line hauling heavy equipment inexplicably breaks. Drilling stops and the derrick is abandoned. But Porky, now convinced there *is* something inhuman lurking about, goes back alone to find it.

What he finds is a creature that had been accidentally drawn up from its underground home with the core samples. It's invisible, but Porky splashes it with red paint and gets a look. He doesn't describe it in detail, simply telling us that he's always been scared of spiders. Despite this, he's drawn to it — its perfect "little girl face" and the pathetic mewling sounds it makes attract his sympathy. He ends up caring for the lost, lonely creature, though this tends to be hard on other people after he finds out what it eats.

As in "Behind the Locked Door," the decision to refrain from describing the creature in detail avoided a potential anticlimax, and quite properly left it to the listener's imagination. All other aspects of the production, especially the narration and sound effects, were exemplary as well. Most notable were the sounds the creature made. Voiced by actor Cecil Roy, the odd mewling managed the seemingly impossible task of generating both sympathy and fear.

Without the option of relying on scenes of graphic bloodletting (something that has nearly destroyed the value of the genre in modern film), radio horror had no choice but to do things right. Good plot construction and characterizations were necessary, not disposable, elements. Men like Arch Oboler and Wyliss Cooper understood this. They knew how to scare you, not just gross you out. It's a rare talent that's tragically disappearing from our culture.

24. Tired of the Everyday Routine? *Suspense, Escape,* Carlton Morse and *The Scarlet Queen*

Suspense began its twenty-year run on June 17, 1942. Billing itself "radio's outstanding theater of thrills," it often managed to live up to this claim, presenting murder mysteries, a smattering of science fiction and horror, and a lot of stories designed to build up an unbearable level of, well, suspense.

Though it first broadcast from New York, production soon moved to Hollywood. *Suspense* would make good use of the movie stars of the day. If you were famous in the 1940s, chances are you appeared on *Suspense*. That was the hook used to lure in listeners. Tune in to CBS each week and hear Humphrey Bogart or Gregory Peck or Jimmy Stewart. William Powell was an escaped convict; Orson Welles was a motorist who sees the same hitchhiker over and over; Joseph Cotton fakes his death to hide from a murder charge.

Suspense was more than just an excuse to get stars on the air. Writers such as John Dickson Carr, Lucille Fletcher and Ray Bradbury turned out potent, intelligent scripts. Producer William Spier made sure the performances and production values matched the scripts in quality. Spier, known as "the Hitchcock of the airways," oversaw every aspect of the show, including music, sound effects and story content. He gave each week's guest star no more than four hours of rehearsal time (making sure they were tense during the live broadcast), and consistently drew great performances out of them. The stars loved it, with many returning multiple times. "If I ever do more radio work, I want to do it on *Suspense*," Cary Grant once said, "where I get a good chance to act." Producers and directors who followed Spier on the show, including Elliot Lewis and Anton M. Leader, did an equally excellent job.

Stories on *Suspense* often played on the theme of an ordinary man unexpectedly thrust into a life-threatening situation. "Dead Earnest," with Pat O'Brien, was about a man thrown into a cataleptic coma when hit by a car. He carries a letter in his jacket pocket describing his catalepsy (it's a recurring condition) and instructing that he not be embalmed even if he appears dead. Unfortunately, his jacket is left at the accident scene and picked up by the owner of a nearby thrift shop. The man is declared dead. The authorities try to call his wife, but she's not home. The jacket sells quickly, and a woman finds the letter inside. Uncertain if it's for real, she tries to find out where the jacket originally came from. In the meantime, the "corpse" is sent to the morgue for embalming. A man's life, put at risk by a quirk of fate, now depends on the efforts of a stranger. The woman with the letter is racing against a clock she doesn't even know is ticking.

It's a great story, rapidly cutting from one scene to another without confusing the listeners. Natural sounding dialogue helps establish realistic everyday characters caught up in a horrific situation. The scenes involving the doctors and morgue attendants are particularly well-done; they're played as competent professionals who have no idea they're about to kill a man. The tension builds in a steady and frighteningly believable manner to a nerve-rattling finale.

"Chicken Feed," with Ray Milland, starts with a man taking a drive. Stopping at a small-town café, the man (named Ralph Clark) realizes he's forgotten his wallet. He has no I.D. and no money — not even a nickel for a phone call. A suspicious local cop locks him up, where he's tormented by a pair of drunks who share his cell. Then a prisoner in the neighboring cell, a notorious bank robber named Phillips, breaks out. He takes Clark with him, mistaking him for an accomplice planted in the jail who'll guide Phillips to a hideout. They get away in Clark's car, driving out of town. Clark breaks away from Phillips on foot, running for several miles through the woods before stumbling across an isolated gas station.

This turns out to be the hideout Phillips had been looking for. Clark is captured by Phillips' accomplice. When the bank robber arrives soon after, the accomplice kills him for the reward money. He tries to kill Clark as well, but the bullet he fires is stopped by a nickel hidden deep in Clark's watch pocket. Clark gets hold of the gun and calls the police. For lack of a nickel, he'd been imprisoned, beaten, kidnapped and shot at. Then a nickel he didn't know he had saved his life.

Occasionally, the stories veered into something more bizarre. Orson Welles starred in a two-part adaptation of Curt Siodmak's novel *Donovan's Brain*, in which a disembodied brain gains telepathic control over another person. "The House in Cyprus Canyon" and "The Hitchhiker" were supernatural thrillers. A two-part adaptaion of *Othello*, with Richard Widmark and Elliot Lewis, aired in 1953. *Suspense* ran for 945 episodes before its end in 1962, giving plenty of opportunity for talented radio professionals to try something a little different.

Well-known comedians guest starred frequently, usually playing heavies. Bob Hope, Jack Benny, Lucille Ball and Red Skelton were all allowed to commit a murder or two, and all were quite good in these roles. Danny Kaye kills a rival for the girl he loves in "Too Perfect Alibi," timing his exit and return to a dinner party so that everyone is convinced he was there the entire time. When his girl is convicted and sentenced to die for his crime, he tries to confess. No one believes him — witnesses from the party assumed he was just being noble in trying to save the girl.

The most famous *Suspense* episode is "Sorry, Wrong Number," starring Agnes Moorehead. Repeated seven times, the popular tale involved an invalid who overhears a phone conversation she's accidentally plugged into. Two men are plotting to commit a murder that night. The invalid tries to call the authorities, but rude operators[1] and disbelieving police leave her frustrated and increasingly hysterical. She is, of course, unaware that it's her own murder she heard being planned.

Moorehead is typically superb, as is sound man Berne Surrey. "A mood can be projected expertly in the mere dialing of a telephone," Moorehead once said, and Surrey's skill certainly backed up this statement. He was considered once of the best in the business, using sound to advance each week's plot, both mechanically and emotionally. After several broadcasts of "Sorry, Wrong Number," he and Moorehead developed a tight synergy, with the actress dialing an imaginary phone while Surrey supplied the sound.

Late in its run, when television had begun to bleed away radio's audience, *Suspense* depended less frequently on famous guest stars. Right until the end, though, *Suspense* told its stories well.

My vote for the best radio series of all time — and I'll fight anyone who disagrees, one at a time or all at once — is *Escape*. Also aired on CBS, *Escape* was never as well-known or popular as *Suspense*. It jumped back and forth between a total of eighteen time slots, almost never had a sponsor,[2] and sometimes disappeared for a year at a time before returning to the air. It rarely had a movie star playing the lead. But it was produced and performed by seasoned veterans of the medium — people who had learned how to use radio to tell breathtakingly good stories.

Escape concentrated mostly on pure adventure yarns, usually adapted from short stories (or, less often, novels), but occasionally using well-written original scripts. It premiered on July 7, 1947, with Rudyard Kipling's "The Man Who Would Be King." The next week was "Operation Fleur-de-Leis," about an OSS agent organizing a resistance cell in occupied France. Starring Jack Webb, this episode was presented in a matter-of-fact, almost emotionless style similar to what Webb would soon be using regularly on *Dragnet*. It was a style that gave the denouement, involving the execution of a traitor, a lot of emotional impact.

That was the key to *Escape*'s artistic success. The stories usually shared a similar theme — someone placed in a dangerous location or situation — but the individual tone of each episode would be tailored to provide the best dramatic fit for its specific plot. "Operation Fleur-de-Leis" emphasized the emotional detachment a soldier must maintain to perform his often ruthless duty. "The Vanishing Lady" and "The Sire de Maletroit's Door" were heavy with melodrama. "A Tooth for Paul Revere" was whimsical, while "Shipment of Mute Fate" was awash in pure dread. Finales were happy or sad, straightforward or ironic, depending on what was most appropriate that week. Story was everything.

Few of those involved in producing *Escape* are well-remembered. That in itself is tragic, as these were men and women who could creatively dope-slap even those few actually talented people working in television today. William M. Robson and Norman Macdonnell served as the producer-directors. Les Crutchfield, John and Gwen Bagni, Gil Doud and others provided the excellent scripts. William Conrad and Paul Frees, two of radio's busiest actors in the late 1940s and 1950s, alternated on the opening narration, and often had roles in the stories. Other regular actors were also among the best in the medium: John Dehner, Ben Wright, Harry Bartell, Parley Baer, Vic Perrin, Jack Kruschen and Georgia Ellis were but a few. Some, like Conrad and Frees, had distinctive voices, though this never prevented them from believably playing a specific role. Others, like Harry Bartell, would sound like a completely different person every time you heard him. They all played lead roles in some episodes, supporting roles in others. Once again, it depended on what best fit the story.

Escape knew how to use words and music to grab listeners right from the start. Most episodes opened with the questions, "Tired of the everyday routine? Ever dream of a life of romantic adventure? Want to get away from it all? We offer you ... Escape!" Moussorgky's *Night on Bald Mountain* played (as the theme music), while William Conrad or Paul Frees hinted at the coming adventure. "You are seated around a green felt table with a dozen desperate men," we are told; or, "You are trapped in the dank darkness of a ruined plantation house"; or, "You have shipped aboard a South Seas schooner, with the ghost of its dead captain in command." It was an introduction designed to personalize each story. It sounds contrived when read on paper, but it avoided contrivance when heard on radio simply because the adventure that followed was told so well.

Escape adapted stories by famous authors such as H.G. Wells, Arthur Conan Doyle and Joseph Conrad, as well as lesser-known writers. They also drew on more ancient sources, telling of Robin Hood's adventures in one episode and recounting the events of one of Sinbad's voyages in another.

It was a half-hour show, making the decision to adapt mostly short stories a wise one.[3] The writing staff wasn't often required to condense or excise anything from the original tales. They were also smart enough to stick close to the source material, restructuring the plots only enough to make them workable on radio. Most stories concentrated on one major character, allowing the use of first-person narration to provide exposition and preserving much of the original prose. Episodes like "The Fall of the House of Usher" or "The Most Dangerous Game" are completely faithful to the stories upon which they are based, bringing these classics to life in a whole new way.

Sometimes changes were made for the radio version of a story. These would never be arbitrary, but would instead demonstrate an understanding of radio drama. Carl Stephenson's short story "Leiningen vs. the Ants" starts with a visit by a government official to the title character's South American plantation. The official warns Leiningen of an approaching horde of ants, urges him to evacuate, then himself leaves. The rest of the story, told in the third-person, recounts Leiningen's battle to fight off the ants.

On radio, the official remains at the plantation with Leiningen, providing first-person narration. Otherwise, the play follows Stephenson's story closely. Leiningen, arrogant but also brave and resourceful, uses a moat and a gasoline-filled ditch to attempt to divert the ants away from his land. Despite his efforts, the ants implacably continue forward.

Finally, the only hope for Leiningen and his men requires that someone run across ant-covered ground and open a dam's water valve in order to flood the plantation. Leiningen himself makes the attempt. At this point, when the plantation owner personally takes action rather than directing others, the official's narration fades and Leiningen tells the story directly. He describes the run to the dam and the fiery pain as ants swarm over him and bite into his flesh. Nearly eaten alive, he turns the valve. Flood waters wipe out the horde. As Leiningen loses consciousness, the official takes up the tale once more to confirm a proud man's victory over nature.

Adding the official to the plot is what made it work so well on radio. Had Leiningen narrated the entire story, his pride and arrogance would have overshadowed his other traits, making him too distasteful a person to work as the protagonist. Instead, we perceive him through someone else's eyes, giving us a more balanced view. This didn't make him likable, but it did make us root for him. The official's first-person account thus served the same purpose as the prose story's third-person narration. Of course, William Conrad's excellent performance as Leiningen, mixing hubris with intelligence, reinforced all this.

Escape's last broadcast came on September 25, 1954, after airing 229 shows, including some repeats.[4] One episode, repeated several times, is as terrifying as anything done on *Quiet, Please*. "Three Skeleton Key" is about three men trapped in an isolated lighthouse by a horde of starving rats. Sound effects man Cliff Thorness won an award for his efforts on this episode, crunching berry baskets and rubbing a wet cork on glass to simulate the squeaking of the hungry vermin. The episode is so thick with claustrophobia and pure fear that it's a wonder the sound is still able to pour out through the speakers.

"Command" is an intelligent western, juxtaposing the responsibilities of an officer leading a cavalry troop with the point of view of the soldiers who were just following orders. "Blood Bath" involves betrayal and survival in a South American jungle, with the piranhas, electric eels and pythons proving less dangerous than man's greed. "Yellow Wake" was about mutiny on a 19th century whaler. "Judgment Day at Crippled Creek" deals with vigilante justice, and "Plunder of the Sun" is one of many plots centering on a search for lost treasure.

The variety of plots and characters continued until the end. *Escape* was superlative storytelling, and perhaps the best example of just how much we lost when radio drama died.

Jack, Doc and Reggie couldn't stay out of trouble if they tried. It was fortunate, then, that they very much enjoyed getting into trouble. It would have been a rough life for them otherwise.

The three men met in China in the late 1930s, helping the nationalists fight the Japanese. They're separated during a battle, but they'd already arranged to meet in San Francisco on the next New Year's Eve.

Jack and Reggie make the rendezvous. At first, it seems like Doc isn't going to show up. When he does arrive, he announces that he's on the run from the cops, accused of a murder he didn't commit. Without hesitation, his two friends go on the lam with him.

This was the birth of the A-1 Detective Agency and the beginning of *I Love a Mystery*, an adventure serial that would run on several networks through much of the 1940s. Carlton E. Morse was creator, director and sole writer of the show. Best known during the 1930s for creating the soap opera *One Man's Family*, Morse demonstrated a flair for writing complex mysteries and solid adventure.

The three heroes were inspired creations. Jack Packard was the strong-voiced leader. Reggie York was a cultured Englishman, though as capable as his partners of holding his own in a fight. Doc Long was a Texan, speaking in a Southern drawl, who liked pretty girls almost as much as he liked barroom brawls. All three were broadly drawn characters with distinctive personalities, designed to play well off one another dramatically.[5] Any one of the three by himself probably would have become tiresome over the course of an extended serial. But put two or three of them together and the audience is soon having as much fun as they are.

Morse dropped his protagonists into one wild adventure after another. A master of the serial format, Morse designed most of the individual 15-minute episodes to unfold in approximately real time, building tension gradually as information is gathered, clues are found and dead bodies are frequently discovered. Morse's strongest talent may have been his sense of pacing — he knew exactly how much information to give away in any one episode.

As on *The Shadow*, individual storylines had great titles: "The Fear That Creeps Like a Cat," "The Thing That Cries in the Night," "Temple of Vampires," "The Decapitation of Jefferson Monk." Unfortunately, in most cases only bits and pieces of individual storylines still exist. The modern listener can hear enough to recognize just how good Morse was at telling a story, then tear his hair out in frustration when the recording abruptly ends.

Two storylines, "The Thing That Cries in the Night" and "Bury Your Dead, Arizona" still exist in their entireties.[6] The first of these is set almost entirely in a mansion owned by Randolph Martin, an oddly-named old woman determined to preserve her family's good name at all costs. This isn't easy, since her grandson Job is a drunk and her three granddaughters (Faith, Hope and Charity) are all pretty much nuts. Also, the chauffer is blackmailing several of the siblings.

Soon after the A-1 detectives arrive, the chauffer is murdered. Charity, who speaks in a soft, perpetually terrified voice, claims a mysterious person or persons is out to destroy the family. To top everything off, a baby's cry is heard each time just before something violent happens. The thing is, there hasn't been a baby in the house for twenty years.

Jack's convinced there's a rational explanation. He's right, of course. He and his partners were frequently running up against seemingly supernatural threats, only to eventually find a rational explanation for it all. In this case, the solution involves dysfunctional relationships, insanity and a radio actress who specializes in baby sounds. Nearly everyone is knocked out at least once, and there's one more murder before the killer is revealed and plunges to a grisly death off the roof of the mansion.

Jack, Doc and Reggie then hop a freight train, ending up in the isolated town of Bury Your Dead, Arizona. Once again, they go up against seeming magic when a villain known as the Maestro apparently turns a girl into a tiger.

I Love a Mystery ran from 1939 to 1942, again from '43 to '44, then once more from '49 to '52. Several different actors played the lead roles, with the 1949 run re-using scripts from the earlier broadcasts. In 1948, Morse brought his three protagonists back in *I Love Adventure*, which consisted of 13 self-contained half-hour episodes. All of these are available on tape or MP3, though the series is much weaker than *I Love a Mystery*. Morse worked best in the serial format.

In 1945, Morse wrote and produced a syndicated series appropriately titled *Adventures by Morse*. The protagonists, Captain Bart Friday and his sidekick Skip Turner, are basically clones of Jack and Doc. This is hardly a problem, though. Morse was simply playing to his strengths, and *Adventures by Morse* is every bit as good as *I Love a Mystery*. Captain Friday investigated weird goings-on in a cemetery in "City of the Dead." He hunted a Nazi war criminal across a thick swamp in "It's Dismal to Die." He deals with corpses that seem to get up and walk away in "Dead Men Prowl." He even saves the world from a cult that plans to release a deadly virus in "Land of the Living Dead." Each storyline[7] is thick with tension. Individual episodes often build up to terrifying cliffhangers. Captain Friday opened each episode with: "If you like high adventure, come with me. If you like the stealth of intrigue, come with me. If you like blood and thunder, come with me." Few writers did blood and thunder better than Carlton Morse, and we went quite willingly with the good captain.

Captain Philip Carney loved his ship. The ketch *Scarlet Queen*, he mused, had "a fresh young body ... bold, teasing. Dressed in only a crown and painted in scarlet red.... The *Scarlet Queen* ... the woman my particular world revolved around."

It may seem as if Carney desperately needs to get out more, but he was first and foremost a sailor, not truly at home anywhere but at sea. Unfortunately, all ships must put into port on occasion. It was Carney's bad luck that his ports-of-call always seemed to be literally dripping with smugglers, pirates and assassins — all bent on making his life difficult.

The Voyage of the Scarlet Queen premiered on the Mutual Network on November 6, 1947. It never found the audience it deserved, running for just 38 episodes. Featuring great characters, solid plots and wonderful sound effects, it was a show worthy of commercial success.

Each week's episode opened with the sound of wind in the rigging and waves breaking on the bow, heard just under the theme music. We'd hear the first mate shouting orders to the crew, then the voice of the captain providing us a few cryptic hints of things to come.

"Log entry: The ketch *Scarlet Queen*; Philip Carney, master. Position: 120 degrees 29' east, 14 degrees north. Wind light, sky overcast. Remarks: Departed port of Manila 9 AM after canceling shore leave for crew. Reason for unscheduled departure: The Barefoot Nymph and the Mother Hubbard Jacket."

Nearly all the episodes had great titles like that — "The Pegleg Skipper and the Iberian Blade," "The Fat Trader and the Sword from Apohaejiam," "The Lonely Sultan of Isabella de Bassilan." The stories lived up to the romantic promise of the opening, mixing together mystery elements in the hardboiled tradition with a sharp sense of adventure.

Elliot Lewis directed the series and also starred as Philip Carney. Lewis was one of radio's true greats — his understanding of how to use the medium to tell stories was probably equal to Orson Welles or William Spier. As an actor, he could do either drama or comedy equally well.[8] As a director and/or producer, he could meld all the elements of radio together seamlessly.

On *Scarlet Queen* he used heavily layered sound effects, running sound men Ray Kemper and Bill James ragged with the effort needed to keep up with the story. The end result was incredible — whether the setting was the *Queen* at sea, a crowded bar in Shanghai, or a deserted pier at midnight, the sound effects always provided both technical accuracy and dramatic ambiance.

Gil Doud and Bob Tallman wrote the scripts. The two scribes had a talent for establishing believable and interesting characters in just a few words. Carney would provide first-person narration, describing one man as "...heavy featured, half a head shorter than me, carrying as his cargo a little too much to drink." Another man, an obese merchant named Ah Sin, was a "brocade-wrapped mountain of flesh ... the child-like features lost in the billowing fat.... He still looked Chinese but still sounded like Charles Laughton." Carney's description of settings was as succinct and effective as those of people. The end result was a lot of fast-paced story fit into each half-hour episode.

The anchor to all this was Lewis' portrayal of Carney. Tough, smart and quick-tempered, Carney was loyal to both his ship's owner and his crew. He was capable of either thinking or fighting his way out of a dangerous situation — though when his temper flares he'd probably prefer to fight.

The premiere episode found Carney in San Francisco, outfitting the *Queen* for a long voyage. The *Queen*'s owner, a Chinese businessman named Kang, is sending Carney out to locate and recover a sunken treasure — artifacts from Chinese history valued at $10,000,000. Kang simply wants to preserve his country's heritage, but a competitor for the treasure, a Portuguese named Constantino, is in it for the money. It will be goons and con artists working for Constantino who usually bring Carney trouble in each episode.

Trouble starts right way. Carney's first mate is kidnapped, tortured for information and murdered. Carney is quickly embroiled in a complex net of overlapping double crosses. Along the way, he meets Red Gallager, a beefy sailor who may or may not be on his side.

In the end, the killers are caught and the *Queen* sets sail. Red Gallager is the new first mate, though several episodes will air before either Carney or the show's listeners finally realize he can be trusted.

Gallager was played by Ed Max. He's another inspired characterization — a loud-mouthed, capable sailor whose tough-guy demeanor doesn't quite hide his own share of brains. He and Carney soon develop a comradely rapport that adds strength to the series.

Each episode took the *Queen* to her next port-of-call as she crisscrossed Asian waters, gathering information and collecting needed equipment while vainly trying to lose Constantino's thugs. Most adventures would involve a confrontation with these thugs; occasionally, there'd be an encounter with pirates or smugglers not directly connected with Carney's primary mission.

In "Ah Sin and the Balinese Beaux Arts Ball" (October 16, 1947), the *Queen* arrives in Bali to purchase underwater salvage equipment. The merchant selling the equipment is Ah Sin, the obese Chinese mentioned earlier. Carney discovers that Ah Sin has already received a generous counteroffer from a representative of Constantino. The merchant "invites" Carney and Gallager to a garden party at his home — Constantino's man will also be there and Ah Sin wants all his eggs in one basket while negotiations proceed. Ah Sin's bodyguard, a Texan named Mangin, backs up the invitation with a six-gun, inducing the two sailors to accept.

Constantino's man, named Gaulter, double-crosses everyone (including Constantino), locking Carney and Gallager up as he tries to get hold of the salvage equipment himself. The two sailors get loose and also free Ah Sin and Mangin, who were held prisoner elsewhere. Ah Sin, who has been shamed by a perceived loss of face, doesn't want to be rescued, but his Texan bodyguard is eager to get back into the fray.

In the end, Carney catches up with Gaulter back at Ah Sin's home and beats him into unconsciousness. We catch a glimpse of Carney's darker side here; his temper has flared red hot and he screams at everyone — Gallager included — to stay away from him as he stands over Gaulter. It takes a minute or so for him to calm down enough to once again recognize friend from foe.

Catching Gaulter at Ah Sin's home has restored the merchant's face. In gratitude, he chokes out the sentence, "I ... *give* to you your supplies."

Like many individual episodes, this one had its share of violence and betrayal. Though it ended well for Carney, it wasn't until the *Queen* put back to sea that all was once again right with the world. This was another standard conceit of the show. No matter how dirty things got on land, the wind in the *Queen*'s sails and the spray leaping over the bow would wash Carney's emotions clean.

"[The mainsail] flapped hopefully for a number of seconds," relates Carney, "and settled back comfortably under the wind that filled it. The jib came up, then the mizzen. And the *Scarlet Queen* slashed into the swells as if impatient, as though the wind and sea she had was not enough for her to work with." Carney and his crew were off to a new adventure.

25. Dramatizing Reality: *Dragnet*

Jack Webb started in radio as an announcer and disc jockey in 1945. Before long, he'd become a busy radio actor, hosting both a morning jazz music program and a comedy show. He came to national prominence in 1947 when he starred in *Pat Novak for Hire*.

Pat Novak was something that only became possible after the vocabulary and images of hard-boiled fiction had been established in the popular consciousness. A private eye show, it took every stereotype of the genre and amped them up to near-parody level. Webb and writer Richard Breen created the ultimate hard-boiled world in which everybody is a little bit crooked and *everybody* speaks in a series of ironic one-liners. Radio historian John Dunning points out that, "the series existed, in fact, simply to push the one-liners."[1] The plots were a mish-mash of murders, frame-ups and double crosses, with just about everybody except the series regulars ending up dead by the finale. Trapped within this formula was Pat Novak, a guy who, as he puts it, "rent[s] boats and wrap[s] small sins in $20 bills." If you have an unusual odd job — delivering a package after hours or finding a missing girlfriend — then Pat's your man. It's a dangerous life, admits Pat, who narrated each episode. "Sooner or later, you draw trouble a size too big," and then you're staring up at your headstone.

Every story begins with Pat taking on one of his odd jobs. It was often something that sounded easy. All he'd have to do was pick up a package or deliver an envelope. Before long, usually within a few minutes, things start to go badly. Pat is beaten up or knocked out. He wakes up next to a dead body, himself suspected of murder. To clear himself, he must find out what's going on.

Webb narrates the show via an unending staccato of wisecracks. "The street was deserted as a warm bottle of beer." Describing a hit-and-run victim: "The old man couldn't have made it with a pocket full of aces." When the old man dies: "He slipped out of my arms and stopped paying taxes." When Pat is knocked out: "I hit the floor and made Rip Van Winkle look like an insomnia victim." When angry: "I was seeing more red than the bleachers at a bull fight."

Whenever Pat's in trouble, he goes to his only friend for help. Jocko Madigan used to be a doctor. Now he's a drunk, but, according to Pat, "the only honest man I know." Prying Jocko away from his bottle usually takes a few minutes of arguing, but the former surgeon then starts helping with the legwork.

The other regular character is Lt. Hellman. Pat and Hellman loathe each other, and the cop is always eager to pin a murder on his nemesis. Pat knows this, giving urgency to the need to clear himself of whatever murder or murders he's currently suspected of. "He'd bury me so deep in San Quentin," comments Pat, "he'd be bringing me air in paper bags." One of the several brutal beatings regularly inflicted on Pat during an episode often is delivered by Hellman.

Pat's desperate investigations inevitably lead him into yet another dangerous situation, in which whatever bad guys haven't yet killed each other are in the middle of one last big double cross. That's the part where everybody else gets killed. A final bit of narration ties everything together, explaining the sequence of events in terms that sorta kinda make sense if you're in a generous mood.

Clever writing and Webb's sardonic, rapid delivery of his dialogue made it all work, endowing the show with dark but potent humor.

Webb played Novak from 1946 to the spring of 1947, with the show originating out of San Francisco and initially airing only on the West Coast. When Webb left for Hollywood, he was replaced by Ben Morris, who was a fine actor but couldn't bring the character to life. It was a role owned soley by Jack Webb. *Pat Novak* soon went off the air.

Webb continued to stay busy in radio, appearing on numerous programs and starring in a couple of short-lived private eye shows. He did five more months of *Pat Novak* in 1948, this time aired nationally. At the same time, he took on some movie work. It was while playing a crime lab technician in *He Walked by Night* that he got the idea for a new kind of radio show.

The technical advisor on *He Walked by Night* was Los Angeles police officer Marty Wynn. "Webb and Wynn," writes John Dunning, "shared a belief that pure investigative procedure was dramatic enough without the melodrama of the private eye."[2]

Webb took this idea and ran with it. In 1949 he convinced NBC to let him make an audition record. Then he obtained the cooperation of the L.A. police, promising to portray them in a positive light.

The result was *Dragnet*, which would have an eight-year run on radio and several successful incarnations on television. With *Dragnet*, Webb quickly proved that he and Marty Wynn were right. A police investigation really was dramatically viable. Each show began with the simple but memorable theme music, then an announcer (Hal Gibney or George Fenneman) would assure us the story we were about to hear is true and then give a brief overview of this week's case. "You're a detective-sergeant. You're assigned to homicide detail. A confessed murderess is paroled from the state prison for women. After seven months, the parole office loses contact with her. Your job — find her." Webb, in character as Sgt. Joe Friday, would then pick up the narration, delivering it in a calm, documentary style.

Friday and his partner would go to work on the case. They check records, question witnesses, canvass neighborhoods and arrange stakeouts. Police work is presented as unglamorous, repetitive and often grueling. *Dragnet* made it not just interesting, but fascinating.

First of all, it was basic sound storytelling. The plots unfolded logically, and the listener had no trouble following the action.

It was realistic. The cops used proper police terminology. The sound effects, from footsteps to the rustling paper of a crime report, were done to perfection. Sound men Bud Tollefson and Wayne Kenworthy built up a library of recorded sounds for the show, including police sirens and radio calls, that helped Webb achieve the level of absolute realism he wanted.

Finally, and perhaps most importantly, there was Webb's style as a director and his insistence on how actors should read their lines. Webb demanded that every role be underplayed, with lines read in an almost unemotional monotone. The idea was to take yet another step away from melodrama, keeping everything as realistic as possible. "He told me … [to] speak everything as if you're not acting," recalled Peggy Webber, who played Joe Friday's mom.[3] Webb used some of radio's best actors, such as Harry Bartell and Herb Ellis. But he would forgo the services of equally talented actors like William Conrad, whose deep voice was too individually distinctive. Every character on the show was an everyman.

It was, in retrospect, a brilliant and innovative approach to drama. The monotone style didn't block off emotion, but rather let it seep in naturally. It allowed Webb and the writers[4] to make the characters human.

Friday was a dedicated professional who really cared about his fellow human beings. His first partner, Ben Romero, was played in an easygoing manner by actor Barton Yarborough. When Yarborough died in 1951, Ben Alexander joined the series, playing Detective Frank Smith as a likable fussbudget. Everyone else — victims, witnesses and crooks — were just as human.

Occasionally, a *Dragnet* episode would be a character study rather than a case study, demonstrating just how well the show could generate real emotion. A young man comes into the station and confesses to murder, claiming to have killed the older woman he had been dating. The woman's body is found, but the medical examiner says she drank herself to death. There's no evidence of violence. Questioning the young man, Friday draws out a tale of two sad, self-destructive people. The man is honestly convinced he murdered the woman simply because he could never make her happy. Friday lets him go and later learns he committed suicide.

Most of the time, *Dragnet* took us step-by-step through an investigation. A two-part story from 1952 details the efforts to catch a man pulling early morning robberies of grocery stores. The man wears a mask, and witnesses can't provide good information. Friday detects a possible pattern in the robberies and they catch a guy, but he proves to be a copycat. The masked bandit changes his pattern. The police change their system of stakeouts. Finally, Friday and Smith catch the bandit in the act. After a shootout and chase, he's placed under arrest.

The story covers a lot of ground, even for a two-parter. This was another benefit of the *Dragnet* monotone. Everyone could deliver their lines just a little faster, fitting 35 to 40 minutes of dialogue into each half-hour episode and making even mundane scenes seem inherently exciting.

And so it went until 1957, with the radio series overlapping its television debut. Friday caught murderers, burglars, drug dealers and muggers. Innocent people are victimized, crooks are tracked down, justice is served and life goes on.

When Webb took *Dragnet* to television in 1952, he kept his cast, format and style intact. Television added nothing new or important to the show. It had been created on radio, and it was in that medium that it had been truly innovative.

26. The Law in
Dodge City: *Gunsmoke*

Radio took two separate approaches to the western. The first, typified by *The Lone Ranger*, was a mythologized and somewhat sanitized version of the Old West. The western, in this case, becomes as much a morality play as was *Dick Tracy*. Heroes and villains are clearly delineated, and moral issues simplified. Quality shows like *The Lone Ranger* demonstrate that this is a perfectly legitimate direction for a storyteller to take, but it's as much a fiction in terms of history and the complexities of human nature as it is in plot and character.

The real West was a dirty, blood-soaked place. People lived hard, lonely lives that often broke both body and spirit. Death came suddenly by violence and disease and accident, often leaving no one behind to bury the fallen. Separating the heroes from the villains was often very much a matter of opinion. Greed and bigotry mixed with courage and nobility — sometimes within the heart of a single individual.

One of radio's finest series portrayed this more realistic version of the West, giving listeners stories that emphasized both the best and the worst we can be.

Producer-director Norm Macdonnell and writer John Meston began to develop the idea for a realistic western series in 1950. That year they collaborated on an *Escape* episode, titled "Wild Jack Rhett," about a gunfighter who had come to terms with the inevitability of his own violent end.[1] This was exactly the sort of plot and atmosphere the two men wanted to bring to a regular series.

Their chance came in 1952 when the cancellation of a spy series called *Operation Underground* opened up a time slot at CBS. On April 26, 1952,

Gunsmoke aired its first episode. Set in Dodge City, Kansas, during the 1870s, the show centered on Marshall Matt Dillon's efforts to enforce the law and keep the peace.

It was a commercial and creative success right from the start. Macdonnell assembled his cast and crew from among the best radio people. Rex Kaury provided the music, composing the memorable theme in his bathroom the morning before the first broadcast.[2] Aside from Meston, the writing staff included Les Crutchfield, Antony Ellis, Kathleen Hite and others Macdonnell had worked with before. The sound effects men were Tom Hanley, Ray Kemper and Bill James (the same trio who had done such fine work on *The Voyage of the Scarlet Queen*).

Everything came together perfectly. The stories were often standard western fare in terms of plot — range wars, rowdy cowpokes and brutal outlaws — but the scripts gave a sense of humanity to it all. The characterizations in *Gunsmoke* may very well be the strongest in radio drama. The citizens of Dodge City and its many transients, both the good and the bad, both male and female, were three-dimensional characters that the listener could easily accept as real.

William Conrad played Matt Dillon. Conrad, always a great radio actor, really excelled himself in this role. He and the writers gave Dillon a quiet confidence counterpointed by occasional bursts of fiery temper. Dillon was a man of both violence and conscience. He wouldn't hesitate to kill if forced to do so; and he had long ago accepted that his chosen job would often lead to killing.

A background theme in many *Gunsmoke* episodes was the idea that the first wave of settlers along a new frontier would be forced to sacrifice themselves before the land was tamed. These sacrifices weren't just physical, but moral and spiritual as well. Dillon was very much a part of that first wave. Doing his job would eventually help make the streets of Dodge and the surrounding territories safe for everyone. But it was a job that would set him apart. The constant danger meant he could never risk having a family of his own. He would never be free of the frequent need to point a pistol at a fellow human being and pull the trigger. Dillon was a lonely man, with little in his life to bring him personal happiness. All he really had was his skill with a gun, his sense of societal responsibility, and an understanding of right and wrong.

The rest of the regular cast consisted of Parley Baer as Chester, Dillion's deputy; Howard McNear as Doc Adams; and Georgia Ellis as Kitty. Busy radio stalwarts such as John Dehner, Harry Bartell and Vic Perrin played various other roles each week. It was an interesting mix of characters. Chester was a bit slow, but loyal and dependable. Early in the series,

Doc Adams came off as somewhat ghoulish, cackling with delight when Dillon had to kill a man because Doc was paid a fee for performing the autopsy and arranging burial. As the series progressed, the writers gradually lightened up Doc's character, and he became another of Dillon's few dependable friends.

Kitty was a saloon girl, implicitly a prostitute, though this was never stated aloud. She was yet another lonely person; without husband or family, she did the only work available to her. It was work that made her a social pariah outside the saloon and left her and Dillon unable to follow up on the attraction each felt for the other. Many contemporary movies and television shows glamorize prostitution or ignore its moral and emotional impact on women. *Gunsmoke* was not guilty of this, and Kitty was as much a tragic figure as Dillon. The show did not require us to approve of what she does, only that we quite appropriately sympathize with her plight.

Solid production values backed up the solid performances. As was typical on all the great shows, great care was taken with the sound effects. From the big things (like gun shots) to the little things (Dillon's spurs as he walked, or the jingle of keys against the jail door), each effect was calculated to add to the realism and ambiance. Macdonnell often included moments of dead air, with no sound at all, to emphasize the particular effect that followed.

The sound of hoofbeats opened an episode that aired on February 23, 1953. Dillon and Chester ride into the small town of Pierceville, finding it inexplicably deserted. Soon they're captured by a group of outlaws. The entire town, in fact, has been taken hostage. The gang, led by a man named Brill, came to town that morning and started trouble. Brill's brother was killed in the ensuing gunplay, and Brill wants to know who did it. The outlaw leader threatens to start shooting people unless the killer is revealed. To make his point, he guns a man down and has several others executed.

Dillon and the townspeople have all been put in the same large warehouse. Dillon, Chester and one other man (named Bill) knock out two guards and escape. Once outside, Bill kills an outlaw with a thrown axe. He has never killed before and, in just a few lines of dialogue that demonstrates just how well *Gunsmoke* humanized its characters, he must pause to pull himself together. Now armed, the three men get the jump on the outlaws, capturing the lot. The episode concludes with Dillon's stark narration: "I was there when they tried [Brill], and I was there when they hanged him."

This provides closure to the episode without lessening its strong aura of tragedy. Yes, justice was served in the end, but innocent lives were snuffed out forever.

Not every episode ended with an emotional downer. Just as often, the finale saw people content or love requited. But *Gunsmoke* didn't back away from tragedy, and the emotional slant of each episode was always turned in the best dramatic direction for the individual stories. This added tension and uncertainty — listeners never knew if a sympathetic character would live or die. More importantly, it also overlaid a sense of optimism over the entire series. No matter what happened, Marshall Dillon always maintained his moral center. He always worked to make things better.

Gunsmoke ran until June 18, 1961; like *Dragnet*, it overlapped its television incarnation by several years.

Norm Macdonnell created another intelligent western in 1956. *Fort Laramie*, starring Raymond Burr, was about the lives of cavalry troopers. Regrettably short-lived (there were 40 episodes produced), the show offered a strong mixture of adventure stories and character studies.

In 1958, *Gunsmoke* writer Antony Ellis created *Frontier Gentleman*. This starred John Dehner as J.B. Kendell, a reported from the *London Times* who travels the West looking for stories. Once again, listeners were provided with intelligent storytelling and sharp characterizations. The western on radio had grown up. Unfortunately, few people were still listening.

27. From the Far Horizons: Science Fiction on Radio

Science fiction on radio followed a pattern of growth similar to what had happened in the pulps. The genre had been a staple of radio almost from the beginning, with horror and mystery anthology shows occasionally delving into S-F themes. Most regular science fiction series were aimed at children. There was *Superman*, of course, as well as *Buck Rogers*; *Flash Gordon*; *Tom Corbett, Space Patrol*; and several others. The quality of these shows varied, but all used science in the same way — like the tales in the early issues of *Amazing Stories*.

Most of these shows were space operas, with the word "science" tossed in to justify impossible gadgets like anti-gravity belts, invisibility pills and death rays.[1] They worked on the same "gee-whiz" level as stories by E.E. Smith and Philip Nowlan. No concern was shown for real-life physics and astronomy, nor was there much effort put into characterizations. Plots were straightforward battles against evil, told with a dime-novel simplicity.

More adult science fiction turned up from time to time on shows like *Escape* or *The Mysterious Traveler*. But it wasn't until April 8, 1950, that a regular series devoted to the best the genre had to offer made it to the air.

Dimension X, a half-hour show on NBC, concentrated mostly on adapting short stories by established writers. "We went the adaptation route," said producer Van Woodward, "simply because that's where the best stories are."[2] Woodward and his writers certainly recognized the best when they saw it. Over the course of fifty broadcasts, ten Ray Bradbury stories were used, as well as four by Robert Heinlein and a brace by Isaac Asimov. Jack Williamson, Clifford Simak, Kurt Vonnegut and other skilled S-F writers were also represented.

Most of the adaptations remained very faithful to the original tales—as with *Escape*, the decision to use mostly short stories meant little (if any) of the plot had to be condensed or cut. The writers, usually Ernest Kinoy or George Lefferts, captured the best elements of each story in terms of plot, science and characters. The result was a level of gripping and intelligent storytelling not usually found in the genre outside of prose.

Also like *Escape*, the *Dimension X* stories dealt with a variety of themes and emotions, demonstrating how versatile science fiction can be. "Dr. Grimshaw's Sanitarium" and "The Professor Was a Thief" are both mad scientist stories, though the first is pretty grim and the second pretty funny. "Time and Time Again" is an unusual time travel yarn. A number of stories offered post-apocalyptic settings, while several dealt with space travel and/or contact with alien races. In nearly every case, realistic characterizations and dialogue backed up the plot.

Dimension X did showcase some original scripts, with two of the best being those written by Ernest Kinoy. "Shanghied" is a good straightforward adventure about a man kidnapped and taken aboard a starship that leaves for a voyage meant to last fifteen years. "The Martian Death March" follows native Martians as they escape from the reservation in which colonists from Earth had placed them. It's a bit heavy-handed in its parallel to Native American history, but good dialogue and a strong insistence that we are all our brother's keepers make it a sincerely emotional piece.

Dimension X was produced on a tiny budget,[3] but skilled writers, actors and sound men made it work. Each week the sound from the radio meshed with the imaginations of listeners to quite literally create whole new worlds.

The show was short-lived, lasting only through September 1951. Three and a half years later, producer William Welsh[4] brought many of the same creative people, including writers Lefferts and Kinoy, back to NBC to try again.

X Minus One first aired on April 24, 1955. By then, radio's audience was steadily hemorrhaging into the vast wasteland of television. Consequently, *X Minus One* received a minuscule budget, one even smaller than its predecessor's. To cope, the show soon dropped live music and went to recorded cues. Despite this and other cost-cutting decisions, the series maintained the same high standard set by *Dimension X*.

In fact, the first fourteen episodes reused scripts from *Dimension X*—hardly a problem considering the quality of those scripts. To obtain new material, the show gave an on-air plug to *Galaxy* science fiction magazine. In return, the series could buy the rights to stories published in *Galaxy* for just $50. The same good taste in selecting stories that served well on *Dimension X* continued to serve on the newer show.

"A Gun for Dinosaur" is about a time-traveling safari out to bag a tyrannosaur. "Shock Troop" is an unusual story about microscopic aliens trying to colonize a human body. "A Saucer for Loneliness" is a heart-rending tale of loneliness and empathy. Episodes like "The Girls from Earth," "The Native Problem" and "One Thousand Dollars a Plate" manage the difficult task of telling a funny S-F story without sliding into parody.

X Minus One featured a great opening, with announcer Fred Collins counting down "X minus five ... four ... three ... two ... X minus one ... Fire!" The blast that followed was the roar of rocket exhaust overlaid with human voices, making an eerie sound that penetrated directly into the listener's imagination. "From the far horizons of the unknown," said Collins, "come transcribed tales of new dimensions in time and space. These are stories of the future, adventures in which you'll live in a million could-be years on a thousand maybe worlds!"

The story that followed didn't play down to you at all — it was assumed the listener would be able to follow the often fantastic plots and would enjoy hearing stories that made him or her think.

"Cold Equations" (from August 25, 1955) starts out with a one-man space ship setting out for a distant planet. The pilot carries a serum needed to save the lives of several sick men stationed at a scientific outpost.

Soon after taking flight, the pilot finds a stowaway on board. It's a young woman, eager to join her husband on the planet, but her very presence on the ship proves disastrous. Her extra weight means the ship doesn't have enough fuel to make it to the planet and land safely.

The only solution seems to be to shove her out an airlock. The pilot can't sacrifice himself, because the woman can't fly the ship. He can't go down with her, because men on the planet will die without the serum.

Desperate, he radios his mother ship for help, but none can be given. It's all simple math — a cold equation that says too much weight means too little fuel.

The whole situation could have been nothing more than contrived melodrama, but in skilled hands it became a frank examination of both physical and moral courage. Based on an excellent short story by Tom Godwin, the adaptation followed the original plot closely and preserved much of the story's dialogue. The only major difference was changing the stowaway from a teenager trying to reach her brother to an adult woman in search of her husband. This did little to alter the emotional intensity of the plot, and "Cold Equations" is nearly as powerful on radio as it is in print.

X Minus One managed to air 125 episodes, with some repeats, before its cancellation in January 1958. As with the western, science fiction on radio had only just begun to realize its full potential before dramatic radio died.

28. The End of Radio

By the late 1940s, radio had two decades of storytelling experience behind it. Excellent drama and adventure could be found across the dial. There was *The Six Shooter* with Jimmy Stewart and *Box Thirteen* with Alan Ladd. Humphrey Bogart and Lauren Bacall set sail on the *Bold* Venture. Detectives from literature, such as Sherlock Holmes, Nero Wolfe and Sam Spade, were well represented.

Detectives created specifically for radio also abounded. One of the best was an insurance investigator with a "two-fisted expense account." *Yours Truly, Johnny Dollar* began in 1949, at first as an average tough-guy detective show about an insurance agent. Each episode was narrated by the title character in the form of his expense account: "Item 2, $2.25; taxi fare from the airport to the hotel. I noticed I was being followed almost as soon as we left the airport..."

It was an interesting and effective conceit, but the show didn't really begin to shine until 1955. In October of that year the format changed from a weekly half-hour show to 15-minute episodes each weekday. Individual storylines lasted the whole week, giving the writers 75 minutes in which to build complex plots and flesh out characters. Johnny was now played by Bob Bailey,[1] who gave a nuanced, intelligent performance to back up the strong scripts. Cases dealt with everything from murder to arson to stolen furs to threats against the life of a valuable show dog. *Johnny Dollar* briefly became one of radio's best detective shows.

In late 1956 it returned to the usual weekly format and became merely average once more. It ran until September 30, 1962, becoming the last network dramatic series to go off the air.

Television killed radio. Something new came along and we once again left the old behind.

I earlier referred to television and movies as inherently lazy media. There are instances when they rise above this— there have been good movies and, on rare occasions, good television shows. But the accusation of laziness is largely warranted.

It's really very simple. In order to attract an audience, radio *had* to learn to tell stories effectively. All it had going for it was sound and the imaginations of the listeners. The *only* option was pure storytelling, where the plots made sense and the characters touched our emotions. Nothing else worked. Plot holes were always glaringly obvious. Poorly drawn characters and stilted dialogue always rang false.

Radio provides only partial information — sound, dialogue and narration — but it used this to build complete images by actively engaging our minds. We are personally involved because we're doing as much work in creating the story as the actors and sound men. Consequently, we each experience the story in a unique way.

Television, on the other hand, provides us with everything — both sound and images. We are asked to bring nothing to the stories ourselves. It is a passive, not active, medium. Each of us sees exactly the same thing, and there's no requirement to think or feel. Compare the two mediums and it clearly becomes a case of "less is more."

Consider the well-documented tendency of people zoning out while watching TV. Television puts our brains into a coma even while our eyes remain open. We don't think. We don't feel. We just sort of glaze over.[2]

On television, storytelling is inherently sloppier than it was on dramatic radio. The constant barrage of images replaces logical plotting. The simple obligation to make sense is lost; plot holes are covered up by lightning-quick editing and rapidly shifting camera angles. A poor storyteller can toss in quick edits, explosions, cars and pretty girls to hid his faults— talent is no longer an essential job requirement.

Visual imagery thus replaces proper story development, reduces the time spent on plot exposition and cuts dialogue down to a stream of weak one-liners. Nearly every technological advance in film and television has made things worse. The disappearance of black-and-white photography and the rise of CGI special effects, to cite two examples, have widened the emotional gap between the storyteller and the audience even further. Compare the charm and power of the stop-motion special effects in *King Kong* with the technically perfect but emotionally vapid effects in a modern fantasy film such as *The Mummy Returns*. Compare the engaging black-and-white imagery of *The Third Man* with, well, any contemporary film.

Another side effect of visual storytelling is the increased vulgarization of modern society.³ As moving imagery replaces good plotting, the temptation to lower standards of good taste increases. Violence becomes bloodier. Romance morphs into casual sex. Language becomes cruder.

It all becomes a peculiar exercise in rationalization. Old standards are ignored without concern about the value they might still have. Bad taste comes to be considered innovative. Film and television artists, even those with demonstrable talent, argue vehemently that a graphic sex scene or foul language is a necessary part of their art. A sense of social responsibility or a desire to tell a story without sinking to new levels of vulgarity are missing from their mind sets.

So why did we give up something so obviously valuable for something so obviously lousy? Once again, it relates to our own inherent laziness when seeking entertainment. Most of us just take the path of least resistance. The result, of course, is less effective and satisfying entertainment. But by then we're too zoned out in front of the TV to notice. And zoning out is not equivalent to relaxation.

Assigning blame for the downfall of radio drama and the deterioration of popular entertainment is therefore very easy. It lies at the feet of every single member of Western civilization.⁴ It's not like the TV doesn't have an off button. It's not like you're required by law to see every heavily-advertised movie the first weekend of its release. Or see it at all, for that matter.

You can instead read a book. You can track down a reprint edition of Hogarth's *Tarzan* and spend an evening with your kids learning to appreciate and *enjoy* real artistry. You can buy recordings of the classic radio shows — most of those I've reviewed are available — and treat yourself to a *real* story.

You still have a choice. Either you tune in to the next episode of *Survivor* and watch people strip themselves of all dignity and self-respect as they clutch at their fifteen minutes of fame, or you feel quite properly embarrassed for them (and for yourselves for watching), turn off the TV and do something worthwhile. It may take a little effort, both in the acquisition of material you don't yet have and in the tiny mental tweak needed to put yourself in the right mind set. But it's worth it.

Appendix I: Timeline

1814   The *London Times* begins using a steam-powered printing press able to print 1,100 pages an hour. Mass production of newspapers and periodicals becomes more practical.

1827   Swiss artist Rodolphe Topffer develops picture stories, using sequential images to tell a specific story. The gestation of the comic strip begins.

1830   The first inter-city steam railway — the Liverpool & Manchester line — opens. By making distribution easier, this and other transportation advances help usher in the age of popular literature.

1860   Beadle & Adams publish the first dime novel — *Malaeska, the Indian Wife of the White Hunter*. An enormously effective mass-marketing campaign helps make this new format a commercial success. At first, westerns and frontier stories dominate the market.

1861   The American Civil War begins. Half-a-million men will die over the next four years in large part because of improvements in military technology. This downside to industrialization, though, does not yet sink into public consciousness.

1865   Beadle & Adams publish *The Steam Man of the Prairies*, ushering in the genre of young inventor stories. These early science fiction tales typically treat science and technology as wonderful things that bring nothing but good.

1869   Buffalo Bill Cody becomes the star of a dime novel series. Other real-life figures soon enter the dime novel universe along with him.

1872   The first dime novel series featuring a detective — the Old Sleuth — appears. A response to the growing urbanization of Western society, the dime novel detectives were soon more popular than their western counterparts.

1893   The *New York World* acquires a full-color press, intending to use color illustrations to increase sales.

1895   The *New York World* publishes *Hogan's Alley*. The American comic strip is born.

        That same year, Guglielmo Marconi demonstrates "wireless telegraphy."

1896   Publisher Frank Munsey issues *Argosy*, the first all-fiction pulp magazine. It is an immediate success. Other pulps soon spring up by the score.

1897   *The Katzenjammer Kids*, by Rudolph Dirks, begins running in the *New York Journal*. Dirks is one of several artists who led in developing the visual vocabulary of the comic strip.

1912   *Under the Moons of Mars*, by Edgar Rice Burroughs, appears in *All-Story* magazine. Burroughs' interplanetary fantasy will influence most science fiction for the next two decades. *Tarzan of the Apes* appears in *All-Story* later the same year.

1914   The Great War begins. The horrors of trench warfare and poison gas finally demonstrate to the general public that technology has a definite downside. This and other factors (urban crime and corruption, pollution, etc.) generates a cynicism that will soon effect American literature, especially detective and science fiction.

1920   KDKA in Pittsburgh, the first federally licensed radio station, begins transmitting. Later that year, Westinghouse opens its own station to give people a reason to buy their radios.

1923   *Weird Tales* begins publication.

        Dashiel Hammett's first Continental Op story appears in *Black Mask*, helping to introduce hardboiled detective fiction.

1924   Roy Crane creates *Wash Tubbs*, a humor strip that he will gradually change into an adventure strip over the next few years.

1926   *Amazing Stories*, the first science fiction specialty pulp, begins publication.

        David Sarnoff forms NBC, the first national radio network.

1927   William Paley forms CBS, a rival network to NBC.

1929   *Amos and Andy*, a comedy show broadcast on CBS, becomes a huge hit. The viability of nationally broadcast radio is firmly established.

1931   *The Shadow* magazine begins publication — this is the first of many pulps to feature stories about a single character.

        Chester Gould creates *Dick Tracy*, demonstrating the growing commercial and artistic value of the adventure strip.

1933   *The Lone Ranger* is broadcast from WXYZ in Detroit. The character's popular success will be the cornerstone for building the Mutual Broadcasting System.

1937 The Shadow comes to radio as the main character of his own show. By now, radio, the pulps and comic strips are actively cross-pollinating one another.

1938 Orson Welles' *War of the Worlds* broadcast vividly demonstrates the grip radio had on the public's imagination.

John Campbell becomes editor of *Astounding Science Fiction*, leading the movement to turn science fiction into a viable and important genre.

The first Superman story appears in *Action Comics* #1. Comic books, a direct outgrowth of the comic strip, soon begin to draw younger readers away from the pulps.

1939 Pocket Books begins mass-production of paperback novels—another competitor for the attention of pulp readers.

1940 WNBT in New York becomes the first regularly broadcasting television station.

1941 The United States enters World War II. Ensuing paper shortages hurt both pulps and comic strips. Comic syndicates begin shrinking strips down dramatically to fit more on each page. By the end of the 1940s, the golden age of the adventure comic strip was over.

1947 *Escape* begins its intermittent seven-year run on CBS. Radio begins to fully realize its artistic potential.

1948 Milton Berle becomes television's first celebrity, starring in the *Texaco Star Theater*. Radio listeners steadily begin to stop listening.

1949 Street & Smith cancels its entire pulp line, including *The Shadow* and *Doc Savage*. Some pulps linger on for a few years, but the format is gone by the mid–1950s.

1952 *Gunsmoke* makes its radio debut. Radio drama will be gone in a decade, but it goes out swinging.

1962 With the cancellation of *Suspense* and *Yours Truly, Johnny Dollar*, radio drama no longer has a significant presence in popular culture. Civilization effectively ends.

Appendix II:
Radio Favorites

What follows is a smattering of specific radio episodes or story arcs that typify the strengths of the medium.

From *The Lone Ranger*

"Remember the Alamo" (December 12, 1941). The Ranger helps organize an isolated band of settlers in order to fight off a band of marauders. This episode is another wonderful example of how sound alone can be used to "visualize" complex action.

"Outlaw's Gold" (January 25 & 28, 1946). A two-parter that dances around hard-boiled detective territory. Several sets of bad guys search for a hidden cache of stolen gold. A dizzying series of double crosses keep the story moving fast. The Ranger, despite making the rather absurd mistake of trusting a woman just because she's good looking, manages to out-think the lot of them.

From *The Shadow*

"The Silent Avenger" (March 13, 1938). *The Shadow* normally relied more on plot and melodrama than on characterization, but this story about a shell-shocked war veteran manages to generate a nice level of sincere sympathy for a man who is not entirely responsible for his murderous actions.

"The Voice of Death" (December 8, 1940). A prime example of using sound to generate horror and suspense. A madman transplants vocal cords between different sorts of animals—the meows of cute little kittens come from the jaws of huge, bloodthirsty dogs.

From *The Mercury Theatre*

"The Count of Monte Cristo" (August 29, 1938). The sequence recounting Edward Danton's escape from prison is a model of clear, concise storytelling.

From *The Adventures of Superman*

"The Dead Voice" (September 26, 1946, through October 16, 1946). Dick Grayson, alias Robin the Boy Wonder, receives threatening phone calls from a man who is supposed to be dead. This leads into a solidly written mystery, climaxing on a burning yacht.

"The Mystery of the Flying Monster" (March 7, 1949). A self-contained 30-minute episode that showcases Jackson Beck's extraordinary skill as narrator as he describes Superman's pursuit of an out-of-control spacecraft.

From *Lights Out*

"Murder in the Script Department" (May 11, 1943). A sort-of companion piece to "The Coffin in Studio B." Two typists are trapped in the CBS script department during a blackout. Arch Oboler's ability to gradually feed terror into a given situation is especially notable here.

From *Quiet Please*

"Good Ghost" (October 24, 1948). This first-person yarn about a helpful ghost steadily slides from comedy to horror during the course of the story.

"Shadow of the Wings" (April 7, 1948). This story of a very sick little girl and the Angel of Death could have been sappy, but Willis Cooper's literate script infuses it with real emotion.

From *Suspense*

"Backseat Driver" (February 3, 1949). The comedy team of Fibber McGee and Molly play a couple who, while driving home one night, discover an escaped murderer has hidden himself in the back seat of their car. The tension builds steadily to an effective twist ending.

"Cabin B-13" (November 9, 1943). A woman, recently recovered from a mental breakdown, boards a cruise ship with her new husband. Then her husband disappears and the crew claims her cabin number doesn't exist. A well-constructed mystery with yet another fine ending.

From *Escape*

"Misfortune's Isle" (March 21, 1948). A 19th century Yankee ship captain agrees to attack a den of pirates on a South Pacific island. Excellent dialogue and performances give an otherwise simple adventure yarn a fresh vitality.

"Up Periscope" (August 8, 1951). This one's set in the 1930s. A U.S. Navy veteran hires out as a mercenary, taking command of a Chinese submarine to fight Japanese invaders. His sub is old, his engines unreliable and his crew untrained. But the bounty for sinking Japanese ships makes it all seem worth the risk.

"A Sleeping Draught" (October 1, 1950). A ship captain, transporting convicts to Australia, must trust a murderer in order to save his vessel. A sharp combination of adventure and character study.

"Price of a Head" (October 19, 1952). A drunken thug's one true friend is a headhunter. We find out why in the last minute of the episode.

From *Dragnet*

"Homicide" (June 24, 1949). A cop is killed in a wild gunfight while trying to stop a robbery. An effective use of flashbacks adds immediacy to the stories of various witnesses. Sgt. Friday is then left with the task of tracking down several wounded but still dangerous bandits.

From *Gunsmoke*

"Overland Express" (October 31, 1952). Dillon, Chester and a prisoner are returning to Dodge on a stagecoach when they encounter a still-more-dangerous outlaw. Dillon delivers some dialogue about being resigned to death ever since he pinned on his badge that gives sharp insight into his character.

"Home Surgery" (September 19, 1952). A man living on an isolated ranch has broken his leg and developed gangrene. With no way of reaching a doctor in time, Dillon must perform an amputation. The scene in which Dillon, Chester and the rancher nervously plan the operation is superb.

From *Frontier Gentleman*

"Aces and Eights" (April 20, 1958). The story of Wild Bill Hickock's death is a standard but well-constructed character study of a burned-out gunfighter.

From *Voyage of the Scarlet Queen*

"The Lonely Sultan of Isabella de Basillan" (October 30, 1947). Captain Carney encounters the usual mixture of greed, betrayal and murder at his latest port of call. This one includes a particularly fine bit of characterization and a truly emotional ending.

From *Dimension X*

"Shanghaied" (November 11, 1950). A skillful blend of science fiction and old-fashioned adventure involving a man shanghaied aboard a space ship as it leaves on a 15-year voyage.

"Time and Time Again" (July 7, 1951). The consciousness of a soldier fighting in World War III is transported back in time into his 13-year-old body. Now he has the chance to change history for the better — providing he can get his dad to believe his story.

From *X Minus One*

"Junkyard" (February 22, 1956). Soon after a space ship lands on an unexplored planet, the crewmen gradually begin to forget key bits of technical knowledge. Based on a story by Clifford Simak, this yarn carefully balances humor and suspense. There's a high-impact twist at the end.

"A Gun for Dinosaur" (March 7, 1956). Based on a story by L. Sprague de Camp, this one's about time traveling hunters who take safaris into the past. But if you're going to hunt dinosaur, make sure you can handle a big enough gun.

"The Native Problem" (September 26, 1957). One of several Robert Sheckley stories used by the show that manage the tricky task of interjecting humor into a science fiction tale without turning it into farce or parody.

And while I'm at it, here's a few pulp stories that are worth digging up:

"Red Nails" by Robert E. Howard (*Weird Tales*, July through September 1936). Conan and a swordswoman named Valeria are trapped in a ruined jungle city by a hungry dragon. The city's inhabitants are divided into two factions eternally at war with one another. Magic, sword play and moments of pure horror punctuate an exciting story. One of the best Conan stories.

"Daemon" by C.L. Moore (*Famous Fantastic Mysteries*, October 1946). Every bit as atmospheric as Moore's "Shambleau," but with the emphasis on loneliness and compassion rather than horror.

"Trouble-Chaser" by Paul Cain (*Black Mask*, April 1934). Cain was one of several contemporaries of Dashiel Hammett who helped develop hardboiled fiction into true art. Like the best Hammett stories, "Trouble-Chaser" clearly tells a complex tale of multiple murders without wasting a single word.

"Hands in the Dark" by Walter Gibson (*The Shadow*, May 1932). Atypically, the Shadow doesn't rely much on his agents for help as he continually out-thinks a band of gangsters searching for hidden loot. Towards the end, there's a really nifty gun battle in a dark attic.

"The Suicide Squad — Dead or Alive" by Emile Tepperman (*Ace G-Men Stories*, April 1940). A perfect reminder that many pulp stories were simple fun and made no pretense to be more than that. A city government has been taken over by gangsters. An elite team of G-Men, known as the Suicide Squad because they take on only the most dangerous assignments, arrives to clean things up. After a few thousand words of non-stop shootouts, kidnappings and fist fights, they succeed.

Notes

Introduction

1. That's from page 35 of Sobol's book.

Part I

Chapter 1

1. The *Times* press could print 1,100 copies of a page per hour. By the 1840s, the best presses could do 8,000 copies per hour.

2. The rise of public education was a direct function of the rise of the middle-class. The former would not have existed without the latter.

3. Several of Edgar Allan Poe's early works appeared in story papers when they won second prize in contests where actual money only went to first-prize winners. Not surprisingly, there never were any first-prize winners.

4. Or by Thomas Peckett Prest — nobody is quite sure.

Chapter 2

1. It's ironic that stories that helped define the mythical American West were being written at the same time the decidedly unromantic and often tragic story of the *real* West was unfolding.

2. Before turning to writing, Ingraham had been publicity agent for Cody's Wild West Show. Before that, he'd been a Confederate soldier and a mercenary.

3. Submarines were particularly common after Jules Verne's *Twenty Thousand Leagues Under the Sea* was published.

4. The proportion of child readers to adult readers probably varied depending on the subject matter. The most interesting thing to note is not what children were reading, but that they considered reading one of their primary forms of entertainment. Think about that a minute, then take a baseball bat to the PlayStation.

5. Remember that a successful dime novel series might run for a couple of decades, with a new story each week.

6. "Old" was a common sobriquet. Age was considered synonymous with wisdom and experience.

7. He apparently subcontracted some of this work to other writers, but it's still an admirable record.

8. Oddly, there was also an occasional ghost story included in the series, with Brady encountering spooks as well as crooks.

Chapter 3

1. One last dime novel, *Wild West Weekly*, struggled on until 1927 before also converting into a pulp.

2. Some of the pulps, such as *Tip Top*, were formally dime novels that changed their format.

Chapter 4

1. The pulps kept costs down in part by paying low rates to their contributors. The slicks, higher priced magazines printed on better quality paper, often were able to steal away writers of proven popularity by offering more money.

2. He wrote more than just westerns. Among his other accomplishments, he created the character of Dr. Kildare.

3. He did eventually publish his poetry.

4. Brand's evenhanded treatment of Indians is also demonstrated in a series of interlocking stories published in *Western Story* in 1927–28. These feature Thunder Moon, a white child kidnapped and raised by the Cheyenne. Brand accurately portrays Cheyenne culture and populates the stories with well-drawn, three-dimensional characters, both white and Indian.

Chapter 5

1. Prose for which Hoffman was not obligated to pay.

2. "...a tall, corpulent man...with a malevolence plainly written on his enormous yellowish countenance." Sabatini's best descriptive passages were both stylish and to the point.

3. One of the few weak points of the story is this aspect of Blood's relationship with Arabella. During any of the several times they meet during the course of the story, their chronic misunderstandings of each other could have been cleared away by one or two simple declarative sentences.

4. Sabatini reorganized and rewrote the story considerably for book form, giving the overall narrative a smoother flow.

5. Mundy himself never fessed up to his past — this was uncovered by later biographers.

6. All this only after quelling a mutiny when his British crew has second thoughts about their misson.

Chapter 6

1. His taste did fail him from time to time. *Weird Tales* would print its share of clunkers throughout its lifetime.

2. That's quoted from Server's book *Danger Is My Business*, page 43.

3. Smith's stories are rife with names like Avoosl Wuthhoqquan. No pronunciation guide was ever provided.

4. This ability was typical of many successful pulp writers.

5. Kane would have called it justice and would honestly have believed this was true.

6. You actually wouldn't want to invite Conan to a party either, because he'd just hack you to death and steal your gold.

7. In the 1970s, this character was adapted for use in the excellent Conan the Barbarian comics book series published by Marvel Comics. Later, the comic book version of Sonya was the basis for a very, very bad movie.

8. Including some successful work as a sculptor.

9. It's been resurrected several times since then by different publishers and with varying degrees of commercial and critical success. It's become the magazine that wouldn't die.

10. "Yours Truly, Jack the Ripper," from the July 1943 issue, should be considered required reading.

11. One aspect of *Weird Tales*—the occasional tastelessness of the cover illustrations—will be discussed in depth in a later section.

12. He tries to "invent" gunpowder, but never does figure out the proper proportions of the ingredients.

13. Leiber died in 1992, with a large body of work to his credit, aside from the Fafhrd stories.

Chapter 7

1. The quote's from page 197 of Robert Sampson's book *The Solvers*.
2. Daly did stay around long enough to strongly influence Mickey Spillane's Mike Hammer novels. Drivel begets drivel.
3. He's never called that in the stories—it just became a convenient way of identifying him in advertisements.
4. The nickname came from his former Army rank of Captain.
5. The quote's from "The Big Knock-over."
6. As is Hammett's 1932 novel *The Thin Man*, which did not appear in *The Black Mask*.
7. His best short story is "Mistral," which appeared in *Adventure* in 1931.
8. Gardner was a very prolific pulp writer, creating dozens of characters for dozens of magazines.

Chapter 8

1. Possibly the single most annoying word ever.
2. Later called *Electrical Experimenter*, then still later *Science and Invention*.
3. Yes, I am consistently using the term "science fiction" anachronistically.
4. He was a real "doc," with a PhD in chemical engineering.
5. We'll save discussion of the racism inherent in many pulp stories until a later section.
6. Two cents a word.
7. And now called simply *Astounding Stories*.
8. "Who Goes There?" has twice been adapted to film, with both film versions entitled *The Thing*.
9. Campbell had studied physics at M.I.T. and Duke University. He knew scientific accuracy when he saw it.

10. When asked, the two men would often give each other the bulk of the credit for who came up with these ideas.

Chapter 9

1. When reprinted as a novel, it was given the title *A Princess of Mars*.
2. The quote is from page 1 of Sam Moskowitz's excellent history of early pulp science fiction, also entitled "Under the Moons of Mars."
3. The species is make-believe, and not based at all on any real apes.
4. The tigers were changed to lions when the story was reprinted as a novel.
5. This was titled "The Return of Tarzan." The ape man gets both Jane and his title of Lord Greystoke at the end.
6. For the sake of the story, it doesn't matter whether the reader accepts or rejects evolution as fact. Burroughs accepted it, but his presentation of it on Caspak is complete fantasy from any point of view.
7. This was a good spot for the local coast guard to mark on their maps. By the time the first two Tarzan stories are over, at least five shipwrecked/marooned individuals or groups ended up there.

Chapter 10

1. Rohmer's stories were published in the U.S. by the slick magazines, but he had a strong influence on the pulps. To be fair, Rohmer was a good writer, and Fu Manchu was an effective villain.
2. There are a few exceptions to this; but just as there are very rare examples of good slasher movies, there were very, very few well-written Weird Menace stories.

Chapter 11

1. That totals about 15 million words.
2. Gibson's only regular failure to maintain plot continuity was his tendency to have revolvers turn into automatic pistols, then back into revolvers

again — often in the space of a single paragraph.

3. Real life concerns of free will and medical ethics weren't a part of Doc Savage's fictional and morally simple universe.

4. Hogan did not fly in combat, but his knowledge of planes and tactics was strong.

5. It seems rather odd for a spy to be so well known, but I suppose when you're a master of disguise, it really doesn't matter.

6. He flies back in a "borrowed" plane, crash landing in a city street.

7. The Phantom Detective, though of uneven quality, had a commercially successful run of twenty years.

Part II

1. Publisher William Randolph Hearst telegraphed a reporter in Cuba: "You furnish the pictures and I'll furnish the war."

2. The colors were red, blue, yellow and black, which could be blended together to make additional shades and colors.

Chapter 13

1. A few years later, the same situation and court decision was neatly mirrored when *Katzenjammer Kids* artist Rudolph Dirks left Hearst for Pulitzer.

Chapter 14

1. Such syndicates had become the usual way to market comics nationally.

2. Daily strips were printed at almost twice the size as they are nowadays. As was the case on Sundays, artists had more leeway in including detail and varying their layouts.

3. From Marschall's *America's Great Comic Strip Artists*, page 153.

4. Dawson would become a recurring villain.

5. The daily and Sunday features eventually merged into a single entity, entitled *Captain Easy*.

6. Crane's assistant Les Daniels took over *Captain Easy* and also did quality work. The strip ran until 1988.

Chapter 15

1. Dick was a slang term for a detective.

2. Quoted from *The Dick Tracy Casebook*, page 272.

3. Richard Marschall makes the comparison to Medieval morality plays in *America's Great Comic Strip Artists*.

Chapter 16

1. Philip Nowlan, author of the original stories, also scripted the comic through its first decade, with Dick Calkins initially doing the art.

2. The syndicate was actually called Metropolitan Newspaper Service when the Tarzan strip first began, but the name changed soon after.

3. He left for a little over a year in the mid–1940s.

4. It was a Sunday only strip.

5. An island kingdom vaguely located in or near the Mediterranean.

Chapter 17

1. Eventually, Dickie began having some "real life" adventures.

2. Patterson thought the *...and the Pirates* bit sounded appropriately dramatic, but storylines involving piracy actually occurred only a few times during the strip's run.

3. Daily and Sunday continuities merged in 1936.

4. That term is used by Alberto Becattini in the book *Profili Caniff*.

5. Caniff, in turn, provided inspiration to movie makers. Orson Welles and

Frederico Fellini were among those influenced by his work.

6. And *nobody* drew good-looking women as well as Caniff.

7. Only Burma reappeared as frequently.

8. Prior to Peal Harbor, the Japanese were only identified in the strip as "the invaders." This was to avoid making isolationist editors nervous. But there was never any doubt who they were.

9. *Terry* continued until 1973,written and drawn by George Wunder.

10. Caniff's hawkish attitude during the Vietnam War—an attitude clearly conveyed in the strip—had also cost him subscribers.

Chapter 18

1. Like the comic books, the strip was written by Jerry Siegal and drawn by Joe Schuster. They had, in fact, originally intended the feature to be a comic strip.

Part III

---

1. As with the rise of popular fiction, radio depended on a prosperous middle class for its business. The initial impetus for buying radios was to listen to music.

2. It also generated a lot of controversy over its portrayal of stereotypical black characters played by white actors.

Chapter 19

1. When people are unaware that they're making history, they have an annoying habit of not taking notes.

2. Different sources, all well-researched and dependable, disagree on this date, as well as on other details.

3. Actually, for the first few years, he rode double with the Ranger on Silver. Eventually, he acquired his own horse, named Scout.

4. He did have his rather famous trouble with English pronouns.

5. Another WXYZ announcer, Mike Wallace, was also considered for the part. Wallace was instead destined for television as host of the newsmagazine *60 Minutes*.

6. An actual origin episode aired in 1948 to mark the show's fifteenth anniversary.

7. The Lone Ranger Atomic Bomb ring, offered as a premium when these episodes aired, was given out to three million kids.

Chapter 20

1. To my knowledge, no recordings of *Love Story Hour* exist.

2. It aired on the Mutual Broadcasting Network.

3. From *The Shadow: The Making of a Legend*, page 20.

4. Welles couldn't do the Shadow's laugh. A recording of Frank Readick's laugh was used instead.

Chapter 21

1. Once and future Shadows Frank Readick and Bill Johnstone also had roles.

2. Herrmann had a long career in radio, television and film. His many scores include *Citizen Kane, Psycho, Taxi Driver*, and many *Twilight Zone* episodes.

3. Houseman once claimed in an interview that between the radio scripts and administrating the Mercury's continuing stage plays, he often worked in bed all day because he didn't have time to get up and dress.

4. Production moved from New York to California after Welles signed a contract to make a film for RKO. The film he made was *Citizen Kane*, and he cast the Mercury players in most of the key roles.

5. These were still good, but too rushed in their 30-minute time frame to be great.

Chapter 22

1. Remember that he was the *first* superhero, and in 1938 his appearance was strikingly original.

2. A later episode from 1945 practices some revisionist history and tells us that Superman was still Superbaby when he first arrives on Earth.

3. The effect was produced by mixing the sounds of a fired artillery shell and a wind tunnel.

4. From a booklet that accompanied a 1997 CD release of episodes titled *Superman with Batman and Robin on Radio*.

5. The show's talented writers included George Lowther, Jack Johnstone and Ben Peter Freeman.

6. Batman and Robin were frequent guest stars beginning in 1945.

7. In the radio series, kryptonite did not actually kill Superman, but could put him into a coma-like state.

8. Actually, Bud Collyer was on vacation.

9. In 1950, Collyer left the show, replaced by Michael Fitzmaurice.

Chapter 23

1. *Inner Sanctum* ran from 1941 to 1952. Its creator, Himan Brown, was inspired by a creaking basement door.

2. Bill Cosby did a great stand-up routine recalling how badly frightened this episode left him when he heard it as a child.

Chapter 24

1. The phone company was flooded with complaints about these operators every time the episode aired.

2. *Suspense* had been sponsored by Roma Wines and Autolite batteries for much of its run.

3. *Escape*'s rare weak episodes, such as "Beau Geste" and "She," were usually adaptations of novels with too much plot to jam comfortably into 30 minutes.

4. In live radio, a repeat was not a recording of the first broadcast, but another live performance using the same script.

5. This being radio, each of the three also had a distinctive, easily identifiable voice.

6. Radio historian Jim Harmon did a wonderful job producing a recreation of "The Fear That Creeps Like a Cat" on tape in 1992.

7. There were four ten-part and four three-part storylines produced. Recordings of all 52 episodes still exist.

8. He appeared regularly on both *The Jack Benny Show* and *The Phil Harris Show*.

Chapter 25

1. *On the Air*, page 534.

2. *On the Air*, page 209.

3. She's quoted in Leonard Maltin's book *The Great American Broadcast*, page 84.

4. James E. Moser and Jack Robinson wrote many of the scripts.

Chapter 26

1. It was based on a story by Ernest Haycox.

2. Macdonnell had asked for "something that suggested the wide-open spaces" of the American frontier. Kaury's theme did this beautifully.

Chapter 27

1. *Superman* was actually the most down-to-earth series of the lot.

2. He's quoted in *Science Fiction on Radio*, page 28.

3. $2000 a week, about a third of what most half-hour shows of that time cost.

4. Welsh had taken over from Van Woodward for the last twenty episodes of *Dimension X*.

Chapter 28

1. Charles Russell, Edmond O'Brien and John Lund had all played the part before 1955.

2. I know this isn't *always* true, but the exceptions are rare enough to prove the rule.

3. Film and television aren't the only factors involved in this, but they're certainly important ones.

4. Except me, of course.

Bibliography

Becattini, Alberto, and Antonio Vianov, eds. *Profili Caniff: Milt Caniff, American Stars & Stripes*. Glamour International Production, 2001.

Becker, Stephen. *Comic Art in America*. New York: Simon & Schuster, 1959.

Bleiler, E.F., ed. *Eight Dime Novels*. New York: Dover Publications, 1974.

Brand, Max. *The Legend of Thundermoon*, introduction by Edgar L. Chapman. Lincoln, NE: University of Nebraska Press, 1996.

_____. *Untamed*, introduction by Jack Nachbar. Boston: Gregg Press, 1978.

Clute, John, and Peter Nicholls. *Encyclopedia of Science Fiction*. New York: St. Martin's Press, 1993.

Collins, Max Allen, and Dick Locher, eds. *The Dick Tracy Casebook*. New York: St. Martin's Press, 1989.

Daniels, Les. *Superman: The Complete History*. San Francisco: Chronicle Books, 1998.

Deandrea, William. *Encyclopedia Mysteriosa*. New York: Prentice Hall, 1994.

Dunning, John. *On the Air: The Encyclopedia of Old-Time Radio*. New York: Oxford University Press, 1998.

Homer. *The Odyssey*. Translated and edited by Albert Cook. Norton Critical edition, 2nd edition. New York: W.W. Norton, 1993.

Gibson, Walter B. *The Shadow Scrapbook*. New York: Harcourt Brace Jovanovich, 1979.

Gies, Frances. *The Knight in History*. New York: Harper and Row, 1984.

Harmon, Jim. *The Great Radio Heroes*, revised edition. Jefferson, NC: McFarland, 2001.

_____. *Radio Mystery and Adventure and Its Appearances in Film, Television and Other Media*. Jefferson, NC: McFarland, 1992.

Hoppenstand, Gary, ed. *The Dime Novel Detective*. Bowling Green, OH: Bowling Green University Popular Press, 1982.

Hutchison, Don. *The Great Pulp Heroes*. Oakville, ON: Mosaic Press, 1995.

Kaye, Marvin, and John Gregory Betancourt, ed. *The Best of Weird Tales, 1923*. Berkeley Heights, NJ: Bleak House, 1997.

Koch, Howard. *The Panic Broadcast.* New York: Avon, 1970.

Maltin, Leonard. *The Great American Broadcast.* New York, Dutton, 1997.

Mandar, Jerry. *Four Arguments for the Elimination of Television.* New York: Quill, 1978.

Marigay, Jean. *Vampires: Restless Creatures of the Night.* New York: Harry N. Abrams, 1994.

Marschall, Rick. *America's Great Comic Strip Artists.* New York: Stewart, Tabori & Chang, 1997.

Moskowitz, Sam, ed. *Under the Moons of Mars: A History and Anthology of "the Scientific Romance" in the Munsey Magazines, 1912–1920.* New York: Holt, Rinehart & Winston, 1970.

Nachman, Gerald. *Raised on Radio.* Berkeley, CA: University of California Press, 1998.

Nolan, William. *The Black Mask Boys.* New York: The Mysterious Press, 1985.

Penzler, Otto. *The Private Lives of Private Eyes: Spies, Crimefighters & Other Good Guys.* New York: Grosset & Dunlap, 1977.

Perkins, George, et al, eds. *Benet's Reader's Encyclopedia of American Literature.* New York: HarperCollins, 1991.

Pronzini, Bill, and Jack Adrian, eds. *Hard-Boiled: An Anthology of American Crime Fiction.* Oxford: Oxford University Press, 1995.

Robinson, Frank. *Science Fiction of the 20th Century: An Illustrated History.* Portland, OR: Collectors Press, 1999.

_____, and Lawrence Davidson. *Pulp Culture: The Art of Fiction Magazines.* Portland, OR: Collectors Press, 1998.

Robinson, Jerry. *The Comics: An Illustrated History of Comic Strip Art.* New York: G.P. Putnam's Sons, 1974.

Rothel, David. *Who Was That Masked Man?: The Story of the Lone Ranger.* New York: A.S. Barnes & Company, 1981.

Ryan, Alan, ed. *Vampires: Two Centuries of Great Vampire Stories.* New York: Doubleday & Company, 1987.

Salzman, Jack, and Pamela Wilkinson, eds. *Major Characters in American Fiction.* New York: Henry Holt & Company, 1994.

Sampson, Robert. *Deadly Excitements.* Bowling Green, OH: Bowling Green University Popular Press, 1989.

_____. *Yesterday's Faces: A Study of Series Characters in the Early Pulp Magazines,* 6 volumes. Bowling Green, OH: Bowling Green University Popular Press, 1983–93.

Sawyer, Ruth. *The Way of the Storyteller.* New York: Penguin Books, 1942.

Server, Lee. *Danger Is My Business: An Illustrated History of the Fabulous Pulp Magazines.* San Francisco: Chronicle Books, 1993.

Sobol, Joseph Daniel. *The Storyteller's Journey: An American Revival.* University of Illinois Press, 1999.

Tollin, Anthony. *The Shadow: The Making of a Legend.* GAA Corporation, 1996.

Van Hise, James, ed. *The Fantastic World of Robert E. Howard.* James Van Hise, 1997.

_____. *Pulp Heroes of the Thirties,* 2nd edition. James Van Hise, 1997.

_____. *Pulp Masters*, expanded edition. James Van Hise, 2002.

Weinberg, Robert. *The Weird Tales Story*. Berkeley Heights, NJ: Wildside Press, 1999.

Widner, James F., and Meade Frierson III. *Science Fiction on Radio: A Revised Look at 1950–1975*. A.F.A.B., 1996.

Wills, Garry. *Lincoln at Gettysburg: The Words That Remade America*. New York: Simon & Schuster, 1992.

Index